WR

Ronald Blythe
history and lite
Age of Illusion
in Winter (197*
Emma, by Jane Austen; *William Hazlitt: Selected*
Writings and *Far From The Madding Crowd* by Thomas
Hardy for the Penguin English Library. He has
received the Heinemann Award and the Society of
Authors Travel Scholarship.

Writing in a War

STORIES, POEMS, AND ESSAYS OF THE
SECOND WORLD WAR

INTRODUCED AND
CHOSEN BY
RONALD BLYTHE

PENGUIN BOOKS

For
John Heath-Stubbs

Penguin Books Ltd, Harmondsworth, Middlesex, England
Penguin Books, 625 Madison Avenue, New York, New York 10022, U.S.A.
Penguin Books Australia Ltd, Ringwood, Victoria, Australia
Penguin Books Canada Ltd, 2801 John Street, Markham, Ontario, Canada L3R 1B4
Penguin Books (N.Z.) Ltd, 182–190 Wairau Road, Auckland 10, New Zealand

—

First published in 1966
Revised edition 1982

—

Copyright © Ronald Blythe, 1966, 1982
All rights reserved

—

Made and printed in Great Britain by
Cox & Wyman Ltd, Reading
Set in Monotype Fournier

We in our haste can only see the small components of the
    scene
We cannot tell what incidents will focus on the final screen.
A barrage of disruptive sound, a petal on a sleeping face,
Both must be noted, both must have their place;
It may be that our later selves or else our unborn sons
Will search for meaning in the dust of long deserted guns,
We only watch, and indicate and make our scribbled pencil
    notes.
We do not wish to moralize, only to ease our dusty throats.

DONALD BAIN

Contents

CONTENTS

CONTENTS

CONFESSIONS AND CONCLUSIONS

CONTENTS

Introduction

THIS anthology seeks to capture the special precision of the poetry of the Second World War and to evoke the deliberate mixture of realism and sensibility which dominated the prose of those violent years. It was, in France and Britain particularly, a highly literary war; if everybody did not burst out writing (and reading), it often seemed that they did. Writers generally believed that they were witnessing a dissolution of the old civilized scene and that they had a duty to preserve the great basic values which had created this scene. They also felt that they must resist the new facelessness forced upon Europe by fascist politics and military expediency; that salvation and hope began with the discovery of one's own identity and its maintenance against all the pressures of the emergency.

The war demanded a temporary suspension of personal identity but, as all wars do, it inevitably offered a great profusion of those experiences by which identity is fed: foreign travel, sexual freedom, bereavement, pain, separation, comradeship and those close groupings which, far from turning many individuals into a regiment or a ship's company or a bomber's crew, brings each man face-to-face with his own essential solitude. The writers of 1939–45 fully accepted engagement in the struggle but rejected the suspension of private life advocated by the various propaganda machines. This was the condition by which their conscience permitted them to fight, as well as forsake the indignation of the poets of 1916–18. Their work was not addressed to great audiences or to the nation, but to another individual. Eventually, as the war intensified and its strangely fragmented pattern added to the impression of world insanity, the quiet urbanity of its literature provided a climate in which the urgent dialogue of the human condition could take place. These writers saw themselves, and with considerable modesty, as healthy cells in a rotting tissue. Their duty was to create other such cells.

Although there was a so-called 'boom' in poetry, with the thirties poets' new work being eagerly read for both moral and technical guidance, and many new writers finding print under the cryptic shelter of a movement called the New Apocalypse, for a considerable period after the war had ended there was only a hazy assessment of its real poetic statement. It was a statement which was awaited with some impatience when the war began. 'Where are the war-poets?' asked the *Times Literary Supplement* in 1940. The popular press asked the same question, only with patriotic indignation. Soon there were accusations; it was implied that while everybody else had taken up their action stations, the poets had not – and they who had been so noisy about Spain! Yet even people like Cyril Connolly, who was so near to the literary heart of the war, became apprehensive about a hush which continued until after the fall of France, when everything pointed to the abyss. Had the poets, like Gide, taken a vow of silence until the war was over? If they had, commented Connolly bitterly, 'they will disappear and their disappearance provide further evidence that the human race has outstayed its welcome.' He urged them to 'flower like the almond blossom'.

Some writers had already decided that almond blossom might stand a better chance in a less gloomy climate and had transplanted themselves to New York and California, most notably W. H. Auden. Their apparent flight to what Connolly called 'a land rich in incident' gave great offence. This was not purged by the shocking logic of E. M. Forster's remark that it was better to be a swimming rat than a sinking ship. Auden himself had no reason to apologize. He had been fighting his war against the fascists – at home and abroad – a whole decade before Mr Chamberlain came to the microphone on 3 September 1939, and he was to leave behind for the war-poets proper invaluable techniques for the expression of their faith. And T. S. Eliot also recognized during the blackest months of the war the absolute priority of the Word in a gobbledegook universe and could tell Stephen Spender at this time that 'it is very important that as many writers as possible should remain detached, and not have any official position'. Spender's official position was in the Auxiliary Fire Service. From it he looked back in grief and disillusionment to the brief Apollonian Germany of the late twenties which had so terribly given way to the Dionysian Germany of Hitler. What was it which allowed nations to accept the convention of the war-time, peace-time cycle?

> Why cannot the one good
> Benevolent feasible
> Final dove descend?

he asked.

It was a rhetorical question for Sidney Keyes, Alun Lewis, Keith Douglas, Richard Spender, Herbert Corby, G. S. Fraser, Henry Reed, R. N. Currey, F. T. Prince, Rayner Heppenstall and the many other young writers in uniform. They had by the very fact of accepting a uniform made a choice which Alex Comfort summed up as 'refusal or death'. Their brief adult experiences had been circumscribed by corrupt politics. Sidney Keyes, one of the most important and prolific of the Second World War poets, was not quite twenty-one when he died in North Africa. The thirties poets had left their 'singing feasts' in order to practise what they preached – in Spain. The forties poets refused to preach at all and thus, beyond the normal duties of the fighting man, they felt they had few obligations beyond those governing their relationship with another human being, and that they were free to use the little time at their disposal in discovering themselves. The great thing was not to pretend, or proffer solutions, or to be histrionic. Each poet spoke as wholly and truthfully as he could from out of the one inviolate spot of an otherwise violated order, his own identity. This he found more threatened by the inanities of the barracks, war-time bureaucrats and those countless inroads upon the dignity of the person which a national emergency prescribes, than by the terrible etiquette of the battlefield. There he could only marvel at the way military primitivism worked afresh for every new generation of victims.

> How can I live among this gentle
> obsolescent breed of heroes, and not weep?

asks Keith Douglas.

> There's no prescribed or easy word
> For dissolution in the Army books ...

says Sidney Keyes.

> Softly the civilized
> Centuries fall,
> Paper on paper,
> Peter on Paul ...

notes Alun Lewis in a poem of such feathery valediction that it is like the leave-taking of ghosts. F. T. Prince, watching soldiers bathing, sees two great Renaissance pictures come to life before his eyes, Michelangelo's mercenaries being called away suddenly from their innocent splashings to kill or be killed, and Pollaiuolo's 'brother-naked' warriors hacking at each other. Here, as recurring as its heroism, is 'war's sorrow and disgrace'.

Sidney Keyes particularly, and most of the Second World War poets to a degree, accepted Rilke's belief that each man carries his own death within him. It was of Keyes that R. N. Currey said that he went 'further than any poet of the First War in his realization that mankind was at war because it was not yet ready for peace, because men were proud and greedy and destructive at heart'.

The other great influence on these identity-claiming poets was Hölderlin, born the same year as Wordsworth but spiritually if not physically killed by the *mal-de-siècle* which followed the moment of hopefulness released over Europe by the French Revolution. Hölderlin's disillusionment sprang from what his translator J. B. Leishman describes as the 'vast gulf between the actual and the ideal'. Vulgarians, particularly nationalists, were soon to smudge these two states together and call them 'destiny', a pretty word for action and power. 'Sacred Destiny' was what Hölderlin called it in 1796 but five years later he is forced to realize that life and art are only seen in their true fullness when destiny, that claptrap term so convenient for national leaders, is 'suspended'. Hölderlin's tragic life presented to the poets of 1939–45 a romantic analogy of their own bitterly realistic position. They had to make swift decisions as to what was politically genuine and what was part of the corrosive ritual, and on the whole they felt they had to do this without cynicism. Hölderlin's

Menon's Laments For Diotima, one of the world's great elegies, and a defence of the personal life, taught them, in the words of his translator, how poetry in becoming more personal also becomes more universal.

Shortly after writing his *Laments* Hölderlin went mad and wandered abstractly through a Europe where glory was rapidly giving place to something called '*la gloire*'. A century and a half of ardent nationalism and militarism faced the world. One day the poet was discovered in the grounds of a château near the Loire and was questioned by the owner.

'You are a Greek, perhaps?'

'No! – on the contrary, I am a German!'

'On the contrary? – Is the German the opposite of the Greek?'

'Yes ... We all are! You, the Frenchman, are too; the Englishman, your enemy, is too – we all are!'

The Second World War poets recognized the difference with humility. The sublime heritage was in the gutter and each and all were culpable. All they could do in the short time which was left was individually to repudiate the state myths and, as Hölderlin requested,

> ... proffer their hands to each other
> Before the sociable light has yet
> Quite gone and the night is upon them.

A strict privacy, though a witty one, also marked William Empson's reaction to the war. While refusing to be stampeded by the quake, natural or national, he equally refused to be shaken to bits by it – 'It seemed the best thing to be up and go'. The mannerisms curl off into essentials, just like Chinese Chippendale.

For T. S. Eliot, in his early fifties when the war began, it was a time of assessment. Three hundred years of English Christianity separate him from the ancestor who left East Coker for New England. What now?

> So here I am, in the middle way, having had twenty years –
> Twenty years largely wasted, the years of *l'entre deux guerres*
> Trying to learn to use words ...

He also says that 'Home is where one starts from', a reminder of origins and that each man bears a unique responsibility for the then and now. The magnificent *Four Quartets* appeared during the darkest years of the war: with *Little Gidding* in 1942 comes a very different kind of patriotism.

> We die with the dying:
> See, they depart, and we go with them.
> We are born with the dead;
> See, they return, and bring us with them.
> The moment of the rose and the moment of the yew-tree
> Are of equal duration. A people without history
> Is not redeemed from time, for history is a pattern
> Of timeless moments. So, while the light fails
> On a winter's afternoon, in a secluded chapel
> History is now and England.

David Gascoyne, the only important surrealist poet of the thirties, also used Christian themes for his war poetry, and Edith Sitwell's profoundly moving *Still Falls the Rain* sees her as a mourner at the crucifixion of cities during air-raids. But it was Dylan Thomas who translated statistics into loss by offering the poor insignificant victims of the bombings – 'A child of a few hours', 'A man aged a hundred' – a similar rich and sonorous devotion to their earthly existence as that offered by the seventeenth-century Henry King to his dead wife in the *Exequy*. Henry Moore was to complement this poetry with his *Shelter Sketchbook* (1943) in which his hieratic treatment of the citizens of mid twentieth-century London repeats over and over again the profound outline of the entombed. A majesty emanates from these classic cocoons as, in Dylan Thomas's words, they await 'the incendiary eve of deaths and entrances'. Countless other human beings reduced to war's bundles in the sealed trains criss-crossing Europe to the final solution schedules, and on the Eastern Front and in the fetid depths of ships, awaited it too.

Dylan Thomas was twenty-four when the war began. His biographer, Constantine FitzGibbon, has described how he found it a personal affront. He had a premonition of a short life, that he would die before he was forty, and now this little span, so essential to his art, was to be interfered with by 'them' – meaning not the Nazis but the various government departments. It was vaguely from this detestation of state meddling in private lives that the idea of *Milk Wood* began to take shape. Thomas's fabulous voice, reading poems and giving talks on the B.B.C., and encrusting the uproar in numerous dismal blacked-out Fitzrovian pubs, was a key sound of these years, while his work released some poets from the precise conditions which Eliot, Auden and their followers had laid upon the language. The singing note returned. There was a fresh lyricism, and the heady love affair with words soon produced prose variants in the stories of Glyn Jones, V. S. Pritchett and Fred Urquhart. The Irish W. R. Rodgers, with his *Awake! and other poems* (1941), was to add to this exultation of language, rich words which contrasted so vividly with the war's special poverty. This word-spree was to continue throughout the forties, feeding itself on austerity in some paradoxical fashion, to reach its apogee in the lively twentieth-century-Jacobean of Christopher Fry's plays and his translations of Anouilh and Giraudoux.

*

In January 1940 the first number of *Horizon* appeared and was greeted with groans of disappointment. 'A magazine should be the reflection of its time and one that ceases to reflect this should come to an end,' declared its editor. Then let it die, wept its subscribers who had bought up every copy, and who had asked for bread and had been given H. E. Bates. Not that he was negligible by any means but his glassily finished stories could be read everywhere. Yet the germ of *Horizon's* future importance was present in this otherwise cautious issue, buried in a little travel-essay by Cyril Connolly and only to be observed in retrospect. This essay, *The Ant Lion*, is ostensibly about Albi, the little Provençal town which was the centre of the Albigensian heresy and the home of Toulouse-Lautrec. In essence it is a statement of *Horizon's* non-parochial intention. Modern wars choke the lines of communication between writers, national literature is inflated and the validity of enemy art denied. While Britain waited for Hitler to invade, Connolly had his own warning to give – 'An island fortress must always be on its guard against provincialism!' His readers – probably the most enthusiastic any magazine has ever had – took due note of this and soon *Horizon*,

with its indulgent baroque retrospection following it like an expertly
stocked baggage-train, and its international high-table atmosphere,
came to epitomize for them a Europe really worth saving. They were
pleasantly seduced by its editor's notoriously skilful lament for the
lost *douceur de vivre*. Constant mention of painters, poets, architects
and musicians working away 'above' the war, as it were, reminded
them of the unity of real civilization. *Horizon* regularly infiltrated
the smug Home Front by letting in the ideas of Aragon, Moravia,
Cavafy, Barea, Croce, Mallarmé, Éluard, Malraux, Pasternak, Miro,
Camus, Bartók, Gide, Sartre, Picasso and others.

Connolly celebrated the dingy months of victory with an intro-
spective masterpiece, *The Unquiet Grave*. The book is a private
distillation of melancholy which, exuded drop by aphoristic drop,
gets the reader wonderfully drunk; it is a Brocks' Benefit Night of the
1939–45 soul, with the great darkness fitfully illuminated by a fine
display of adroit scholarship and high imagination, and at the heart
it reveals Connolly's celebrated analysis of *Angst*, its causes and its
cures. With this anthology–autobiography the forties search of the
self achieved full circle.

A profusion of other little magazines shared the scene – in spite
of every discouragement, niggardly paper rations, bombed offices,
breakdowns in distribution and, above all, the fact that nearly everybody connected with their production had full-time national work
as well. The most popular was *Penguin New Writing*, which began
publication in 1936, but which established itself in a much broader
sense after 1940. While lacking the curious glamour of *Horizon*,
under the editorship of John Lehmann it maintained a distinguished
and inimitable climate of its own with stories, essays and poems, as
well as film, ballet, art and theatrical criticism of a high level. To be
published in *New Writing* was to have arrived. Copies of it travelled
the world in small-packs and kit-bags, along with its subsidiary
Penguin Parade. The most exotic of the little magazines was undoubtedly J. M. Tambimuttu's *Poetry London*, with its glowing
lyre-bird covers by Graham Sutherland, Henry Moore and John
Craxton, its lavish menu-size format and lucky-dip contents.
Tambi's descent on London and his subsequent reign over a large
collection of poets and pubs were not the least wonders of the war.

A grimly comic description of him is given by the late Julian Maclaren-Ross in *Memoirs of the Forties* (1965). Other magazines included Reginald Moore's *Modern Reading*, Alex Comfort's *New Road*, Robert Herring's *Life and Letters Today*, Geoffrey Grigson's *New Verse*, Wrey Gardiner's *Poetry Quarterly* and Neville Braybrooke's *Wind and the Rain*.

Another group of editors, notably Patricia Ledward, Keidrych Rhys and R. N. Currey, made periodical collections of war poetry. These often included a single fine poem by an unknown writer never to be heard of again in the literary sense. Excellent but isolated short stories and essays would frequently appear in this way from one or other of the ironically named 'theatres' of war, an imaginative fragment struck from some otherwise non-creative hand by a collision in unique circumstances.

*

The fiction of these years only really takes on some vaguely cohesive pattern in the development of the novel if the dates are stretched from *Brighton Rock* (1938) to *Lucky Jim* (1953). It is only in this way that it is possible to trace the progress of the anti-hero and eventually to see the mannered climate of Christian guilt swept away by an ill-mannered gale of social protest. Journalists dubbed the protestants Angry Young Men. The real note was one of deliberately graceless laughter at the bloodless niceties of British life. Some sharp reaction to the now infamous romanticism of the forties was inevitable. This romanticism had grown out of a valid anxiety during the early war years for novelists to conserve traditional liberal values. In 1941 Walter Allen observed a halt amongst artists of all kinds in associating themselves with the thirties idea of art and action. A period of reflection had set in. Allen recommended a fresh consideration of Flaubert's withdrawal doctrine. Flaubert was a most unfashionable writer just then, and he made the important point that the much ridiculed Flaubertian ivory tower was not a shelter from the world, but a quiet eminence from which the writer could view his world.

The artist should be in his work, like God in creation, invisible and all-powerful; he should be felt everywhere and seen nowhere (wrote

Flaubert). And the art should be raised above personal affections and nervous susceptibilities. It is time to give it the precision of the physical sciences by means of pitiless method.

But when one looks back on the results of these four or so years of creative dedication and, so far as could be claimed from war work and war pressures, the novelists' vocational position, it is to see them not so much as en-towered observers as a group of literary Simeon Stylites, each aloft on his pillar above the revolution, and able to convey very little of the tumult below.

Graham Greene, in *The Power and the Glory* (1940), became the first and eventually the foremost novelist of the last twenty-five years to draw elaborate moral conclusions from lives ruined by sin-consciousness. His Mexican whisky priest and his seedy Scobie from *The Heart of the Matter* (1948) could hardly be called sinners at all in a world which contained Himmler and Josef Kramer or – in a different sense – the airmen who dropped the bomb on Hiroshima. Yet each of these novels was immediately seen to contain a direct relevance to what was happening in national spheres of evil. Greene sees both heaven and the jungle as man's natural states, and man's tragedy that he has to fluctuate between both.

Henry Green, too, was a writer who offered an accurate vision of the war existence in microcosmic terms. His novels did what nobody else's did, they moved from class to class with a new kind of conviction. They had brief meaningful titles which told one exactly what the story was about, *Caught*, *Loving*, *Party Going*; but the characters constantly act out of character. Henry Green defied the neat pigeon-holing of humanity and challenged surface judgements. His novels have something of the oriental subtlety and refinement of William Empson's poetry. *Caught* (1943) is about the Fire Service and is remarkable for its accurate use of working-class dialogue.

1940 saw Dylan Thomas's *Portrait of the Artist as a Young Dog*, C. P. Snow's *Strangers and Brothers*, Charles Morgan's *The Voyage* as well as Graham Greene's *The Power and the Glory*, but saved its top honours for Arthur Koestler's *Darkness at Noon*, perhaps the greatest novel to have come out of the war. Both 1941 and 1942 were lean years for fiction, although one brilliant dialogue continued as imperturbably as ever with Ivy Compton Burnett's *Parents and Children* (1941). This was also the year of Rex Warner's Kafkaesque study *The Aerodrome*, and of Elizabeth Bowen's stories, *Look At All Those Roses*. In 1942 came the famous novel which turned Gerald Kersh into a barrack-room myth, *They Die With Their Boots Clean*. 1942 also witnessed the beginning of the American 'Deep South School' influence on British fiction with Carson McCullers' *Reflections in a Golden Eye*, followed a few months later by her *The Heart is a Lonely Hunter*. Further American stories arrived on the scene, all full of extraordinary emotional material, vivid dialogue and colour, Eudora Welty's *A Curtain of Green* (1943), *The Robber Bridegroom* (1944), *The Wide Net* (1945); the first stories of J. D. Salinger and, most potent of all though not Deep South, Edmund Wilson's *Memoirs Of Hecate County* (1945).

At the time the really good short story seemed to be a rare event. Critics—including George Orwell and Stephen Spender—constantly attacked the form, declared that it was tepid and too concerned with tidiness, and looked back longingly to Lawrence and Turgenev. But hindsight shows the war years unusually rich in first-rate short stories, and that it is these, rather than the novels, which retain their spell. The work of James Hanley, Frank Sargeson, William Sansom, Elizabeth Bowen, Glyn Jones, V. S. Pritchett, Alun Lewis, Fred Urquhart and Julian Maclaren-Ross touches the nerve of the period with an exactitude which often escapes the novel.

The most distinguished fiction of the second half of the war includes Rayner Heppenstall's *Saturnine* (1943), C. S. Forester's *The Ship* (1943), L. P. Hartley's *The Shrimp and the Anemone* (1943), Nigel Balchin's *The Small Back Room* (1943), Rosamund Lehmann's *The Ballad and the Source* (1944), Joyce Cary's *The Horse's Mouth* (1944), Mervyn Peake's *Titus Groan* (1945), Aldous Huxley's *Time Must Have A Stop* (1945) and George Orwell's terrible fairy-tale, *Animal Farm* (1945). Not one of these books, or any lesser novel of these times, attempted to offer some really great answer to what was happening; there is also a general avoidance of the 'great description' of events. Among the victim-heroes there is no Good Soldier Schweik – although 1939–45 was a Schweik Age if ever there was one – and among the novelists there was no Mottram, no Remarque or Jules Romains. Perhaps World War One had set a precedent of poetry during battle and fiction afterwards. Perhaps the uniquely barbarous way in which World War Two ended – Belsen and the atom bomb – suddenly drove the whole subject beyond what were believed to be up until this point in human conduct, the barrier-less limits of the artist's comment. But whatever it was which caused so many of the best novelists to occupy themselves as they did while hell gaped, it is significant that the best-known attempt to produce a 'great' Second World War novel was made by Norman Mailer with *The Naked And The Dead*. Walter Allen, considering this question at the time, wrote that 'The brands of liberalism and rationalization held by the bulk of present day writers are incapable of assimilating large-scale evil'. But in France Jean-Paul Sartre's 'Immortality is a dreadful alibi' was the accusation made about writers who neglected the crucial debates of their day for art and the private vision.

At the end of the war, British writers hurried to liberated Paris to see for themselves the superior literary landscape which was rum-oured to exist there, and they were overwhelmed by what they found. Guido de Ruggiero's definition of *Angst* – 'the flashing spark of shock between two unknowns, the individual and God' – had to face Sartre's definition of Existentialism. It was the old melancholy versus the new hell. The flourishing state of French writing as well as giving pleasure to the liberators gave cause for heart-searching too. It was immediately observed that although the French were undernourished and made tense by the risk of torture, they did not suffer from the crushing fatigue which afflicted the British writer, who was worn-out by having to double the essentially lonely terms of his vocation with the various forms of gregariousness demanded by what the newspapers called 'a nation in arms'. Paulhan, the dis-tinguished French poetry critic, and an anti-Puritan, could look at the Paris scene just before the victors arrived and say that 'art benefits by being clandestine and subversive'. In the work of British writers during the Second World War it is possible to see a continuous – and emotionally exhausting – effort to subvert the immanence of their artist-nature from the demands made on it, not only by the state, but by unique appeals to their conscience.

RONALD BLYTHE

The City

Mysterious Kôr

ELIZABETH BOWEN

FULL moonlight drenched the city and searched it; there was not a niche left to stand in. The effect was remorseless: London looked like the moon's capital – shallow, cratered, extinct. It was late, but not yet midnight; now the buses had stopped the polished roads and streets in this region sent for minutes together a ghostly unbroken reflection up. The soaring new flats and the crouching old shops and houses looked equally brittle under the moon, which blazed in windows that looked its way. The futility of the black-out became laughable: from the sky, presumably, you could see every slate in the roofs, every whited curb, every contour of the naked winter flower-beds in the park; and the lake, with its shining twists and tree-darkened islands would be a landmark for miles, yes, miles, overhead.

However, the sky, in whose glassiness floated no clouds but only opaque balloons, remained glassy-silent. The Germans no longer came by the full moon. Something more immaterial seemed to threaten, and to be keeping people at home. This day between days, this extra tax, was perhaps more than senses and nerves could bear. People stayed indoors with a fervour that could be felt: the buildings strained with battened-down human life, but not a beam, not a voice, not a note from a radio escaped. Now and then under streets and buildings the earth rumbled: the Underground sounded loudest at this time.

Outside the now gateless gates of the park, the road coming down-hill from the north-west turned south and became a street, down whose perspective the traffic lights went through their unmeaning performance of changing colour. From the promontory of pavement outside the gates you saw at once up the road and down the street: from behind where you stood, between the gate-posts, appeared the lesser strangements of grass and water and trees. At this point, at this moment, three French soldiers, directed to a hostel they could not find, stopped singing to listen derisively to the water-birds wakened up by the moon. Next, two wardens coming off duty emerged from their post and crossed the road diagonally, each with an elbow cupped inside a slung-on tin hat. The wardens turned their faces, mauve in the moonlight, towards the Frenchmen with no expression at all. The two sets of steps died in opposite directions, and, the birds subsiding, nothing was heard or seen until, a little way down the street, a trickle of people came out of the Underground, around the anti-panic brick wall. These all disappeared quickly, in an abashed way, or as though dissolved in the street by some white acid, but for a girl and a soldier who, by their way of walking, seemed to have no destination but each other and to be not quite certain even of that. Blotted into one shadow, he tall, she little, these two proceeded towards the park. They looked in, but did not go in; they stood there debating without speaking. Then, as though a command from the street behind them had been received by their synchronized bodies, they faced round to look back the way they had come.

His look up the height of a building made his head drop back, and she saw his eyeballs glitter. She slid her hand from his sleeve, stepped to the edge of the pavement and said: 'Mysterious Kôr.'

'What is?' he said, not quite collecting himself.

'This is –

> Mysterious Kôr thy walls forsaken stand,
> Thy lonely towers beneath a lonely moon –

– This is Kôr.'

'Why,' he said, 'it's years since I've thought of that.'

She said: 'I think of it all the time –

> Not in the wastes beyond the swamps and sand,
> The fever-haunted forest and lagoon,
> Mysterious Kôr thy walls –

– a completely forsaken city, as high as cliffs and as white as bones, with no history –'

'But something must once have happened: why had it been forsaken?'

'How could anyone tell you when there's nobody there?'

'Nobody there since how long?'

'Thousands of years.'

'In that case, it would have fallen down.'

'No, not Kôr,' she said with immediate authority. 'Kôr's altogether different; it's very strong; there is not a crack in it anywhere for a weed to grow in; the corners of stones and the monuments might have been cut yesterday, and the stairs and arches are built to support themselves.'

'You know all about it,' he said, looking at her.

'I know, I know all about it.'

'What, since you read that book?'

'Oh, I didn't get much from that; I just got the name. I knew that must be the right name; it's like a cry.'

'Most like the cry of a crow to me.' He reflected, then said: 'But the poem begins with "Not" – *Not in the waste beyond the swamps and sand* – And it goes on, as I remember, to prove Kôr's not really anywhere. When a poem says there's no such place –'

'What it tries to say doesn't matter: I see what it makes me see. Anyhow, that was written some time ago, at that time when they thought they had got everything taped, because the whole world had been explored, even the middle of Africa. Every thing and place had been found and marked on some map; so what wasn't marked on any map couldn't be there at all. So *they* thought: that was why he wrote the poem. *The world is disenchanted*, it goes on. That was what set me off hating civilization.'

'Well, cheer up,' he said; 'there isn't much of it left.'

'Oh, yes, I cheered up some time ago. This war shows we've by no means come to the end. If you can blow whole places out of existence, you can blow whole places into it. I don't see why not. They say we can't say what's come out since the bombing started. By the time we've come to the end, Kôr may be the one city left: the abiding city. I should laugh.'

'No, you wouldn't,' he said sharply. '*You* wouldn't – at least, I hope not. I hope you don't know what you are saying – does the moon make you funny?'

'Don't be cross about Kôr; please don't, Arthur,' she said.

'I thought girls thought about people.'

'What, these days?' she said. 'Think about people? How can anyone think about people if they've got any heart? I don't know how other girls manage: I always think about Kôr.'

'Not about me?' he said. When she did not at once answer, he turned her hand over, in anguish, inside his grasp. 'Because I'm not there when you want me – is that my fault?'

'But to think about Kôr *is* to think about you and me.'

'In that dead place?'

'No, ours – we'd be alone there.'

Tightening his thumb on her palm while he thought this over, he looked behind them, around them, above them – even up at the sky. He said finally: 'But we're alone here.'

'That was why I said "Mysterious Kôr".'

'What, you mean we're there now, that here's there, that now's then? . . . *I* don't mind,' he added, letting out as a laugh the sigh he had been holding in for some time. 'You ought to know the place, and for all I could tell you we might be anywhere: I often do have it, this funny feeling, the first minute or two when I've come up out of the Underground. Well, well: join the Army and see the world.' He nodded towards the perspective of traffic lights and said, a shade craftily: 'What are those, then?'

Having caught the quickest possible breath, she replied: 'Inexhaustible gases; they bored through to them and lit them as they came up; by changing colour they show the changing of minutes; in Kôr there is no sort of other time.'

'You've got the moon, though: that can't help making months.'

'Oh, and the sun, of course; but those two could do what they liked; we should not have to calculate when they'd come or go.'

'We might not have to,' he said, 'but I bet I should.'

'I should not mind what you did, so long as you never said, "What next?"'

'I don't know about "next", but I do know what we'd do first.'

'What, Arthur?'

'Populate Kôr.'

She said: 'I suppose it would be all right if our children were to marry each other?'

But her voice faded out; she had been reminded that they were

28

homeless on this his first night of leave. They were, that was to say in London without any hope of any place of their own. Pepita shared a two-roomed flatlet with a girl friend, in a by-street off the Regent's Park Road, and towards this they must make their half-hearted way. Arthur was to have the sitting-room divan, usually occupied by Pepita, while she herself had half of her girl friend's bed. There was really no room for a third, and least of all for a man, in those small rooms packed with furniture and the two girls' belongings: Pepita tried to be grateful for her friend Callie's forbearance – but how could she be, when it had not occurred to Callie that she would do better to be away tonight? She was more slow-witted than narrow-minded – but Pepita felt she owed a kind of ruin to her. Callie, not yet known to be home later than ten, would be now waiting up, in her house-coat, to welcome Arthur. That would mean three-sided chat, drinking cocoa, then turning in: that would be that, and that would be all. That was London, this war – they were lucky to have a roof – London, full enough before the Americans came. Not a place: they would even grudge you sharing a grave – that was what even married couples complained. Whereas in Kôr...

In Kôr... Like glass, the illusion shattered: a car hummed like a hornet towards them, veered, showed its scarlet tail-light, streaked away up the road. A woman edged round a front door and along the area railings timidly called her cat; meanwhile a clock near, then another set further back in the dazzling distance, set about striking midnight. Pepita, feeling Arthur release her arm with an abruptness that was the inverse of passion, shivered; whereat he asked brusquely: 'Cold? Well, which way? – we'd better be getting on.'

Callie was no longer waiting up. Hours ago she had set out the three cups and saucers, the tins of cocoa and household milk and, on the gas-ring, brought the kettle to just short of the boil. She had turned open Arthur's bed, the living-room divan, in the neat inviting way she had learnt at home – then, with a modest impulse, replaced the cover. She had, as Pepita foresaw, been wearing her cretonne house-coat, the nearest thing to a hostess gown that she had; she had already brushed her hair for the night, rebraided it, bound the braids in a coronet round her head. Both lights and the wireless had been on, to make the room both look and sound gay: all alone, she had come to that peak moment at which company should arrive – but so seldom does. From then on she felt welcome beginning to wither in her, a flower of the heart that had bloomed too early. There she had sat like an image, facing the three cold cups, on the edge of the bed to be occupied by an unknown man.

Callie's innocence and her still unsought-out state had brought her to take a proprietary pride in Arthur; this was all the stronger, perhaps, because they had not yet met. Sharing the flat with Pepita, this last year, she had been content with reflecting the heat of love. It was not, surprisingly, that Pepita seemed very happy – there were times when she was palpably on the rack, and this was not what Callie could understand. 'Surely you owe it to Arthur,' she would then say, 'to keep cheerful? So long as you love each other –' Callie's calm brow glowed – one might say that it glowed in place of her friend's; she became the guardian of that ideality which for Pepita was constantly lost to view. It was true, with the sudden prospect of Arthur's leave, things had come nearer to earth: he became a proposition, and she would have been as glad if he could have slept somewhere else. Physically shy, a brotherless virgin, Callie shrank from sharing this flat with a young man. In this flat you could hear everything: what was once a three-windowed Victorian drawing-room had been partitioned, by very thin walls, into kitchenette, living room, Callie's bedroom. The living-room was in the centre; the two others opened off it. What was once the conservatory, half a flight down, was now converted into a draughty bathroom, shared with somebody else on the girls' floor. The flat, for these days, was cheap – even so, it was Callie, earning more than Pepita, who paid the greater part of the rent: it thus became up to her, more or less, to express good will as to Arthur's making a third. 'Why, it will be lovely to have him here,' Callie said. Pepita accepted the good will without much grace – but then, had she ever much grace to spare? – she was as restlessly secretive, as self-centred, as a little half-grown black cat. Next came a puzzling moment: Pepita semed to be hinting that Callie should fix herself up somewhere else. 'But where would I go?' Callie marvelled when this was at last borne in on her. 'You know what London's like now. And, anyway' – here she

laughed, but hers was a forehead that coloured as easily as it glowed –
'it wouldn't be proper, would it, me going off and leaving just you
and Arthur; I don't know what your mother would say to me. No,
we may be a little squashed but we'll make things ever so homey. I
shall not mind playing gooseberry, really, dear.'

But the hominess was by now evaporating, as Pepita and Arthur
still and still did not come. At half-past ten, in obedience to the rule
of the house, Callie was obliged to turn off the wireless, whereupon
silence out of the stepless street began seeping into the slighted room.
Callie recollected the fuel target and turned off her dear little table
lamp, gaily painted with spots to make it look like a toadstool,
thereby leaving only the hanging light. She laid her hand on the
kettle, to find it gone cold again and sighed for the wasted gas if not
for her wasted thought. Where are they? Cold crept up her out of
the kettle; she went to bed.

Callie's bed lay along the wall under the window: she did not like
sleeping so close up under glass, but the clearance that must be left
for the opening of door and cupboards made this the only possible
place. Now she got in and lay rigidly on the bed's inner side, under
the hanging hems of the window curtains, training her limbs not to
stray to what would be Pepita's half. This sharing of her bed with
another body would not be the least of her sacrifice to the lovers'
love; tonight would be the first night – or at least, since she was an
infant – that Callie had slept with anyone. Child of a sheltered middle-
class household, she had kept physical distances all her life. Already
repugnance and shyness ran through her limbs; she was preyed upon
by some more obscure trouble than the expectation that she might
not sleep. As to *that*, Pepita was restless; her tossings on the divan,
her broken-off exclamations and blurred pleas had been to be heard,
most nights, through the dividing wall.

Callie knew, as though from a vision, that Arthur would sleep
soundly, with assurance and majesty. Did they not all say, too, that
a soldier sleeps like a log? With awe she pictured, asleep, the face
that she had not yet, awake, seen – Arthur's man's eyelids, cheek-
bones and set mouth turned up to the darkened ceiling. Wanting to
savour darkness herself, Callie reached out and put off her bedside
lamp.

At once she knew that something was happening – outdoors, in the street, the whole of London, the world. An advance, an extraordinary movement was silently taking place; blue-white beams overflowed from it, silting, dropping round the edges of the muffling black-out curtains. When, starting up, she knocked a fold of the curtain, a beam like a mouse ran across her bed. A searchlight, the most powerful of all time, might have been turned full and steady upon her defended window; finding flaws in the black-out stuff, it made veins and stars. Once gained by this idea of pressure she could not lie down again; she sat tautly, drawn-up knees touching her breasts, and asked herself if there were anything she should do. She parted the curtains, opened them slowly wider, looked out – and was face to face with the moon.

Below the moon, the houses opposite her window blazed black in transparent shadow; and something – was it a coin or a ring? – glittered half-way across the chalk-white street. Light marched in past her face, and she turned to see where it went: out stood the curves and garlands of the great white marble Victorian mantelpiece of that lost drawing-room; out stood, in the photographs turned her way, the thoughts with which her parents had faced the camera, and the humble puzzlement of her two dogs at home. Of silver brocade, just faintly purpled with roses, became her house-coat hanging over the chair. And the moon did more: it exonerated and beautified the lateness of the lovers' return. No wonder, she said to herself, no wonder – if this was the world they walked in, if this was whom they were with. Having drunk in the white explanation, Callie lay down again. Her half of the bed was in shadow, but she allowed one hand to lie, blanched, in what would be Pepita's place. She lay and looked at the hand until it was no longer her own.

Callie woke to the sound of Pepita's key in the latch. But no voices? What had happened? Then she heard Arthur's step. She heard his unslung equipment dropped with a weary, dull sound, and the plonk of his tin hat on a wooden chair. 'Sssh-sssh!' Pepita exclaimed, 'She *might* be asleep!'

Then at last Arthur's voice: 'But I thought you said –'

'I'm not asleep; I'm just coming!' Callie called out with rapture, leaping out from her form in shadow into the moonlight, zipping on her enchanted house-coat over her night-dress, kicking her shoes on, and pinning in place, with a trembling firmness, her plaits in their coronet round her head. Between these movements of hers she heard not another sound. Had she only dreamed they were there? Her heart beat: she stepped through the living-room, shutting her door behind her.

Pepita and Arthur stood the other side of the table; they gave the impression of being lined up. Their faces, at different levels – for Pepita's rough, dark head came only an inch above Arthur's khaki shoulder – were alike in abstention from any kind of expression; as though, spiritually, they both still refused to be here. Their features looked faint, weathered – was this the work of the moon? Pepita said at once: 'I suppose we are very late?'

'I don't wonder,' Callie said, 'on this lovely night.'

Arthur had not raised his eyes; he was looking at the three cups. Pepita now suddenly jogged his elbow, saying, 'Arthur, wake up; say something; this is Callie – well, Callie, this is Arthur, of course.'

'Why, yes, of course this is Arthur,' returned Callie, whose candid eyes since she entered had not left Arthur's face. Perceiving that Arthur did not know what to do, she advanced round the table to shake hands with him. He looked up, she looked down, for the first time: she rather beheld than felt his red-brown grip on what still seemed her glove of moonlight. 'Welcome, Arthur,' she said. 'I'm so glad to meet you at last. I hope you will be comfortable in the flat.'

'It's been kind of you,' he said after consideration.

'Please do not feel that,' said Callie. 'This is Pepita's home, too, and we both hope – don't we, Pepita? – that you'll regard it as yours. Please feel free to do just as you like. I am sorry it is so small.'

'Oh, I don't know,' Arthur said, as though hypnotized; 'it seems a nice little place.'

Pepita, meanwhile, glowered and turned away.

Arthur continued to wonder, though he had once been told, how these two unalike girls had come to set up together – Pepita so small, except for her too-big head, compact of childish brusqueness and of unchildish passion, and Callie, so sedate, waxy and tall – an unlit candle. Yes, she was like one of those candles on sale outside a church; there could be something votive even in her demeanour. She was unconscious that her good manners, those of an old-fashioned country doctor's daughter, were putting the other two at a disadvantage. He found himself touched by the grave good faith with which Callie was wearing that tartish house-coat, above which her face kept the glaze of sleep; and, as she knelt to relight the gas ring under the kettle, he marked the strong, delicate arch of one bare foot, disappearing into the arty green shoe. Pepita was now too near him ever again to be seen as he now saw Callie – in a sense, he never *had* seen Pepita for the first time: she had not been, and still sometimes was not, his type. No, he had not thought of her twice; he had not remembered her until he began to remember her with passion. You might say he had not seen Pepita coming: their love had been a collision in the dark.

Callie, determined to get this over, knelt back and said: 'Would Arthur like to wash his hands?' When they had heard him stumble down the half-flight of stairs, she said to Pepita: 'Yes, I was glad you had the moon.'

'Why?' said Pepita. She added: 'There was too much of it.'

'You're tired. Arthur looks tired, too.'

'How would you know? He's used to marching about. But it's all this having no place to go.'

'But, Pepita, you – '

But at this point Arthur came back: from the door he noticed the wireless, and went direct to it. 'Nothing much on now, I suppose?' he doubtfully said.

'No; you see it's past midnight; we're off the air. And, anyway, in this house they don't like the wireless late. By the same token,' went on Callie, friendly smiling, 'I'm afraid I must ask you, Arthur, to take your boots off, unless, of course, you mean to stay sitting down. The people below us – '

Pepita flung off, saying something under her breath, but Arthur, remarking, 'No, I don't mind,' both sat down and began to take off his boots. Pausing, glancing to left and right at the divan's fresh cotton spread, he said: 'It's all right is it, for me to sit on this?'

'That's my bed,' said Pepita. 'You are to sleep in it.'

Callie then made the cocoa, after which they turned in. Prelimi-

nary trips to the bathroom having been worked out, Callie was first
to retire, shutting the door behind her so that Pepita and Arthur
might kiss each other good night. When Pepita joined her, it was
without knocking: Pepita stood still in the moon and began to tug
off her clothes. Glancing with hate at the bed, she asked: 'Which
side?'

'I expected you'd like the outside.'

'What are you standing about for?'

'I don't really know: as I'm inside I'd better get in first.'

'Then why not get in?'

When they had settled rigidly, side by side, Callie asked: 'Do you
think Arthur's got all he wants?'

Pepita jerked her head up. 'We can't sleep in all this moon.'

'Why, you don't believe the moon does things, actually?'

'Well, it couldn't hope to make some of us *much* more
screwy.'

Callie closed the curtains, then said: 'What do you mean? And –
didn't you hear? – I asked if Arthur's got all he wants.'

'That's what I meant – have you got a screw loose, really?'

'Pepita, I won't stay here if you're going to be like this.'

'In that case, you'd better go in with Arthur.'

'What about me?' Arthur loudly said through the wall. 'I can
hear practically all you girls are saying.'

They were both startled – rather than abashed. Arthur, alone in
there, had thrown off the ligatures of his social manner: his voice
held the whole authority of his sex – he was impatient, sleepy, and
he belonged to no one.

'Sorry,' the girls said in unison. Then Pepita laughed soundlessly,
making their bed shake, till to stop herself she bit the back of her
hand, and this movement made her elbow strike Callie's cheek.
'Sorry,' she had to whisper. No answer: Pepita fingered her elbow
and found, yes, it was quite true, it was wet. 'Look, shut up crying,
Callie: what have I done?'

Callie rolled right round, in order to press her forehead closely
under the window, into the curtains, against the wall. Her weeping
continued to be soundless: now and then, unable to reach her handkerchief, she staunched her eyes with a curtain, disturbing slivers of

moon. Pepita gave up marvelling, and soon slept: at least there is
something in being dog-tired.

A clock struck four as Callie woke up again – but something else
had made her open her swollen eyelids. Arthur, stumbling about on
his padded feet, could be heard next door attempting to make no
noise. Inevitably, he bumped the edge of the table. Callie sat up: by
her side Pepita lay like a mummy rolled half over, in forbidding,
tenacious sleep. Arthur groaned. Callie caught a breath, climbed
lightly over Pepita, felt for her torch on the mantelpiece, stopped to
listen again. Arthur groaned again: Callie, with movements soundless as they were certain, opened the door and slipped through to
the living-room. 'What's the matter?' she whispered. 'Are you ill?'

'No; I just got a cigarette. Did I wake you up?'

'But you groaned.'

'I'm sorry; I'd no idea.'

'But do you often?'

'I've no idea, really, I tell you,' Arthur repeated. The air of the
room was dense with his presence, overhung by tobacco. He must
be sitting on the edge of his bed, wrapped up in his overcoat – she
could smell the coat, and each time he pulled on the cigarette his
features appeared down there, in the fleeting, dull reddish glow.
'Where are you?' he said. 'Show a light.'

Her nervous touch on her torch, like a reflex to what he said,
made it flicker up for a second. 'I am just by the door; Pepita's
asleep; I'd better go back to bed.'

'Listen. Do you two get on each other's nerves?'

'Not till tonight,' said Callie, watching the uncertain swoop of
the cigarette as he reached across to the ash-tray on the edge of the
table. Shifting her bare feet patiently, she added: 'You don't see us
as we usually are.'

'She's a girl who shows things in funny ways – I expect she feels
bad at our putting you out like this – I know I do. But then we'd
got no choice, had we?'

'It is really I who am putting you out,' said Callie.

'Well, that can't be helped either, can it? You had the right to
stay in your own place. If there'd been more time, we might have
gone to the country, though I still don't see where we'd have gone

there. It's one harder when you're not married, unless you've got the money. Smoke?'

'No, thank you. Well, if you're all right, I'll go back to bed.'

'I'm glad she's asleep – funny the way she sleeps, isn't it? You can't help wondering where she is. You haven't got a boy, have you, just at present?'

'No. I've never had one.'

'I'm not sure in one way that you're not better off. I can see there's not so much in it for a girl these days. It makes me feel cruel the way I unsettle her: I don't know how much it's me myself or how much it's something the matter that I can't help. How are any of us to know how things could have been? They forget war's not just only war; it's years out of people's lives that they've never had before and won't have again. Do you think she's fanciful?'

'Who, Pepita?'

'It's enough to make her – tonight was the pay-off. We couldn't get near any movie or any place for sitting; you had to fight into the bars, and she hates the staring in bars, and with all that milling about, every street we went, they kept on knocking her even off my arm. So then we took the tube to that park down there, but the place was as bad as daylight, let alone it was cold. We hadn't the nerve – well, that's nothing to do with you.'

'I don't mind.'

'Or else you don't understand. So we began to play – we were off in Kôr.'

'Core of what?'

'Mysterious Kôr – ghost city.'

'Where?'

'You may ask. But I could have sworn she saw it, and from the way she saw it I saw it, too. A game's a game, but what's a hallucination? You begin by laughing, then it gets in you and you can't laugh it off. I tell you, I woke up just now not knowing where I'd been; and I had to get up and feel around this table before I even knew where I was. It wasn't till then that I thought of a cigarette. Now I see why she sleeps like that, if that's where she goes.'

'But she is just as often restless; I often hear her.'

'Then she doesn't always make it. Perhaps it takes me, in some way – Well, I can't see any harm: when two people have got no place, why not want Kôr, as a start? There are no restrictions on wanting, at any rate.'

'But, oh, Arthur, can't wanting want what's human?'

He yawned. 'To be human's to be at a dead loss.' Stopping yawning, he ground out his cigarette: the china tray skidded at the edge of the table. 'Bring that light here a moment – that is, will you? I think I've messed ash all over these sheets of hers.'

Callie advanced with the torch alight, but at arm's length: now and then her thumb made the beam wobble. She watched the lit-up inside of Arthur's hand as he brushed the sheet; and once he looked up to see her white-nightgowned figure curving above and away from him, behind the arc of light. 'What's that swinging?'

'One of my plaits of hair. Shall I open the window wider?'

'What, to let the smoke out? Go on. And how's your moon?'

'Mine?' Marvelling over this, as the first sign that Arthur remembered that she was Callie, she uncovered the window, pushed up the sash, then after a minute said: 'Not so strong.'

Indeed, the moon's power over London and the imagination had now declined. The siege of light had relaxed; the search was over; the street had a look of survival and no more. Whatever had glittered there, coin or ring, was now invisible or had gone. To Callie it seemed likely that there would never be such a moon again; and on the whole she felt this was for the best. Feeling air reach in like a tired arm round her body, she dropped the curtains against it and returned to her own room.

Back by her bed, she listened: Pepita's breathing still had the regular sound of sleep. At the other side of the wall the divan creaked as Arthur stretched himself out again. Having felt ahead of her lightly, to make sure her half was empty, Callie climbed over Pepita and got in. A certain amount of warmth had travelled between the sheets from Pepita's flank, and in this Callie extended her sword-cold body: she tried to compose her limbs; even they quivered after Arthur's words in the dark, words *to* the dark. The loss of her own mysterious expectation, of her love for love, was a small thing beside the war's total of unlived lives. Suddenly Pepita flung out one hand: its back knocked Callie lightly across the face.

Pepita had now turned over and lay with her face up. The hand that had struck Callie must have lain over the other, which grasped the pyjama collar. Her eyes, in the dark, might have been either shut or open, but nothing made her frown more or less steadily: it became certain, after another moment, that Pepita's act of justice had been unconscious. She still lay, as she had lain, in an avid dream, of which Arthur had been the source, of which Arthur was not the end. With him she looked this way, that way, down the wide void pure streets, between statues, pillars and shadows, through archways and colonnades. With him she went up the stairs down which nothing but moon came; with him trod the ermine dust of the endless halls, stood on terraces, mounted the extreme tower, looked down on statued squares, the wide, void, pure streets. He was the password, but not the answer: it was to Kôr's finality that she turned.

Deaths and Entrances

DYLAN THOMAS

On almost the incendiary eve
    Of several near deaths,
When one at the great least of your best loved
    And always known must leave
Lions and fires of his flying breath,
    Of your immortal friends
Who'd raise the organs of the counted dust
    To shoot and sing your praise,
One who called deepest down shall hold his peace
    That cannot sink or cease
    Endlessly to his wound
In many married London's estranging grief.

On almost the incendiary eve
    When at your lips and keys,
Locking, unlocking, the murdered strangers weave,
    One who is most unknown,
Your polestar neighbour, sun of another street,
    Will dive up to his tears.
He'll bathe his raining blood in the male sea
    Who strode for your own dead
And wind his globe out of your water thread
    And load the throats of shells
    With every cry since light
Flashed first across his thunderclapping eyes.

On almost the incendiary eve
    Of deaths and entrances,
When near and strange wounded on London's waves
    Have sought your single grave,
One enemy, of many, who knows well

Your heart is luminous
In the watched dark, quivering through locks and caves,
   Will pull the thunderbolts
To shut the sun, plunge, mount your darkened keys
   And sear just riders back,
   Until that one loved least
Looms the last Samson of your zodiac.

Ceremony After a Fire Raid

DYLAN THOMAS

I

MYSELVES
The grievers
Grieve
Among the street burned to tireless death
A child of a few hours
With its kneading mouth
Charred on the black breast of the grave
The mother dug, and its arms full of fires.

Begin
With singing
Sing
Darkness kindled back into beginning
When the caught tongue nodded blind,
A star was broken
Into the centuries of the child
Myselves grieve now, and miracles cannot atone.

Forgive
Us forgive
Us your death that myselves the believers
May hold it in a great flood
Till the blood shall spurt,
And the dust shall sing like a bird
As the grains blow, as your death grows, through our heart.

Crying
Your dying
Cry,
Child beyond cockcrow, by the fire-dwarfed

Street we chant the flying sea
In the body bereft.
Love is the last light spoken. Oh
Seed of sons in the loin of the black husk left.

II

I know not whether
Adam or Eve, the adorned holy bullock
Or the white ewe lamb
Or the chosen virgin
Laid in her snow
On the altar of London,
Was the first to die
In the cinder of the little skull,
O bride and bride groom
O Adam and Eve together
Lying in the lull
Under the sad breast of the head stone
White as the skeleton
Of the garden of Eden.

I know the legend
Of Adam and Eve is never for a second
Silent in my service
Over the dead infants
Over the one
Child who was priest and servants,
Word, singers, and tongue
In the cinder of the little skull,
Who was the serpent's
Night fall and the fruit like a sun,
Man and woman undone,
Beginning crumbled back to darkness
Bare as the nurseries
Of the garden of wilderness.

III

Into the organpipes and steeples
Of the luminous cathedrals,
Into the weathercocks' molten mouths
Rippling in twelve-winded circles,
Into the dead clock burning the hour
Over the urn of sabbaths
Over the whirling ditch of daybreak
Over the sun's hovel and the slum of fire
And the golden pavements laid in requiems,
Into the bread in a wheatfield of flames,
Into the wine burning like brandy,
The masses of the sea
The masses of the sea under
The masses of the infant-bearing sea
Erupt, fountain, and enter to utter for ever
Glory glory glory
The sundering ultimate kingdom of genesis' thunder.

A Refusal to Mourn the Death, by Fire, of a Child in London

DYLAN THOMAS

NEVER until the mankind making
Bird beast and flower
Fathering and all humbling darkness
Tells with silence the last light breaking
And the still hour
Is come of the sea tumbling in harness

And I must enter again the round
Zion of the water bead
And the synagogue of the ear of corn
Shall I let pray the shadow of a sound
Or sow my malt seed
In the least valley of sackcloth to mourn

The majesty and burning of the child's death.
I shall not murder
The mankind of her going with a grave truth
Nor blaspheme down the stations of the breath
With any further
Elegy of innocence and youth.

Deep with the first dead lies London's daughter,
Robed in the long friends,
The grains beyond age, the dark veins of her mother,
Secret by the unmourning water
Of the riding Thames.
After the first death, there is no other.

Among those Killed in the Dawn Raid was a Man aged a Hundred

DYLAN THOMAS

When the morning was waking over the war
He put on his clothes and stepped out and he died,
The locks yawned loose and a blast blew them wide,
He dropped where he loved on the burst pavement stone
And the funeral grains of the slaughtered floor.
Tell his street on its back he stopped a sun
And the craters of his eyes grew springshoots and fire
When all the keyes shot from the locks, and rang.
Dig no more for the chains of his grey-haired heart.
The heavenly ambulance drawn by a wound
Assembling waits for the spade's ring on the cage.
O keep his bones away from that common cart,
The morning is flying on the wings of his age
And a hundred storks perch on the sun's right hand.

1940

BRYHER

At midday on 28 September 1940 I reached H.D.'s apartment at 49 Lowndes Square, after a rough flight from Lisbon and a night at some seaside hotel. I have never discovered where the seaplane actually landed us although I think it may have been Poole. Hilda was out having lunch but she returned shortly after my arrival, less surprised to find me sitting on my suitcase than I was to be in London, and she remarked by way of greeting, 'Osbert told me you would be coming over with the invasion barges. Did you?' Everything, as she opened the door, seemed very strange.

I arrived in a belligerent frame of mind and I did not have 'a good war'. I had had to leave my home, my dogs, my library and many friends; it seemed unlikely that I should see them again. What use was it to me now that I had known the war to be inevitable? 'I warned you,' I kept repeating, 'why didn't you listen to me?' It made people angry and words could not bring back the things that I had lost. The five and a half years between my arrival in London and my return to Switzerland on 5 April 1946 was a time of almost complete frustration, endurable only because I shared it with friends.

By the time I got to England, most Londoners were living in a state of bewilderment and guilt. 'It's your own fault,' I hastened to assure them, 'you lost the Czech army in 1938 and the goodwill of the thousands who have since been liquidated and what did you do with the time you gained?' They were angry, they did not want to have their guilt confirmed (who does?) and they walked away murmuring their sacred slogan, 'If only the leaders could have got together round a conference table' without the least realization that international promises seldom hold unless backed by force. Just what use were words against a ruthless enemy magnificently equipped? 'Realize that human life does not matter to your antagonists,' I insisted, 'if you believe in freedom you must be prepared to defend it.' I was more than unpopular, I was considered to be treacherous, although I cannot imagine why it was treachery to point out the truth.

The Government had had almost eighteen months (if the period of the 'phony war' were taken into consideration) to prepare for battle but what had they done? They had neither imported foodstuffs in sufficient quantity, drawn up a proper and comprehensive rationing scheme such as we had in Switzerland nor pushed the construction of aircraft to the full. They had flung away much of the nation's foreign reserves in panic selling after the Fall of France. The measures that they were imposing about the time of my arrival were planned in haste, often wasteful and largely unfair.

I had lived for a year under the Swiss regulations. The authorities there had prepared their scheme scientifically and at leisure several years previously. Our blackout had been inspected before Munich, food control came into force on the outbreak of war and functioned perfectly. Quality was stressed rather than quantity and they had stockpiled immense reserves. It was said in England that we gave the children in England an adequate diet but that was propaganda. The ones I met were always hungry and their parents undernourished. Of course this is not the picture that was presented to the world but it comes from direct observation and was for me a depressing lesson; control the Press and other methods of influencing public opinion and a nation can be persuaded into believing whatever a government wishes. I often wonder today when I read about the rejection of order by the young if this is not due to memories inherited from parents who were adolescent during the war and suffered so much from austerity and restraint? 'Your rebellion goes back to the forties,' I think, as they stroll noisily down the streets in their dirty clothes, 'it does not belong to the sixties at all.'

The English had no clear picture of invasion. Unfortunately for myself, I had, and I was anxious about my friends. I was never so afraid during the raids as I had been on that day in Switzerland when we had been warned to be ready to resist the German army, no doubt because I had seen what had happened to people whom the Nazis had tortured. I begged my cousin Hilda (H.D.), who was an American by birth, to rejoin her relatives there. I knew the war would hit her harder than it would hit us, she was so sensitive to noise, so thin and tall that it was obvious she was already suffering from the lack of protein in our diet. 'Now?' she said, wrinkling up her Ionic nose (I have seen so many Greek statues that might have been portraits of her), 'Now? Of course not.'

So I walked across the park to the American Consulate in Grosvenor Square and handed back the immigration visa that had carried me across Portugal. 'Don't you want to use it?' they politely inquired.

'If I did, would you want me as a citizen?' A particularly loud burst of gunfire shook the room at that moment and we all laughed. I believed that invalids and elderly people ought to leave if they had the opportunity but I was less sure about the children unless there were special circumstances. It is difficult for the young to fit into a community later on when they have missed a national experience. I might have considered going to New York myself in sheer disgust at the Munich muddle but I was not going to desert my friends.

The next step was to find a job. I was a trained observer of European politics, I had various *tuyaux* abroad that could have been most useful I was told when it was too late, I spoke French and German fluently and had brought a recommendation from the consul at Montreux. I should like to think that my warnings had so irritated the Establishment that they would have nothing to do with me but I suspect my work had never been noticed and that it was merely my long residence in Europe that was against me. Once, and once only, in the middle of the war, I was offered a job in Australia! By that time, life was extremely difficult and I saw no reason why I should leave my friends, they were all I had, to spend an indefinite period in an unknown land and I refused it. So seeing that a deeper than usual knowledge of the Continent had become a blind alley and that help was needed at *Life and Letters To-day*, a monthly magazine devoted to literature and edited by my friend, Robert Herring, where all but two of the staff were now in the army, I went back to familiar work. I had previously collected material for the paper from different countries in Europe but now as the editorial side had never been my métier, I answered letters and did odd jobs.

Life was strange and familiar at the same time, yet in spite of the bombing I found the Second War so much easier to bear than the First. We were all 'in it' and there was not the dreadful gap between soldiers and civilians that had caused so much stress in 1914.

There were even a few links during the first month between Switzerland and England. The porter stopped me as I was going out, a couple of days after my arrival. 'They say you have come over from Montreux, madam, what's the town like now?'

I was a little surprised at his interest. Vaud seemed far away but it had always been a favourite place with tourists. 'Oh, it's much as usual except that the roads are empty. Only cars needed for essential work get petrol.'

'Has the market place changed?'

'No, they still sell vegetables there, they are not rationed.'

'It looked so beautiful. Of course, I only saw it upside down.'

I believe the correct expression is 'stunned with surprise' and I can think of no better words to express my feelings. 'Upside down?'

'I was an acrobat.' No poet ever spoke more proudly. 'We played all the towns along the coast.' He knew his lake, we always spoke of it locally as 'the coast'. He grasped my hand and shook it as it had never been shaken before, not even when I was young by my fencing master. It was as if some iron instrument of torture from the Middle Ages had gripped it. 'I'm English, of course, but I was born at Geneva in a tent.'

I have always been sorry that I did not stop to ask him more about his experiences but I was still bewildered by my journey and in a hurry to collect my identity card and ration book. Before I could find him again, he had gone to a more important job than guarding our doors. Yet I often wonder what happened to him when I walk now beside the market place on a summer day when they are putting up the side shows for some fête. The dusty ground looks so hard, the gables so dangerous, and how do the swans and the shouting, excited children appear to a man swinging head downwards from a rope? It is a corner of Montreux that has scarcely changed since I was ten. There are tall new buildings to the left and right of it but the steamer comes into the landing place, the stalls are crowded on a market day, and there are still roundabouts and pedlars at the summer fair.

The acrobat was not my only contact with home. I had to buy something at a neighbouring store after a night of particularly noisy raids and happened to mention that I had just got back to England. 'Montreux! You come from Montreux,' the assistant said, 'aren't you lucky? I went there on my honeymoon and last night when a bomb came down in the next street, I clutched Hubby and said, "If we've got to die, let's remember that balcony where we stood and looked at the lake with all the stars shining above our heads."'

Switzerland was a bright ribbon across their otherwise drab lives, and these strangers were full of sympathy. It was otherwise with my friends; for some reason that I do not understand even today, they would not allow me to speak about my home. Osbert Sitwell apart, they did not even want to know how I had reached London although it had been rather more than an adventurous journey. I did not want commiseration but the barrier puzzled me. I had spent five summers in the Alps as a child and I had lived afterwards for eighteen years in Vaud. The day that we were threatened with invasion it became a part of me. I have three countries, England, Switzerland and America and I am proud of them all. I had come to London simply because at a time of adversity and danger, I wanted to be with my friends.

I remembered a bit of advice from the First World War. Never register all the members of a household at the same shop. One part of Lowndes Square was in Westminster but our side was in Chelsea so as soon as I got my ration book I took it not to Hilda's grocer but to a large neighbouring store. It was there that I met Susy, a few days after my arrival. She was standing behind the bread counter with tears literally streaming down her cheeks. There had not been any raid the previous night or news of any battle but I muttered a word of sympathy. 'Oh, madam, it's this wartime bread, mee plate stuck in it and it broke.'

'Dear me, how very unfortunate.'

'Yes, madam, it means a day's pay getting the fitting and the new set will cost me more than my Christmas bonus. You see, madam, us business girls have got to have our teeth.'

The bread, though unrationed, was appalling. Again I wished (oh, how often I was to wish) that the Swiss could have organized our food system. Our loaves in Vaud had been limited in quantity but excellent. Help was essential for Susy so, cursing the Establishment, I hurriedly pressed on her a little financial aid. I got a dazzling smile from her a few days later and we were firm friends until she died, shortly after the war. She would probably have lived to a good age if it had not been for its hardships.

Susy was my first new friend but I had soon had others, in 'veg', in 'groceries' and 'pots and pans'. I knew how they had to get up at five thirty of a cold winter morning to make their beds and get a cup of tea before hurrying to a windy corner to get one of the crowded, infrequent buses to their work. I heard what they did on Sundays (mostly they slept), their scruples about their rose bushes, ought they to scrap them and plant lettuces instead, where they would go the next Bank Holiday afternoon. All they asked in return was a comfort I could not give them, some assurance that this time it would not be a 'long war'. Occasionally I could find them an oddment for which they had no time to search. Once one of them pressed a tiny packet of custard powder into my hand. 'She offered me five shillings for it' ('she' was a woman disappearing into the next department) 'but I kept it for you, dear, you really care about my aunt's rheumatic knee.' And it was true. I cared, profoundly cared about a poor old woman hit by this second war through the stupidity of our politicians and thus deprived of the legitimate small comforts due to her age. I was not myself a custard addict but it was an accolade.

My great friends, however, lived in the neighbouring street. Hilda had discovered the 'Warming Pan' some years earlier and usually went there for lunch. Up to 1941, its owners, Selina and Angelina, supplied their clients with soup, meat, two veg and dessert for two shillings and ninepence. They were country people, they bought all the ingredients they could directly from farms and the cooking was plain but excellent. Such places are now extinct. I liked it because, as I said, I could go there without fear. There was a large notice, 'Dogs Welcome', hanging on the door and as I am to those, but only those, who know me intimately, Fido, I felt at ease and knew that I should not be hustled out to eat from my bowl somewhere under the stairs. Up to the time that the restaurant was badly damaged by a bomb, Selina saw that our food was as honest as possible and not composed completely from powders.

My dear, dear Selina. She was a symbol to me of the essential soul of England. She did not encourage casual conversation when we went up to her desk to pay our bills but if I were careful, I could manage to exchange a few words with her. She and her partner had built their business up from scratch and now, just as they were beginning to pay off the debts that had always been a nightmare to them, most of their customers had gone into the country or joined the Women's Services. It is always the middle groups that suffer most in war and the Victorian doctrine that hard work is its own reward flops at once in a time of national disaster.

The raids were heavy throughout October. I went out gloomily one morning with my basket to get our rations and saw a huge crater at the end of Basil Street. Somebody had fetched a large plaster bulldog, I assume from Harrods because they were then on sale there, and stuck it on guard beside the biggest pile of rubble. At that moment *Beowulf*, my war novel, was conceived.

Many years later I tried to get one of the small plaster dogs to serve as a model for the book's jacket. The assistant, a look of horror on his face, assured me that they had never stocked anything so vulgar. 'There wouldn't be any demand for it,' he said, 'I've never been asked for one.'

'Of course not,' I could not resist replying, 'it was merely a national emblem.'

Knowing the circumstances, I could forgive the man his shock but those plaster bulldogs were standing proudly about the streets in 1940. I saw another one in the Edgware Road.

Hilda had taken a small apartment in Lowndes Square some years previously at an annual rent of two hundred and fifty pounds. It is a measure of the present depreciation of money that when I last heard about it some years ago, it was said to be six hundred a year and there was a rumour subsequently that even this had been increased. She had a bedroom, a sitting room with a clear view across to Basil Street because the big block that now occupies what was then a vacant site was not built till after the war, a tiny bathroom, an equally small kitchen and a spare bedroom that she gave over to me. In addition, she had the use of a room for storage purposes in the basement. We slept there for a few nights at the beginning of the Blitz but soon gave it up because, as Hilda sensibly remarked, 'If we are going to be killed, let us be comfortable up to the last moment.'

There was no room for a table in my room but there was a broad window ledge that I could use as a desk during the day; only at night because of the blackout, I had to sit on my bed and balance the typewriter on my knees. It got rather noisy one October evening but I had started on notes for *Beowulf* when there was a thundering knock and the superintendent burst in (he had a master key) with what appeared to be a revolver sticking out of his pocket. The blackout was in order, the curtains were drawn, there was not a crack of light showing anywhere. 'That noise,' he looked at me accusingly, 'that cracking noise?'

'Is it the new weapon?' They had been warning us that the Germans were preparing a surprise and I had been discussing what it could be over supper with Hilda that evening.

'No, it was in here.' He looked round and noticed my machine.

'You were *typing*.'

I nodded.

'Never do that again in a raid. I thought you were signalling.' He slammed the door as he left and I reflected dismally that the way of the artist is hard in war. It is not difficult to write during a Blitz, there is nothing else to do, but merely uncomfortable.

The English refused to publish *Beowulf*. They do not want to remember. It was a documentary, not a novel, but an almost literal description of what I saw and heard during my first six months in London. It sold steadily if not brilliantly after the war in America. I loved my characters, especially Rashleigh, Ruby and Selina. Of course, I altered a few details of their lives but it was otherwise as authentic a record as I could make it.

I never actually met Rashleigh (that was not his real name) but we had corresponded for years and as he earned his living painting miniatures on ivory of the *Victory*, what else could I call him but Horatio? He knew his boats. 'I went in my youth to Australia in a sailing ship and learned all about square-rigged vessels.' His wife, to whom he had been devoted, had recently died as well as a cousin, 'now, alas, no more, save his delightful memory', his daughters were away nursing, his savings had practically disappeared. It would be hard to say which frightened him most, the war or modern painting. Yet I could feel from his letters a complete dedication to art although due to early influences or perhaps the lack of funds to study either in London or abroad he had never progressed beyond neat landscapes seen through Victorian eyes or studies of red sails and coasters in a storm. People complained that he was a conventional figure when they read *Beowulf*. He was, but I did not invent him, I knew him. If we had met, I should have shocked him profoundly. Yet the only law in art is never to despise the seeker and I wrote to him regularly to inquire what was happening to the seascape he was painting and how he was managing on his rations? I like to think that my letters helped him a little till he caught a chill in an air-raid shelter during some heavy raids on the South Coast. The illness turned to pneumonia and, mercifully, he died.

I, also, have laughed at such people and I have always wanted 'the art after tomorrow' but fate gives all of us a different apprenticeship to serve and at the end it is the use we make of it that matters, not our successes.

'London can take it' was not a slogan, it was a statement of fact. The bombing that October seemed continuous. Some people pretended that it was not happening at all, others endured hours of uncomfortable travel daily in order to spend the night in the supposedly safer countryside. The majority of us, however, 'got on with it'. People were not robots, they were afraid, but they expressed their feelings obliquely if at all. Still, I shall never forget a neighbour I met in the hall, he was evidently on his way to some function since he was carrying a grey top hat that I had not seen since Edwardian times. 'I do hope we are not going to be disturbed by the guns all evening,' he remarked as we braced ourselves against the wall when an explosion shook the neighbouring street. I bowed as politely as circumstances permitted and murmured 'Yes,' knowing that he must be under a great emotional strain to have spoken to me. We had never been properly introduced.

The traditions held, if perhaps for the last time. A day or so later, I went into a grocer's shop in search of some small, as yet unrationed article. The alert had sounded but I had not bothered about it. Suddenly the floor heaved up, the assistant and I rolled to the ground as inextricably intertangled as a brace of lobsters, while the dust of ages enveloped us from the ceiling. 'And the next thing, madam?' the grocer inquired as, shaking ourselves, we rose to our feet.

Some scenes defy words and one of these was the Underground. A few days after reaching London I went to visit friends at Edgware and coming back about six, saw one of the strangest spectacles that London can have witnessed during its long history, the camps along the platforms of the Tube stations. Not all things in wartime were bad. One of the taboos that the Blitz was breaking down was that it was wrong to speak to strangers. It is a mistake to suppose that it is the upper groups in a community that are aloof. I have always found that the top and the bottom of the ladder talk freely. The 'professionally lonely' come from the lower middles who consider it to be a status necessity 'to keep themselves to themselves'. Many of these barriers broke with the raids. Cook, secretary, shopkeeper and workman sat on their rugs and sleeping bags, carefully arranged above a layer of old newspapers (I was assured that *The Times* was the thickest and most comfortable) leaving a few inches free here and there so that passengers alighting from the trains could struggle to the dangerous upper levels while they themselves smoked, drank tea, munched sandwiches and told each other stories. They were having, a number assured me, 'the time of their lives'. It was said that one lady slept under an eiderdown covered with blue silk but I did not actually see this myself. There were bundles of valuables that served as pillows, the occasional clock, much passing round of cigarettes. It combined the slight trepidation of a mixed group of holiday adventurers about to start on their first climb and the pseudo-resignation of the parlour maid, waiting for a chance to contradict the cook. Old men in second-hand clothes were in one ring, ladies saving their best furs in the more favoured positions nearer the wall where there was less dust. A few people could not stand the noise and returned to their own beds but these shelters must have fulfilled a need beyond that of safety (was it perhaps for adventure?) because a couple of years later at almost the quietest moment of London's war, there were bunks lined with gay, chintz curtains the length of the platforms and officials spoke with pride about the 'loyal few' who still spent their nights beside the clanging trains. In 1940, the scene was unforgettable. It was a science fiction novel in action although at the time I did not recognize it, not having then discovered the genre.

I sometimes wonder whether I should have survived the war if it had not been for Osbert's friendship and Edith's love. Sacheverell Sitwell was serving in the navy and for that reason I met him only much later. They had invited Robert Herring to stay with them in Derbyshire until he could find fresh quarters as both his house in Chelsea and the office of *Life and Letters To-day* had been badly damaged by bombs. Soon after my arrival I was asked to spend the following weekend with them.

I felt really stupefied with astonishment when I found I could buy a ticket and board a train without producing my passport or stating the purpose of my journey. People were talking calmly to each other about the bombing when I sat down in the railway carriage but I could not help thinking how little they knew about war. They had not seen the French soldiers with the soles looped to their boots by bits of string nor waited in desperate fear at a frontier post. I could forgive the 'little people' for not under-standing the real motives behind Munich but not these middle-aged men, chattering over their newspapers in apparent surprise. They ought to have known better. They had let things slide, murmuring, 'Oh, it will settle itself somehow, there's too much at stake for the Germans really to go to war.' Hoping for the best and doing nothing to achieve it is possibly the deadliest sin there is. How many millions died in Europe because the supposedly solid citizens of a dozen countries thought only of their village interests and never of the world?

The damp, October landscape I watched from the window took me right back to childhood. I saw myself, as if I were still there, sitting on a hassock in the nursery with a picture book on my knees. Two children on rough, brown ponies were galloping across a field of just the same green grass, with a few bramble hedges and a few red leaves at the side which we were passing now in the train. For a second, I wondered why I should recall so vividly a moment that had happened to me forty years earlier? Yet it was the far past that was a poster-coloured reality, the present was a fog. I was only going to be away for two nights yet I already felt the shame that many of us noticed if we were outside London during the raids.

I missed a taxi at the station that Osbert had sent to meet me because it had not occurred to me that taxis were still available. I walked up to Renishaw wondering where it was and what it was like. To say that I was amazed when I saw it would be an understatement. I had only thought about Osbert and Edith as fellow writers, we had never talked about homes. It was true that I had seen some of Osbert's treasures in his house in Chelsea when I had lunched with him there before the war but all I knew about Derbyshire was the address. The range of windows reminded me of those old Italian palaces that are a town in themselves and the formal garden was still a blaze of summer flowers. It was the first and last time that I saw it in its glory because by my next visit the beds were full of cabbages. The butler seemed a little startled that I was carrying my suitcase when he opened the door.

The dining room was full; besides visitors who were staying at Renishaw, people had come over from Sheffield, the nearest big town. I had expected to sit beside Robert Herring because although we had telephoned I had not seen him since landing. Instead I was put next to Charles Morgan and realized afterwards that it was yet another of Osbert's thoughtful acts. Morgan had many friends in France and was desperate for news. It was a relief to be questioned by somebody who knew the Continent and had also prophesied war from early in the thirties. I was also glad to be able to talk about the problems of friends without meeting the resentment that so many had shown me in London. They said I had dodged their tribulations by remaining in Vaud for a year.

Sometimes one meets a person casually and recognizes a relationship due to a mutual admiration for some particular period or place. Neither of us could help our friends, we did not even know where they were. Had they left Paris, were they trapped in some corner of a remote province or already in prison? The deserted roads, the abandoned cars still lying in the ditches that I had seen during my journey, had almost annihilated hope. Almost, not quite; after a drive of sixteen hours during which time we had hardly seen one peasant in the fields, the coach in which we were travelling had drawn up in darkness in front of a little hotel somewhere in a city. I asked the name of the town and they answered 'Cette'. So I had Valéry's name and the memory of his poems to sustain me during the last night I was to spend on French soil for seven years.

I cannot remember our conversation word for word but Charles Morgan was even more pessimistic than I was about the length of the war and its effect upon civilization. We both knew how much had already been destroyed. I kept thinking of Sylvia Beach and Adrienne Monnier in Paris until it was almost as if they were waiting in another room. Europe, we agreed, if it emerged would be a different world. The young would not know what they had lost, the old would be too exhausted to care. A great civilization had been swept away in less than a fortnight and, as I was to observe later, little was salvaged. Paris in the fifties was never the Paris of even the thirties.

We started sentences to encourage each other, they broke off in the middle, we had no facts. All we could do was to sit side by side, a couple of shipwrecked sailors, still dazed by our own rescue and drawn together by a common anxiety about our friends. We never met again.

It was during this visit to Renishaw that my friendship with Edith began. I had met her a few times, always in the midst of a crowded tea party, in the apartment where she had lived for a time in Bayswater. Now, and Edith herself could not have realized how much it meant to me, once the visitors had left she read me poems, sitting outside on the terrace in the pale, October sunshine. It was indescribably peaceful to sit listening to the poems with the sweep of the garden in front of us and the feeling that beyond the poetry there could be something indestructible in the mind. Even now, more than twenty years after the so-called peace, Renishaw is a circlet of golden moments uncovered from a temple's dust.

My own past caught me up. I walked across the edge of a forlorn Hyde Park full of guns and searchlights, to seek consolation in a bookshop. There, turning over the pages of a just-published volume, Koestler's *Scum of the Earth*, I saw the name Walter Benjamin and read of his death on the Spanish frontier. I had believed him to be safe.

The previous April, Sylvia and Adrienne had taken me to meet him at a café near the rue de l'Odéon. He had seemed so much a part of Paris, of that blue, smoky atmosphere where everyone was sipping bitter coffee and arguing about metaphysics. The scholar is truly afraid that action, even if it is harmless, may disturb his contemplation and Adrienne had begun a dialogue with him that evening that had carried them on a chase of some philosophical comet where neither Sylvia nor I could follow them. An artist thinks in a different way, linking present impression to past experience. Suddenly Benjamin had asked us if we thought that he could live in New York? What could we say? Other than Paris, there were few places where he would have felt at home.

I tried to temporize, always a form of cowardice, but after we left, Adrienne asked me whether as Benjamin had received an American visa, he ought to leave at once? As regards my own refugees, I had always told them to go if possible the day they received their papers. This time I trusted to emotion rather than reason and agreed with her she should wait before urging him to leave, to see how things turned out. What would he do, we wondered, in a small bedroom in windswept New York where there were no cafés at that time and few friends? I had heard while still in Switzerland that he had got away from Paris in time, we had tried to send him funds for the further journey to Lisbon but it is possible they never reached him; we supposed that he had landed safely in America. Now I read in a bookshop the bare fact of his death. There was an air raid in progress, guns were thundering in the distance but all I could feel was how lucky we were to be part of a nation fighting back with every weapon it possessed. Yet what did my fellow citizens know of the terror of being chased and tortured for supposed crimes of which the victims had never even heard? Why did the religious institutions of Europe fail to denounce the Nazis early in the thirties? Some clergymen, in particular from some Protestant sects and above all, the Quakers, were heroic in their efforts to rescue the victims but in general the established churches looked the other way. A condemnation by them might have saved thousands of lives and would have given a lead to citizens to accept more refugees into their homes.

The full story of Benjamin's death reached us only after the war.

London grew greyer and dingier. We wondered if the dust could have come from the Great Fire in 1666. Yet I can truthfully say that I was not afraid during the first raids. I had been inoculated against what I called 'this simple terror' by my experience abroad. Yet I had been unable to make the English understand. Whenever I had told them what was happening in Europe, all they replied was, 'Very sad, dear, but if I were you, I would not get mixed up in these foreign disputes.' Now they were getting their answer. In bombs. I myself declared war on the Establishment. Had they not brought us to this sorry pass because unlike the 'Old Contemptibles' they had been afraid of Germany? Around me the deluded but by now awakened populace was amazingly, fantastically heroic. 'We shall never see the Nazis marching through London,' my neighbours declared in the queue although apart from a few Spitfires, I could see nothing myself to prevent them, and these same Spitfires, I was told, had only been developed at the beginning through private enterprise and not with Government aid. I had warned people since 1932, nobody had listened to me so I decided that my moral duty was to grumble. I was reasonably cheerful if uncertain whether we could survive the winter, invasion seemed probable and we did not even have enough weapons to arm the Home Guard. 'By Pike and Mace, or With Bulldog to Victory,' I wrote to a friend in America; 'my chief preoccupation is, if we are to act as powder monkeys in the Blitz, must we wear pigtails? As for myself, it is sheer stupidity to go on breathing and I heard that slogan about "Building a Better Britain" in 1918. Oh, if dinosaurs had been fluid and more adaptable, there need never have been a human race.'

Still Falls the Rain

(The Raids, 1940. Night and Dawn)

EDITH SITWELL

Still falls the Rain –
Dark as the world of man, black as our loss –
Blind as the nineteen hundred and forty nails
Upon the Cross.

Still falls the Rain
With a sound like the pulse of the heart that is changed to the hammer
  beat,
In the Potter's Field, and the sound of the impious feet

On the Tomb:
Still falls the Rain
In the Field of Blood where the small hopes breed and in the human
  brain
Nurtures its greed, that worm with the brow of Cain.

Still falls the Rain –
At the feet of the Starved Man hung upon the Cross.
Christ that each day, each night, nails there, have mercy on us –
On Dives and on Lazarus:
Under the Rain the sore and the gold are as one.

Still falls the Rain –
Still falls the Blood from the Starved Man's wounded Side:
He bears in His Heart all wounds, – those of the light that died,
The last faint spark
In the self-murdered heart, the wounds of the sad uncomprehending
  dark,

The wounds of the baited bear –
The blind and weeping bear whom the keepers beat
On his helpless flesh ... the tears of the hunted hare.

Still falls the Rain –
Then – O Ile leape up to my God: who pulles me doune –
See, see where Christ's blood streames in the firmament:
It flows from the Brow we nailed upon the tree
Deep to the dying, to the thirsting heart
That holds the fires of the world, – dark-smirched with pain
As Caesar's laurel crown.

Then sounds the voice of One who like the heart of man
Was once a child who among beasts has lain –
'Still do I love, still shed my innocent light, my Blood, for thee.'

The Wall

WILLIAM SANSOM

IT was our third job that night.

Until this thing happened, work had been without incident. There had been shrapnel, a few inquiring bombs, and some huge fires; but these were unremarkable and have since merged without identity into the neutral maze of fire and noise and water and night, without date and without hour, with neither time nor form, that lowers mistily at the back of my mind as a picture of the air-raid season.

I suppose we were worn down and shivering. Three a.m. is a meanspirited hour. I suppose we were drenched, with the cold hose-water trickling in at our collars and settling down at the tails of our shirts. Without doubt the heavy brass couplings felt moulded from metal-ice. Probably the open roar of the pumps drowned the petulant buzz of the raiders above, and certainly the ubiquitous fire-glow made an orange stage-set of the streets. Black water would have puddled the City alleys and I suppose our hands and our faces were black as the water. Black with hacking about among the burnt-up rafters. These things were an every-night nonentity. They happened and they were not forgotten because they were never even remembered.

But I do remember it was our third job. And there we were – Len, Lofty, Verno and myself, playing a fifty-foot jet up the face of a tall city warehouse and thinking of nothing at all. You don't think of anything after the first few hours. You just watch the white pole of water lose itself in the fire and you think of nothing. Sometimes you move the jet over to another window. Sometimes the orange dims to black – but you only ease your grip on the ice-cold nozzle and continue pouring careless gallons through the window. You know the fire will fester for hours yet. However, that night the blank indefinite hours of waiting were sharply interrupted – by an unusual sound. Very suddenly a long rattling crack of bursting brick and mortar perforated the moment. And then the upper half of that five-storey building heaved over towards us. It hung there, poised for a timeless second before rumbling down at us. I was thinking of nothing at all and then I was thinking of everything in the world.

In that simple second my brain digested every detail of the scene. New eyes opened at the sides of my head so that, from within, I photographed a hemispherical panorama bounded by the huge length of the building in front of me and the narrow lane on either side.

Blocking us on the left was the squat trailer pump, roaring and quivering with effort. Water throbbed from its overflow valves and from leakages in the hose and couplings. A ceaseless stream spewed down its grey sides into the gutter. But nevertheless a fat iron exhaust-pipe glowed red-hot in the middle of the wet engine. I had to look past Lofty's face. Lofty was staring at the controls, hands tucked into his armpits for warmth. Lofty was thinking of nothing. He had a black diamond of soot over one eye, like the White-Eyed Kaffir in negative.

To the other side of me was a free run up the alley. Overhead swung a sign – 'Catto and Henley'. I wondered what in hell they sold. Old stamps? The alley was quite free. A couple of lengths of dead, deflated hose wound over the darkly glistening pavement. Charred flotsam dammed up one of the gutters. A needle of water fountained from a hole in the live hose-length. Beneath a blue shelter-light lay a shattered coping stone. The next shop along was a tobacconist's, windowless, with fake display cartons torn open for anybody to see. The alley was quite free.

Behind me, Len and Verno shared the weight of the hose. They heaved up against the strong backward drag of the water pressure. All I had to do was yell 'Drop it' – and then run. We could risk the live hose snaking up at us. We could run to the right down the free alley – Len, Verno and me. But I never moved. I never said 'Drop it' or anything else. That long second held me hypnotized, rubber boots cemented to the pavement. Ton upon ton of red-hot brick hovering in the air above us numbed all initiative. I could only think. I couldn't move.

Six yards in front stood the blazing building. A minute before I would never have distinguished it from any other drab Victorian atrocity happily on fire. Now I was immediately certain of every minute detail. The building was five storeys high. The top four storeys were fiercely alight. The rooms inside were alive with red fire. The black outside walls remained untouched. And thus, like the lighted carriages of a night express, there appeared alternating rectangles of black and red that emphasized vividly the extreme symmetry of the window spacing: each oblong window-shape posed a vermilion panel set in perfect order upon the dark face of the wall. There were ten windows to each floor, making forty windows in all. In rigid rows of ten, one row placed precisely above the other, with strong contrasts of black and red, the blazing windows stood to attention in strict formation. The oblong building, the oblong windows, the oblong spacing. Orange-red colour seemed to *bulge* from the black frame-work, assumed tactile values, like boiling jelly that expanded inside a thick black squared grill.

Three of the storeys, thirty blazing windows and their huge frame of black brick, a hundred solid tons of hard, deep Victorian wall, pivoted over towards us and hung flatly over the alley. Whether the descending wall actually paused in its fall I can never know. Probably it never did. Probably it only seemed to hang there. Probably my eyes only digested its action at an early period of momentum, so that I saw it 'off true' but before it had gathered speed.

The night grew darker as the great mass hung over us. Through smoke-fogged fireglow the moonlight had hitherto penetrated to the pit of our alley through declivities in the skyline. Now some of the moonlight was being shut out as the wall hung ever further over us. The wall shaded the moonlight like an inverted awning. Now the pathway of light above had been squeezed to a thin line. That was the only silver lining I ever believed in. It shone out – a ray of hope. But it was a declining hope, for although at this time the entire hemispherical scene appeared static, an imminence of movement could be sensed throughout – presumably because the scene was actually moving. Even the speed of the shutter which closed the photograph on my mind was powerless to exclude this motion from my deeper consicousness. The picture appeared static to the limited surface sense, the eyes and the material brain, but beyond that there was hidden movement.

The second was timeless. I had leisure to remark many things. For instance, that an iron derrick, slightly to the left, would not hit me. This derrick stuck out from the building and I could feel its sharpness and hardness as clearly as if I had run my body intimately over its contour. I had time to notice that it carried a foot-long hook, a chain with three-inch rings, two girder supports and a wheel more than twice as large as my head.

A wall will fall in many ways. It may sway over to one side or the other. It may crumble at the very beginning of its fall. It may remain intact and fall flat. This wall fell as flat as a pancake. It clung to its shape through ninety degrees to the horizontal. Then it detached itself from the pivot and slammed down on top of us.

The last resistance of bricks and mortar at the pivot point cracked off like automatic gun fire. The violent sound both deafened us and brought us to our senses. We dropped the hose and crouched. Afterwards Verno said that I knelt slowly on one knee with bowed head, like a man about to be knighted. Well, I got my knighting. There was an incredible noise – a thunderclap condensed into the space of an eardrum – and then the bricks and the mortar came tearing and burning into the flesh of my face.

Lofty, away by the pump, was killed. Len, Verno and myself they dug out. There was very little brick on top of us. We had been lucky. We had been framed by one of those symmetrical, oblong window spaces.

Building Alive

WILLIAM SANSOM

As on a fleet and smooth naval pinnace, intricate with grey cocks and rope and white-painted enumeration – we six on the Heavy Fire Unit drove swiftly through the quiet Sunday streets. Sometimes at odd corners or through a breach in the skyline of tall buildings the huge buff plume showed itself, calm and clean as sand against a pale bluish sky. We as well felt clean, in our blue flared tunics and silver buttons, too clean for what was coming, conscious of this and awkward at a time when smudged khaki and camouflage net were the equipment for action. The streets were too clean; there were no people, the people were all hidden away cooking their Sunday dinners; one church bell pealed ceaselessly to an empty town caught in the Sunday pause.

Then, gradually, the immaculate polish showed a ruffling, stray scraps of paper suggested the passing of a crowd, a weed of splintered glass sprung up here on the pavements, another and invisible weed seemed to be thrusting the window frames from their sockets and ahead, as this tangle grew denser, the street hung fogged with yellow dust.

Our destination lay within the dust. Once inside it was easy to see, only the outer air had painted it opaque. But it was like driving from the streets of a town into sudden country; nothing metropolitan remained to these torn pavements, to the earthen mortar dust and the shattered brick returning to the clay. The fly-bomb had blasted a pause within the pause of Sunday morning.

Ambulances already. Two or three people stood about, handkerchiefs to their red-splashed faces. In the silence a loud-speaker called for silence. The rich living voices appealed to the dead rubble, coaxing it to make tapping noises. And men with long detecting poles weaved to and fro through the mist like slow shrimpers. We were ordered round the debris to search the broken buildings on either side. At the top of the first flight of stairs, dark and rickety, a

light shone through a crack in the unhinged door. The door came
off easily. A single shadeless electric bulb hung over a tailor's table,
shone weakly and yellow against the large daylit window beyond.
On the table lay a pair of trousers, an iron, slivers of glass and
splashes of red blood, comet-shaped, like flickings from a pen. Every
lightly fixed furnishing of the room had shifted – bales of cloth,
doors, chairs, plaster mouldings, a tall cupboard – all these had
moved closer and now leant huddled at strange, intimate angles.
Plaster dust covered everything. There was no space left in the room,
there was nobody in the room. The blood led in wide round drops
to the door, the tailor must have been 'walking wounded'. Had he
been one of those outside, fingering blindly for the ambulance
doors? The yellow bulb on its single string burned on, the only
life in this lonely Sunday workroom, the only relic of the tailor's
shattered patience.

Then, under the steady burning of this bulb, against its silent
continuing effort, other sounds began to whisper. My number two,
Barnes, looked at me quickly – the building was alive. Our boots had
thudded on the stairs. Now for a moment, no more, they were quiet.
They were silent, the light was silent, but falsely – for beneath these
obvious silences other sounds, faint, intractable, began to be heard.
Creakings, a groan of wood, a light spatter of moving plaster, from
somewhere the trickle of water from a broken pipe. The whole house
rustled. A legion of invisible plaster mice seemed to be pattering up
and down the walls. Little, light sounds, but massing a portentous
strength. The house, suddenly stretched by blast, was settling itself.
It might settle down on to new and firm purchases, it might be
tacking itself further, slowly, slowly grinding apart before a sudden
collapse. I saw Barnes glance at the ceiling; he was thinking of the
four floors still hanging above us; he was thinking perhaps, as I
was, that the raid was still on and that any other explosion within
miles might rock through the earth and shake the whole lot down.
Walking in such houses, the walls and floors are forgotten; the
mind pictures only the vivid inner framework of beams and supports, where they might run and how, under stress, they might
behave; the house is perceived as a skeleton.

Then through the stripped window came further sounds – a

distant explosion from the south, and above this the purposeful drone of a second bomb flying louder every moment. The gallows that would mark its course! To each dreadful roof gallows along the bomb's course a black sock would rise to swing like a sentence rather than a warning of death. The sound approached like a straight line. It approached thus for many people ... everyone on the half-circle of its sound fanning forwards would attach the bomb to themselves. It could drop anywhere. It was absolutely reasonless. It was the first purely fatal agent that had come to man for centuries, bringing people to cross their fingers again, bringing a rebirth of superstition.

Down in the courtyard they were carrying a man out from the opposite block. We caught a glance of him through the twisted framework of an iron footbridge. They had laid him on a blanketed stretcher on the grey rubble. He lay still, bloodless, only his face showing, and that plastered with the same sick grey dust. It lay evenly on him, like a poisonous mask – he looked gassed with dust. Once he struggled, his head turned from side to side. He seemed to be trying to speak. It was as if his real face, clean and agonized, tried to be free and show its pain.

Now – in the long moment it takes these bombs to fly their swift distance – now the drone was already changing its note. The first remote aerial wavering, like a plane engine far up and away, had strengthened and bolted its direction upon our area. It was coming all right. We waited, though there was no time to wait, no real time but only the expansion of a moment so alert, and listened then for the drone to sharpen itself into a spluttering drum-beat of a jet-engine. But beneath this sound, separated from us by widths of sky, the little murmurs of secret life, fearful in their intimacy, could still be heard. And still fixed in a second's glance at the wounded man below, our eyes absorbed the whole courtyard, the waste of rubble between tall, torn office buildings. The iron bridge hung darkly between. Across it a new nest of broken pipes splayed up, a hydra head of snaky lead, but halted, paused like the rest of it. Only the oncoming sound moved deliberately, but this too was fixed, mounted on a straight, straight line that in its regular, unvarying crescendo provided only an emphasis to the stillness of the courtyard. A whole

architecture, all that had ever been built, all the laborious metropolitan history had been returned to its waste beginning. The virgin
scrap, the grey mortar earth, the courtyard wall torn and stripped
into the texture of ancient moon-burnt rock – all these paused,
taking breath. Only the little sounds sucking themselves in hinted
at a new life, the life of leaden snakes, hesitating and choosing in
whispers the way to blossom.

The drone was diving into a roar. We crouched down beneath the
window. My eyes now near the floor found themselves facing a gap
some three inches wide where the outer wall had loosened itself from
the floorboards. The wall was leaning outwards. I saw my hand
steady itself on a book of cloth patterns; the fingers were bleeding,
the hand removed itself instinctively from the cleanish cloth, cut
itself again on more glass on the floor. The bomb was above. We
held our breaths, not in all that sound daring to breathe for fear we
might miss the cut-out. It seemed much darker nearer the floor . . .
the floor grew as dark as childhood. Only the amazing crack in the
wall remained clear, gaping its draughty mouth. The noise grew
deafening, a noise now as heavy as the shadow of a wing. Then in
a burst of anger, it seemed to double up on itself, its splutter roared
double, it was diving, at four hundred miles an hour, without ever
cutting out, heading like all mad anger unrestrained on to the
fragile roofs. . . .

The wall, like a rubber wall in a Disney cartoon, sprang out at my
eyes, bulging round, then snapped back into its flat self. That happened, distinctly. Whether despite the crack it had actually expanded
into so round and resilient a curve, or whether the noise and the
windclap of the explosion jarred this round illusion within my own
round eyes – I do not know. But what happened . . . just as the
silence fell again, just as the glass rain spat again, just as an iron tank
went tumbling down outside, and – it seemed a long time after the
explosion, we were already up at the window – the wall of the
building opposite across the courtyard wobbled and then heaved its
concrete down on the wounded man and his rescuers below, burying
them finally. It seemed, even at that time, extra hard for the man on
the stretcher.

Swiftly the life of the house blossomed. The trickling from the pipes gushed free, cascading noisily into the courtyard. Tiles, plaster gutter fragments and more glass lurched off the roof. A new growth was sprouting everywhere, sprouting like the naked plumbing, as if these leaden entrails were the worm at the core of a birth, struggling to emerge, thrusting everything else aside. But the house held. It must have blossomed, opened, subsided upon itself. We raced down the stairs to the concrete mass below.

As we picked, hopelessly, at the great fragments, it was impossible to forget how hard it was on the man on the stretcher. It seemed, stupidly, that he alone had had no chance.

Daylight Alert

E. J. SCOVELL

When the daylight Alert has sounded, calling us
To what? not fear but application – we seem to have stepped across
A line in time, like a low wall that nettles guard,
Into a place marked off, an orchard or unkempt grave-yard.

The long gust sinks to peace, children who cried recover
Their joy; we stand in grass and look, the low wall is crossed over.
This is another realm where silence is so loud,
The sky shines so, the grass springs thicker, the fruits rush and thud.

Bombs have not fallen on our town; the shoppers scarcely
Lift eyes to the clear sky and fighters crossing straight and sparsely.
Our blood no more than smiles at this *memento mori*
As if it were a skull in flowers or a pale murder story.

Only our souls say in the stillness of their breath:
This is the hour that may be ours, the hour of pain and death.
What are we waiting for? What are we stretched to meet
Here in a walled and haunted plot set in our shopping street?

The hour shuts like a flower or dream when it is ended,
The far wall come upon too suddenly, the All Clear sounded.
It was not death but life we were called to entertain,
Waving to one who flashed so fast by in a royal train;

Called not to death but thought, still called to application,
Standing with empty eyes, dropped hands, at the small railway
station,
On the flowered country platform, we who have come so far
To honour one we never meet – wind, is he? falling star?

74

Days Drawing In

E. J. SCOVELL

The days fail: night broods over afternoon:
And at my child's first drink beyond the night
Her skin is silver in the early light.
Sweet the grey morning and the raiders gone.

A Map of Verona

HENRY REED

Quelle belle heure, quels bons bras me rendront ces régions d'où viennent mes sommeils et mes moindres mouvements?

Rimbaud

A MAP of Verona is open, the small strange city;
With its river running round and through, it is river-embraced,
And over this city for a whole long winter season,
Through streets on a map, my thoughts have hovered and paced.

Across the river there is a wandering suburb,
An unsolved smile on a now familiar mouth;
Some enchantments of earlier towns are about you:
Once I was drawn to Naples in the south.

Naples I know now, street and hovel and garden,
The look of the islands from the avenue,
Capri and Ischia, like approaching drum-beats –
My youthful Naples, how I remember you!

You were an early chapter, a practice in sorrow,
Your shadows fell. But were only a token of pain,
A sketch in tenderness, lust, and sudden parting,
And I shall not need to trouble with you again.

But I remember, once your map lay open,
As now Verona's, under the still lamp-light.
I thought, are these the streets to walk in in the mornings,
Are these the gardens to linger in at night?

And all was useless that I thought I learned:
Maps are out of place, not time, nor can they say

The surprising height and colour of a building,
Nor where the groups of people bar the way.

It is strange to remember those thoughts and try to catch
The underground whispers of music beneath the years,
The forgotten conjectures, the clouded, forgotten vision,
Which only in vanishing phrases reappears.

Again, it is strange to lead a conversation
Round to a name, to a cautious questioning
Of travellers, who talk of Juliet's tomb and fountains
And a shining smile of snowfall, late in Spring.

Their memories calm this winter of expectation,
Their talk restrains me, for I cannot flow
Like your impetuous river to embrace you;
Yet you are there, and one day I shall go.

The train will bring me perhaps in utter darkness
And drop me where you are blooming, unaware
That a stranger has entered your gates, and a new devotion
Is about to attend and haunt you everywhere.

The flutes are warm: in tomorrow's cave the music
Trembles and forms inside the musician's mind.
The lights begin, and the shifting crowds in the causeways
Are discerned through the dusk, and the rolling river behind.

And in what hour of beauty, in what good arms,
Shall I those regions and that city attain
From whence my dreams and slightest movements rise?
And what good Arms shall take them away again?

The Sky

The Sky Makes Me Hate It

WILLIAM CHAPPELL

I

How do you feel after sixteen months of Army life? I asked myself. Exactly how do you feel? Stop now, I said, before I could begin to answer. You were going to reply without thinking or considering. Why not? I said. I can reply without thinking and without considering; and I can give you three answers. All of them would be correct, though none of them would describe exactly how I feel. Today it is no longer possible to be exact about the way one feels.

I could say –

I feel much better, thank you,

or

I do not feel at all, thank you,

or

I feel quite differently, thank you very much.

Don't thank me, I said to myself. You are so ridiculous with words. You do not understand how to handle or present them; and you know, one does not really give question and answer in the mind. Particularly your mind, I said. Your consciousness is never consecutive. You have no real stream of thought; only a slow circular movement that changes form, and is sometimes globular, sometimes elliptical. It churns round and round; pauses and churns on. Through it, and across it, small flashing things move; passing so rapidly it is difficult to tell what shape they are.

Each one of your separate thoughts has nine hundred and ninety-nine little off-shoots, trailing inelegantly out of its small, fecund inside. One thousand births a second, each like a kitten that is drowned before it can open its staring blue eyes.

It is a miracle that you do not appear a kind of cretin to the world; making grunting sounds, lolling your head, and unable to read or spell.

Don't you quite often despair?

Yes, I said. Not so much, however, as I did during my first six months, and when I despair now it is in a different way. Of course, before the war, I did not know how to despair. My life being free, I did not have to think at all. These days I think all the time, and so deeply that I find I am paying no attention to what people are saying to me, though I can feel my face set in an expression of unreal interest as I continue to answer them. It is almost as though it were being done for me by a familiar spirit, so that I might lean back into the warm darkness of my head, and busy myself with the important work of tracking and listening to my thoughts. My mind is altering. Whether it is due to Army life, or whether my mental condition is a general one, a world war-mind, I cannot decide. When I first joined the army I could understand my vague, muddled way of thinking. Now, I cannot understand it at all. I might have undergone a very delicate operation, and been given an unused brain, in which to find my way about. I have to learn to know it and to discover how it functions.

I did not alter during my first few months in the army. I could not even change, as most of the recruits did, that is, by losing weight and looking healthier. My body has always been hard and strong, and I was sunburnt all over a deep golden brown. There was nothing to affect me adversely about my surroundings. I was stationed by the coast on the edge of a town where I had friends. It was summer and the weather was hot, and when it is hot I can be more or less contented anywhere. It was later, at the beginning of the winter, when I was moved to another unit, inland, that I became rather unhappy. It was an unhappiness I could cope with, as I could see all the reasons for it. I was unhappy because I was uncomfortable, and nearly always cold; and I disliked sleeping in one hut with twenty-eight other men; and the food was ugly and unappetizing, and I was tired all the time, and had to do mathematics, which I hated.

II

It was shortly after my arrival at the new station that I began, periodically, to undergo a peculiar new mental condition in which I would suddenly feel as though I were no longer myself. I might be drilling or sitting in the crowded Naafi with people talking all round me and the piano playing; or be on guard, alone in a steely night; or just walking by day through the camp; when abruptly, inside my clothes, my body would dissolve, and harden again to a thin glass centre. My glass bones, and my glass flesh, fragile and brittle, would creep away into a central thinness, avoiding all contact with the outer shell of my clothing. My heavy boots would crash like thunder as I moved. Out of my transparent head, I would look down, and see my boots advancing, neatly, one after the other, with the toes turned in a little; but the feet beneath the polished leather had no substance, and though I could still feel the blisters on my heels, I knew that the feet inside the boots were as unsubstantial as the mists that filled the hollows of the country, and made Japanese landscapes round the camp in the early winter mornings. These strange moments occurred frequently for about six or eight months, and then gradually ceased.

III

Later, I discovered that it made me strangely sad to look at the sky. During the weeks I had spent on the coast it had never affected me deeply, though it had always been a source of pleasure to my eyes. It was there, before me. Like a stage backcloth with pretty lighting effects, it hung behind the edge of the grey horizon.

When I joined my new unit I found the sky immensely important. It dominated the landscape completely, and seemed higher and vaster than I had ever known it. I realized it as an element, aloof, distant, limpid and unsoilable; and so far removed from this small dirty world, whirling like a pebble through space, with the small dirty people balanced on it, wrangling and gesticulating with infinitesimal gestures.

I can remember how I sometimes stood at the first parade, in the still bitter air of the winter dawn, waiting for the command to fall in, changing my rifle from hand to hand to avoid its chill touch that crept through my woollen gloves and froze my fingers. I can remember standing there, shifting my numb feet, and staring down at the floor of the parade ground shaded umber and indigo and thinly sheeted with ice. After a time my reluctant eye would lift its lid of flesh, letting the sight travel forward across the frosted grass, till it climbed the edges of the squat corrugated iron huts and mounted into the sky. There, like a seeing mouth, my eye would peer and nibble at the marbled clouds, seeking a life-vein of light, an artery that it might tear with its probing glance, to suck the gushing radiance from the new-risen sun. It hurt me to look, because I simultaneously desired and dreaded this bright food for my sight.

Now the marbled surface of the sky began to stir, and the night-drowsed men around me moved with it, breaking their muttering groups to re-form into orderly files. The sergeants shouted; a few rifle butts clattered, slipping through numb fingers, and the icy ground rang like iron.

Frozenly 'at ease' I stood, my greedy eyes fixed again on the sky, searching for the heart of the morning to stab it and gulp the life-light blood. The rosy marble cracked. Its patterns dissolved and changed, edges appeared, entrances to cool tunnels of space and beyond them, a piercing distance, now filled with light.

Break – marble paving! My heart cried out. Break! Floor of the gods. And release my sustenance. This glittering poison that I need and hate.

How high is the sky! How far! How delicate! My eyes and my heart exclaimed in thin, jangling whispers. The morning rose, bringing with it a wind that dragged the clouds apart, and as they sank into colourless wisps, drained of their rosy blood (a quota of it swallowed by my sight), a blinding radiance drowned my preying eyes. High up in the magic architecture of the heavens, a flock of starlings wheeled, competing noisily with a distant aeroplane for possession of the morning.

Oh, sweet denizens of space! Winged with speed! cried the heart. Let me into the skies. Better not to look upwards said the mind, dashed to despair by the glory above it. Drag down the feasting glance and bury it here, in this soiled and injured world that dims and swallows all exultation. I will look down and never up, for the sky makes me feel, and then I hate the earth I move on.

Nevertheless, and inevitably, the sky draws my gaze, and I cannot avoid it, for here it is spread in infinite arcs from horizon to horizon.

I can watch the storms gather and break, and take their way around the edge of the distance. The looming mulberry-coloured clouds, dragging behind them trains of rain, pass slowly by, avoiding the centre where I stand. Above my head, day and night, the sky spreads its ethereal canopy, shot with colour and stained with light, patterned with star and cloud, and burnt by the rising and setting of the sun. It points all my moods, lifts up my heart, and underlines my despair.

IV

Before the war, and during my first months in the army, my thoughts streamed from me in a jerky rhythm, outwards, into the world. Now they turn inwards, probing; and I feel in my brain that an endless transformation scene is taking place. A pantomime transformation in which curtains of membrane that are patterned with my life endlessly dissolve and part. My thoughts peck and knock at things which stir somewhere behind the furthest curtains. My mind knows that there is something more than it was aware of to be found behind itself. It claws and scratches gently at the walls of its dimly-lighted caves, sensing, more than seeing, a thin music of words it has never heard before. Suspecting, more than seeing, a suggestion of forms it cannot picture, they are so distant, remote, and unknown. Perhaps, lurking there, is the enormous comprehension that humanity needs; the lack of which makes so pitiful its efforts to manage itself. To tackle decently the handling of its relationships, its loves, lives and deaths.

This turning inwards of my thoughts cannot be happening only to me. I look avidly into the faces of the men who fill the camps and barracks in the district; the faces that crowd my sight in the streets of the town, in the pubs and restaurants and cinemas and on the buses; faces oafish, brutal, cunning, noble, sensitive and beautiful.

In the cathedral I see soldiers moving under the high arches, holding their caps in their hands, with faces solemn because they are in church. Their eyes rove, and their sight climbs from them, like birds, into the vaulted roof. They sit, too, in the back seats, beside the tall pillars, at Evensong. Sometimes praying or singing, or just resting their faces in their hands, staring quietly before them, their eyes sightless with thought, and I feel that in all their minds, whether they realize it or not, something is happening, as in mine.

No one can be genuinely happy at this time. War, as it welds the people of a nation together, makes every life an isolated life. Everyone is lonely. More lonely than they have ever been before in the life of the world. We have all become strangers; and when the war is over we shall have to start learning once more to know each other. The picture I hold, painted on my mind, of people, things and places is the pre-war picture. When I go on leave there is an air of strangeness about everything and everybody, and I cannot fully enjoy the companionship of my friends and my family, for our lives no longer mix. They run for a while parallel; thin, dusky-coloured streams with a narrow space between them. The mind cannot make the stupendous effort needed to bridge the gap; nor can it do anything to stop the running of the stream when it diverges from its place beside the others, and moves off quietly into a deserted country.

The life I lead in the army gives me nothing. My freedom is restricted, my privacy torn, my comfort abolished. New friendships are almost an impossibility, hardly can the first gestures be made before one or the other of the two people involved is moved away and a crowd of strange faces hem each one about. Army life lacks everything, particularly in a static unit. People do not realize it is worse for the spirit to be dreary than endangered; that boredom is more deadly than bombs.

Even in its fighting aspects, the army has none of the terrible beauty of the airman's flight to the stars and his battles in high space. None of the plunging splendour of the sailors' life in the vast steel ships that cut the spreading seas. And army death is sad: a heap of mutilated bodies, littering the scarred earth in ugly anonymity. Yet this life, that is not an individual's life, is making me more of an individual, driving my thoughts into deeper, rarer places than they have visited before. I wait for them to bring up to the surface of my consciousness the knowledge that my mind desires. Behind the self that goes about my army duties, I am occupied feverishly, searching to find this new mind that is forming somewhere within me.

I hate to think that war can do anything good for me, yet it has reached into me and made my thoughts, which were moving quietly in a known direction, turn on themselves and move another way, inwards this time, listening; and then down to my heart, whispering, at present so quietly that I cannot hear the words. It makes me restless and uncomfortable not to recognize the meaning, or the shape, of those words. I cannot tell if the other eyes I see hide the same turmoil that my calm gaze protects from the people around me. It seems to be such a very personal thing. One cannot talk of it, or explain it, even to one's friends. It has to be understood and explained by oneself to oneself.

This chaos within my head is bringing about a ruin of the brain that will eventually disclose a place where order and comprehension have always existed. The mind is being wrecked to reveal the foundations on which it can be rebuilt in clear and understandable patterns.

So I find that I accept this life. Accept the loss of my home, the collapse of my career, the bomb that injured my mother, the wide scattering and disintegration of the web of friendship I had woven so painstakingly for myself; accept it all with an equanimity that amazes me. I have always had a character chameleon-like in its capacity for adjustment to new surroundings. This is more than adjustment. It is an intense preoccupation with my innermost being that protects me from everything, without making me self-centred or egotistical in the smallest degree.

This concentrated stirring of thought continues the whole time. Above it, my life moves quietly as before. I still want the same things. More chocolate; longer hours in bed; easily acquired hot baths; delicious, varied and delicate food; all my own possessions around me. I still do the same things. I read, and talk, and sit in the cinema watching gangsters, palm trees, machines of war, and Marlene Dietrich with equal interest. I am bothered by my feet, sick of khaki, bored and annoyed by my companions, and all the monotonous, slow, fiddle-de-dee of army life. I long for it all to be finished with, and sometimes vaguely envy those who have gone. I suffer the same desires, disappointments and frustrations as all my fellows. I wonder if they partake with me of this inward life that murmurs without cease, its busy, urgent humming, in the hidden places of the brain; and draws me at all times and between the thoughts that run my daily life, into itself?

Sometimes, at night, my mind calls halt to my thoughts and each one becomes immobilized; imprinted on the backs of my eyes as the people and objects one sees through the window of a moving train, are left in the mind's eye, struck to stone in the one gesture that was seen as the train rattled past. The child that climbs a fence and waves a hand; the long grass blown sideways by the wind; the curtain that billows from an open window; the woman in the suburban garden who lifts her arms to the washing-line; the man who pauses on the street corner to light his pipe; the horse in the field that tosses its head, and the girl who moves, bent forward a little, up the side of the hill. As they are caught and immortalized by the mind, so my surface thoughts stand still; I wait, straining my ears, longing and hoping to hear the small cry that will tell me of the birth of my new self. This self which must struggle its way up from the darkness and out of me, reaching immediately forward with clawing hands, its clear, serene, wide-open eyes, reflecting and understanding all the distance of the sky. No longer saddened, but enraptured and possessed, by those crystal heights.

In the Beginning was the Bird

HENRY TREECE

In the beginning was the bird,
A spume of feathers on the face of time,
Man's model for destruction, God's defence.

Before man, a bird, a feather before time,
And music growing outward into space,
The feathered shears cutting dreams in air.

Before birds, a God, a Nothing with a shape
More horrible than mountains or the Plague,
A Voice as large as fate, a tongue of bronze.

Before this, O no before was there.
Where? Among the placeless atoms, mad
As tale the maggot makes locked in the skull.

And so I state a bird. For sanity
My brain's lips blow the tumbled plume.
I see it prophesy the path winds take.

Lincolnshire Bomber Station

HENRY TREECE

Across the road the homesick Romans made
The ground-mist thickens to a milky shroud;
Through flat, damp fields call sheep, mourning their dead
In cracked and timeless voices, unutterably sad,
Suffering for all the world, in Lincolnshire.

And I wonder how the Romans liked it here;
Flat fields, no sun, the muddy misty dawn,
And always, above all, the mad rain dripping down,
Rusting sword and helmet, wetting the feet
And soaking to the bone, down to the very heart . . .

Spitfires

RICHARD HILLARY

NOEL and I spent one night in London. Peter Howes collected us at about ten o'clock and we drove down to Old Sarum. During the drive we talked ourselves into a belated enthusiasm for Army Co-operation, and as we came on to the road skirting the aerodrome and saw the field slanting downhill from the hangars with machines picketed around the edge, we gazed at them with interest. There were an equal number of Hectors and Lysanders, heroic enough names though the machines might belie them in appearance. The Hectors were slim biplanes, advanced editions of the old Hart, but it was the Lysanders, the machines in which it seemed probable that we should be flying for the duration, that really caught our attention. They were squat, heavy, high-winged monoplanes and looked as though they could take a beating. We were less impressed by the two solitary guns, one fixed and firing forward and the other rotatable by the rear gunner.

The road running up to the Mess took us close by Salisbury, and the towering steeple of its cathedral was a good landmark from the aerodrome. The countryside lay quiet in the warm glow of the summer evening. A few minutes' flying to the south was the sea, and across from it France, equally peaceful in the quiet of the evening; within a few weeks Britain's army was to be struggling desperately to get back across that narrow stretch of water, and the France that we knew was to be no more.

The Course was run with great efficiency by a dapper little Squadron Leader by the name of Barker. We were divided into squads and spent from nine o'clock in the morning to seven in the evening alternating between lectures and flying our two types of aircraft.

To our delight, on the second day of the Course Bill Aitken appeared from Cranwell to join us. We had not seen him since together with most of our friends he had been posted to his F.T.S. several months before. He was the same as ever, rather serious, with deep lines across his broad forehead and little bursts of dry laughter. He did his best to answer all our questions, but when we got around to Frank Waldron and Nigel Bicknell he was inclined to become a little pompous. It appeared that the regulations at Cranwell had been somewhat more strictly enforced than in Scotland. Frank and Nigel had set off with much the same ideas as Noel and I up in Scotland, but with more determination as the rules were stricter, and consequently they had come up against more trouble. They had consistently attempted to avoid lectures, and Frank had crowned his efforts by oversleeping for the Wings Exam. He was also violently sick whenever he went up (which was not his fault), so the Air Ministry raised little objection when he applied for a transfer to the Scots Guards.

Nigel, it appeared, had found the restrictions an irresistible attraction, and no notice could appear without him hearing of it; he would solemnly produce pieces of red tape from his pocket and pin them around the board. This did not tend to encourage cordial relations with the higher authorities, and when he finally wrote an extremely witty but hardly tactful letter to the Commanding Officer, pointing out that Volunteer Reservists had joined the R.A.F. to fight the Germans and not to be treated like children, his stock was at its lowest ebb. He was not actually kicked out, but his record sheet was the blackest of the Course and his action resulted in a tightening-up of all restrictions.

'When I left Cranwell,' said Bill, 'he was trying to hook himself a job as Air Force Psychologist.'

It was obvious that Bill did not approve, and one could not blame him. He thought their actions represented something deeper than mere fooling-about, a disinclination to face up to the war and a desire to avoid fighting it for as long as possible. He thought further that there were a dangerous number of young men with pseudo-intellectual leanings in the same direction – this last with a signifi-cant glance at me.

I disagreed with him. I thought he had made a superficial assess-ment and said so. I went further: I prophesied that within six months he would have to take those words back, that those very people who were being so unstable at the moment would prove themselves as capable as anyone of facing an emergency when the time came. 'I doubt it,' he said. 'Anyway you know that war has been described as "a period of great boredom, interspersed with moments of great excitement". The man who believes enough in what he's fighting for to put up with the periods of boredom is twice as important in the winning of a war as the man who rises to a crisis.'

Besides Bill we discovered two other familiar figures, Peter Pease and Colin Pinckney. They had both been in the Cambridge Air Squadron before the war. Peter was, I think, the best-looking man I have ever seen. He stood six-foot-three and was of a deceptive slightness for he weighed close on 13 stone. He had an outward reserve which protected him from any surface friendships, but for those who troubled to get to know him it was apparent that this reserve masked a deep shyness and a profound integrity of character. Soft-spoken, and with an innate habit of understatement, I never knew him to lose his temper. He never spoke of himself, and it was only through Colin that I learned how well he had done at Eton before his two reflective years at Cambridge, where he had watched events in Europe and made up his mind what part he must play when the exponents of everything he most abhorred began to sweep all before them.

Colin was of the same height but of broader build. He had a bony, pleasantly ugly face and openly admitted that he derived most of his pleasure in life from a good grouse-shoot and a well-proportioned salmon. He was somewhat more forthcoming than Peter but of fundamentally the same instincts. They had been together since the beginning of the war and were now inseparable. I was to become the third corner of a triangle of friendship the record of which will form an important part of the rest of this book. It is therefore perhaps well to stress that Peter Pease, and not Peter Howes, is the peak of this triangle.

The work at Old Sarum was interesting. We studied detailed-map reading, aerial photography, air-to-ground Morse, artillery shoots, and long-distance reconnaissance. The Lysander proved to be a ponderous old gentleman's plane, heavy on the controls but easy to handle. It seemed almost impossible to stall it.

Of flying incidents there were few, though once I did my best to kill my observer. We were on our way back from a photography sortie when I decided to do some aerobatics. As our Inter-Comm. was not working, I turned round, pointed at the observer, and then tapped my straps, to ask him if he was adequately tied in. He nodded. I started off by doing a couple of stall turns. Behind me I could hear him shouting away in what I took to be an involuntary access of enthusiastic approval. After the second stall turn I put the machine into a loop. On the dive down he leaned forward and shouted in my ear. I waved my hand. On the climb up, I saw him out of the corner of my eye letting himself low down into the rear seat. Then we were up and over. I straightened up and looked back. There was no sign of my observer. I shouted. Still he did not appear. I had a sudden feeling of apprehension. That shouting – could it mean . . . ? I peered anxiously over the side. At that moment a white face emerged slowly from the back cockpit, a hand grabbed my shoulder and a voice shouted in my ear: 'For Christ's sake don't do a slow roll, I'm not strapped in!'

He had taken my signals for a query whether I was strapped in. His cries had been not of joy but of fear, and when we had started down on our loop he had dived rapidly to the bottom of the cockpit, clutching feverishly at the camera on the floor for support and convinced that his last hour had come.

I headed back for the aerodrome and, after making a quick circuit, deposited him gingerly on the field, landing as though I had dynamite in the back.

Noel nearly cut short a promising flying career in a Hector. He opened up to take off with the pasteboard instructions for his second Morse exercise on his knee. As the machine gathered speed across the aerodrome the card had dropped from his knee on to the floor. He bent to pick it up, inadvertently pushing the stick further forward as he did so. The long prop touched the ground and the machine tore its nose in and somersaulted on to its back. It did not catch fire. As the ambulance shot out from the hangars, I remember muttering to myself: 'Pray God don't be a bloody fool and undo the straps.' Fortunately he did not and escaped with a badly cut tongue and a warning from the C.F.I. that a repetition of the episode would not be treated lightly.

A surprising number of people have managed to kill themselves by putting on their brakes too hard when coming in to land, toppling on to their backs, and then undoing the straps – to fall out on their heads and break their necks.

Every night at nine o'clock the Mess was crowded with Army and Air Force officers, men who commonly never bothered to listen to the news, parked round the radio with silent expressionless faces, listening to the extermination of France and the desperate retreat of the British Expeditionary Force.

Privately we learned that Lysanders were hopping across the Channel two or three times daily in an effort to drop supplies to the besieged garrison in Calais, sometimes with a solitary one-gunned Hector for fighter support. As the Lysander was supposed to operate always under a covering layer of fighters, we could imagine how desperate the situation must be.

Then came Dunkirk: tired, ragged men who had once been an army, returning now with German souvenirs but without their own equipment; and the tendency of the public to regard it almost as a victory.

After days on the beaches without sight of British planes these men were bitter, and not unnaturally. They could not be expected to know that, had we not for once managed to gain air superiority behind them, over Flanders, they would never have left Dunkirk alive. For us the evacuation was still a newspaper story, until Noel, Howes, and I got the day off, motored to Brighton, and saw for ourselves.

The beaches, streets, and pubs were a crawling mass of soldiers, British, French, and Belgian. They had no money but were being royally welcomed by the locals. They were ragged and weary. When Howes suddenly met a blonde and vanished with her and the car for the rest of the day, Noel and I soon found ourselves in various billets acting as interpreters for the French. They were very tired and very patient. It had been so long. What could a few more hours matter? The most frequent request was for somewhere to bathe their feet. When it became obvious that there had been a mix-up, that some billets looked like being hopelessly overcrowded and others empty, we gave up. Collecting two French soldiers and a Belgian dispatch rider, we took them off for a drink. The bar we chose was a seething mass of sweating, turbulent khaki. Before we could even get a drink we were involved in half a dozen arguments over the whereabouts of our aircraft over Dunkirk. Knowing personally several pilots who had been killed, and with some knowledge of the true facts, we found it hard to keep our tempers.

In fairness to the B.E.F. it must be said that by no means all returned as rabble. A story of the Grenadier Guards was already going the rounds. In columns of three they had marched on to the pier at Dunkirk with complete equipment, as though going for a route march. A Territorial officer, seeing them standing at ease, advanced and started to distribute spoons and forks for them to deal with the food that was being handed out. His efforts were summarily halted by the acid comment of a young Grenadier subaltern:

'Thank you,' he said, 'but the Grenadiers always carry their own cutlery.'

The French were less bitter, possibly out of politeness, but more probably because while they had seen few British aircraft, they had seen no French. But it was our Belgian dispatch rider who surprised and delighted us by endorsing everything we said.

'How could we expect to see many British Fighter planes?' he asked. 'There was a heavy fog over the beaches and they were up above.'

One fight, however, he had seen – a lone Spitfire among four Junkers. For him, he said, it had been symbolic, and he admitted having prayed. If that Spitfire came out on top, then they would all be rescued. His prayer was answered. It shot down two Germans, crippled a third, and the fourth made off.

We sat on till well into the night, talking, arguing, singing, getting tight; they, tired and relaxed, content to sit back, their troubles for the moment over, we taut and expectant, braced by our first real contact with the war, eager to get started.

Finally, through an alcoholic haze, we made our farewells and staggered out into the street. Somehow we located both Howes and the car and set off back for Old Sarum. We were late and Howes drove fast. There was no moon. Coming out of a bend, he took the bank with his near-side front wheel, skidded, touched the brake, and hit the bank again. We were still travelling fast. For a moment we hung on two wheels, and then we turned over, once, twice. There was a crash of splintering glass, a tearing noise as two of the doors were torn off, and then, but for the sound of escaping petrol, silence. That week I had bought myself a new service cap and I could see it wedged under Noel's left knee.

'Get off my cap, blast you!' I shouted, thus destroying the silence and bringing down on my head a storm of invective, from which I gathered that none of us was seriously hurt. It turned out that we hadn't even a scratch. 'It looks,' said Howes, 'as though Fate doesn't want us to go out this way. Maybe we have a more exciting death in store for us.' Looking back, unpleasantly prophetic words.

A day or so later all leave was cancelled, no one was allowed further than half an hour's call from the aerodrome, and the invasion scare was on. An order came that all officers were to carry side arms, and at the station armoury I was issued with an antiquated short-nosed Forty-five and six soft-lead bullets. I appealed to the armament sergeant.

'Sorry, sir,' he said, 'but that's the regulation. Just content your-self with six Jerries, sir.'

That in itself would not have been so bad if only the ammunition fitted, which I soon found it did not. With only six bullets there was little temptation to waste any of them practising, but one day by low cunning I managed to get myself another twelve and loosed off. The first round fired but the second jammed. I had .455 bullets for a .45 revolver.

The Government's appeal to the people to stay put and not to evacuate, printed on the front page of every newspaper, roused England to the imminence of disaster. It could actually happen. England's green and pleasant land might at any moment wake to the noise of thundering tanks, to the sight of an army dropping from the skies, and to the realization that it was too late.

In Government departments, city offices, and warehouses, in farms, schools, and universities, the civilian population of England woke up. It was their war. From seventeen to seventy they came forward for the Home Guard. If they had no arms – and usually they hadn't – they drilled with brooms. The spirit was there, but the arms and the organization were not.

At Old Sarum we had completed our six weeks and were ready for drafting to our Squadrons. Then the inevitable happened, though at that time it seemed more like a miracle. It started as a rumour, but when the whole Course was called together and the chief instructor rose to his feet, rumour became reality.

Owing to the sudden collapse of France and our own consequent vulnerability it had been decided that a number of us were to go to Fighter Squadrons. The Air Ministry had ordered fifteen to be transferred. We each looked at our neighbour as though he was suddenly an enemy. There were twenty of us, and the five who were to continue in Army Cooperation were to be drawn from a hat. It was my worst moment of the war, and I speak for all the others.

Bill Aitken and Peter Pease were both drawn, together with three others. The rest of us almost groaned with relief. But it seemed hard on Peter, though he made no complaint. It would mean his separation from Colin and the loss of a potentially great fighter pilot.

For Bill it did not matter: he was older, that type of flying appealed to him, and he was admirably suited for it. I think he was not too disappointed. The fighter pilots were to go to an Operational Training Unit in Gloucestershire close to the Welsh border, for a fortnight. Then our training would be complete and we would be drafted to Fighter Squadrons.

Of us all, I think Noel was the most elated. His face wore a permanent fixed grin which nothing could wipe off.

'Spitfires at last,' he kept repeating.

'Spitfires or Hurricanes,' I said meanly.

He continued to grin.

'Don't give a damn. They're both good enough for me.'

We were to leave at once. At the last moment one other man was required and Peter Pease was selected; so it was in a contented frame of mind that we set off.

To our delight our instructors were No. 1 Squadron, back from France and being given a rest. There is little need for me to say much about them, for through Noel Monk's account in *Squadrons Up* of the part they played at Maastricht Bridge and elsewhere at the front, they must be about the best-known Squadron in the R.A.F.

'Bull' Halahan was still their Commanding Officer, and Johnnie Walker was in charge of flying. They were the first decorated pilots of this war that we had seen and we regarded them with considerable awe. They were not unaware of this and affected a pointed nonchalance. The Bull was so much what one had expected as to be almost a caricature. A muscled stocky figure with a prominent jaw and an Irish twinkle in his eye, he would roll into the lecture room and start right in with whatever he had to say.

These men treated us as junior members of a Squadron. They were friendly and casual, but they expected cooperation and they got it. It was a pleasant change from Training Command. Time was short and we had much to learn.

We learned many things then new, though perhaps no longer true, so swiftly do fighter tactics change. We learned for the first time the German habit of using their fighter escorts in stepped-up layers all around their bombers, their admitted excellence in carrying out some prearranged manoeuvre, and their confusion and ineffectiveness once this was in any way disturbed.

We learned of the advantage of height, and of attacking from out of the sun; of the Germans' willingness to fight with height and odds in their favour and their disinclination to mix it on less favourable terms; of the vulnerability of the Messerschmitt 109 when attacked from the rear and its almost standardized method of evasion when so attacked – a half roll, followed by a vertical dive right down to the ground. As the Messerschmitt pilots had to sit on their petrol tanks, it is perhaps hard to blame them.

We learned of the necessity to work as a Squadron and to understand thoroughly every command of the Squadron Leader whether given by mouth or gesture.

We learned that we should never follow a plane down after hitting it, for it weakened the effectiveness of the Squadron; and further was likely to result in an attack from the rear. This point was driven home by the example of five planes over Dunkirk all of which followed each other down. Only the top machine survived.

If we were so outnumbered that we were forced to break formation, we should attempt to keep in pairs, and never for more than two seconds fly on a straight course. In that moment we might forget all we had ever learned about Rate-1 turns and keeping a watchful eye on the turn-and-bank indicator. We should straighten up only when about to attack, closing in to 200 yards, holding the machine steady in the turbulent slipstream of the other plane, and letting go with all eight guns in short snap-bursts of from two to four seconds.

We learned of the German mass psychology applied even to their planes, of how they were so constructed that the crews were always bunched together, thus gaining confidence and a false sense of security.

We learned the importance of getting to know our ground crews and to appreciate their part in a successful day's fighting, to make a careful check-up before taking off, but not to be hypercritical, for the crews would detect and resent any lack of confidence at once.

And we learned, finally, to fly the Spitfire.

I faced the prospect with some trepidation. Here for the first time was a machine in which there was no chance of making a dual circuit as a preliminary. I must solo right off, and in the fastest machine in the world.

One of the Squadron took me up for a couple of trips in a Miles Master, the British trainer most similar to a Spitfire in characteristics.

I was put through half an hour's instrument flying under the hood in a Harvard, and then I was ready. At least I hoped I was ready. Kilmartin, a slight dark-haired Irishman in charge of our Flight, said: 'Get your parachute and climb in. I'll just show you the cockpit before you go off.'

He sauntered over to the machine, and I found myself memorizing every detail of his appearance with the clearness of a condemned man on his way to the scaffold – the chin sunk into the folds of a polo sweater, the leather pads on the elbows, and the string-darned hole in the seat of the pants. He caught my look of anxiety and grinned.

'Don't worry; you'll be surprised how easy she is to handle.'

I hoped so.

The Spitfires stood in two lines outside 'A' Flight Pilot's room.

The dull grey-brown of the camouflage could not conceal the clear-cut beauty, the wicked simplicity of their lines. I hooked up my parachute and climbed awkwardly into the low cockpit. I noticed how small was my field of vision. Kilmartin swung himself on to a wing and started to run through the instruments. I was conscious of his voice, but heard nothing of what he said. I was to fly a Spitfire. It was what I had most wanted through all the long dreary months of training. If I could fly a Spitfire, it would be worth it. Well, I was about to achieve my ambition and felt nothing. I was numb, neither exhilarated nor scared. I noticed the white enamel undercarriage handle. 'Like a lavatory plug,' I thought.

'What did you say?'

Kilmartin was looking at me and I realized I had spoken aloud. I pulled myself together.

'Have you got all that?' he asked.

'Yes, sir.'

'Well, off you go then. About four circuits and bumps. Good luck!'

He climbed down.

I taxied slowly across the field, remembering suddenly what I had been told: that the Spitfire's prop was long and that it was therefore inadvisable to push the stick too far forward when taking off; that the Spitfire was not a Lysander and that any hard application of the brake when landing would result in a somersault and immediate transfer to a 'Battle' Squadron. Because of the Battle's lack of power and small armament this was regarded by everyone as the ultimate disgrace.

I ran quickly through my cockpit drill, swung the nose into wind and took off. I had been flying automatically for several minutes before it dawned on me that I was actually in the air, undercarriage retracted and half-way round the circuit without incident. I turned into wind and hauled up on my seat, at the same time pushing back the hood. I came in low, cut the engine just over the boundary hedge, and floated down on all three points. I took off again. Three more times I came round for a perfect landing. It was too easy. I waited across wind for a minute and watched with satisfaction several machines bounce badly as they came in. Then I taxied rapidly back to the hangars and climbed out nonchalantly. Noel, who had not yet soloed, met me.

'How was it?' he said.

I made a circle of approval with my thumb and forefinger.

'Money for old rope,' I said.

I didn't make another good landing for a week.

The flight immediately following our first solo was an hour's aerobatics. I climbed up to 12,000 feet before attempting even a slow roll.

Kilmartin had said, 'See if you can make her talk.' That meant the whole bag of tricks, and I wanted ample room for mistakes and possible blacking-out. With one or two very sharp movements on the stick I blacked myself out for a few seconds, but the machine was sweeter to handle than any other that I had flown. I put it through every manoeuvre that I knew of and it responded beautifully. I ended with two flick rolls and turned back for home. I was filled with a sudden exhilarating confidence. I could fly a Spitfire; in any position I was its master. It remained to be seen whether I could fight in one.

We also had to put in an oxygen climb to 28,000 feet, and air-firing exercise, formation attacks, and numerous dog-fights.

The oxygen climb was uneventful but lengthy. It was interesting to see what a distance one ended up from the aerodrome even though climbing all the way in wide circles. Helmet, goggles, and oxygen mask gave me a feeling of restriction, and from then on I always flew with my goggles up, except when landing. The results of this were to be far-reaching.

The air-firing exercise was uneventful, but as short as the oxygen climb had been long. We were given a few rounds in each gun and sent off to fire them into the Severn. All eight guns roared out from a quick pressure on the fire button on the control stick. The noise through the enclosed cabin was muffled, but the recoil caused a momentary drop in speed of 40 miles per hour.

For our formation attack practices we usually needed six machines. We flew in two sections of three with an instructor heading each. One section would fly along in V formation representing the enemy and the other would make an attack. The attacking section would also fly in V formation until the enemy was sighted. Then the section leader would call out over the radio telephone, 'Line astern!' and the pilots to right and left of him would drop behind.

A section in the line astern is in its most manoeuvrable formation. The leader would then come up on the enemy formation, taking care to keep well out to one side (usually to starboard) and a few hundred feet above them. When still some distance off, he would call out, 'Echelon starboard!' and the two following machines would draw out to his right, still keeping fairly tight formation. When about 300 yards astern and to starboard of the enemy, he would call out, 'Going down!' and all three machines, still in echelon formation, would dive down and come up behind the target aircraft. At about 250 yards' range they would open fire (theoretically), and close in more slowly to about 100 yards when the leader would call out, 'Breaking away!' and with an abrupt movement of stick and rudder go tearing downwards and sideways beneath the enemy machines, thus giving the rear gunners, if they were still alive, a double factor to allow for when taking their aim. The other two machines would follow and form up again in line astern, this time to port of the enemy and in a position to repeat the attack. We came up in echelon to avoid cross fire – assuming the target aircraft to be bombers – and we broke away downwards to avoid presenting the bellies of our machines to the rear gunners. If the target aircraft were fighters, we broke away upwards, as they had no rear gunners, and by doing so we at the same time gained height.

When we were sent up for a dog-fight, two of us would go off together for forty minutes and endeavour in every way possible to 'Shoot' each other down. One learned most from this exercise, of course, when an instructor was in the plane; but there were many pilots and few instructors, so this was a rarity. On one occasion I went up with Kilmartin. We climbed to 10,000 feet, and he intimated that he would attempt to get on my tail. He succeeded. In frenzied eagerness I hurled my machine about the sky. Never, I felt, had such things been done to a plane. They must inevitably dislodge him. But a quick glance in my mirror showed that he was quietly behind me like a patient nursemaid following a too boisterous charge. Only once did I nearly succeed. I did a particularly tight turn and inadvertently went into a spin which took me into a cloud. For a moment I had lost him, but I had lost myself too, and thus restored the *status quo*.

When we re-established contact, he signalled to me to get on his tail and stay there. I carried out the first part of my orders admirably and started to pursue him round in ever-tightening circles. I attempted to get him in my sights, but could not quite succeed in doing so. But that did not prevent me from wondering why he calmly allowed me to follow him without taking any evasive action: these circles were becoming monotonous and making me dizzy. I glanced in my mirror and understood. I was dead long ago, and I could almost imagine that I saw him smile. I was very glad it was a practice.

I landed considerably mortified and prepared for some withering comments. Kilmartin climbed out of his machine with a sly grin at the corner of his mouth.

'Do you feel as dead as you should?' he asked.

I nodded.

'That's all right,' he said. 'I meant you to. Now I'll give you a few tips for the next time.'

He told me then of the uselessness of all aerobatics in actual combat. Their only value was to give a pilot a feeling of mastery over his machine in any position, upright or inverted. To do a loop was to present a slow-moving sitting target to your opponent, who need only raise the nose of his machine slightly to keep you permanently in his sights. A slow roll was little better. For complete evasion the two most effective methods were a half roll and a controlled spin – especially if you had been hit, for it gave an impression of being out of control. For the rest it was a question of turning inside your opponent (sometimes pulling up and above him, the more effectively to dive down again), of thinking quickly and clearly, of seizing every opportunity and firing at once, and of a quick break-away. All this and more he impressed upon me, and I did my best to carry it out on my subsequent flights. These were less one-sided, but then I never flew with him again.

On these dog-fights we would also practise beam attacks, probably the most effective and certainly the most difficult means of bringing down an enemy machine. The attacking Spitfire would overhaul his target, well out to the side and about 500 feet or so above. When some little way ahead he would bank and turn in, to let the other machine come through his sights almost at right angles, and with a double deflection (twice the diameter of his sights) he would let go in a long burst. He thus opened fire in front of the enemy's nose and raked him all the way down the side where he had the least protection and the smallest field of fire, while himself presenting a very small and awkwardly moving target for the gunners. He could then drop in behind and deliver another attack from the rear.

But my clearest memory of the Course was the bridge. It was across the Severn and linked England to Wales. It was a narrow bridge with close-set arches and it was the occasion of a long-brewing quarrel for Noel and me.

Noel, Peter Howes, and I had been together now for some time and were beginning to get on one another's nerves. There was soon to be a parting of the ways. It happened at the very end of our training, when we were about to join our Squadrons, and was to have consequences which none of us could foresee, which all three of us vaguely sensed, but yet could do nothing to stop. With Howes it took the form of withdrawing into himself, of saying little and of avoiding our company. For Noel and me, fundamentally closer together and considerably quicker-tempered, it could not end like that. There had to be a show-down: the bridge provided it.

Noel, low-flying down the Severn, came to the bridge and flew under it. He came back and told me. From then on the bridge fascinated and frightened me. I had to fly under it. I said as much to Peter Pease. He gave me a long quizzical stare.

'Richard,' he said, 'from now on a lot of people are going to fly under that bridge. From a flying point of view it proves nothing: it's extremely stupid. From a personal point of view it can only be of value if you don't tell anybody about it.'

He was right of course.

To fly under the bridge now simply to come back and say that I had done so would be sheer exhibitionism. It would prove nothing. Yet I knew I would fly under it. I had to for my own satisfaction, just as many years before I had had to stand on a 25-foot board above a swimming-pool until I dived off.

There was a strongish wind blowing, and as I came down to a few feet above the river I saw that I had on quite an amount of drift. The span of the arch looked depressingly narrow: I considered pulling up but forced myself to hold the stick steady. For a moment I thought I was going to hit with the port wing, and then I was through.

It was later in the Mess and we were playing billiards when Noel asked me if I had done it. By now we could not even play billiards without the game developing into a silently bitter struggle for supremacy. As Noel nearly always won, he could not have chosen a worse moment to speak.

'Well, did you?' he asked.

I played a deliberate shot and didn't answer.

He laughed.

'Surely our little winged wonder isn't getting soft? I was expecting to hear how narrowly you missed death.'

I put down my cue.

'Listen, Noel,' I said, 'for months you've been smugly satisfied that you're a better pilot than I am, and just because I soloed before you here you have to go off and make a bloody fool of yourself under some bridge just to prove that you're still a hell of a pilot. You make me sick.'

He looked at me bitterly.

'Well, little Lord Fauntleroy, this *is* a new angle. And from you, the biggest line-shooter I've ever known. All right. Stick around the hangars cadging extra flights and crawling to the instructors. Maybe they'll give you a good assessment yet.' And with that he slammed red into a corner pocket to win the game and I stalked out of the room and slammed the door.

Next day Squadron vacancies were announced. I walked down to the Adjutant's office with Peter Pease and Colin Pinckney. 603 (City of Edinburgh) Squadron had three vacancies. It was out of the battle area (the first battle over Dover had already been fought), but it was a Spitfire Squadron and we could all three go together. We put our names down.

Noel decided to go to Northolt to 609 Squadron to fly Hurricanes, and Peter Howes to Hornchurch to 54 Squadron.

The following day we left. I was to drive up with Peter Pease and we were to make an early start. I piled my luggage into his car and prepared to climb in after it. Then I hesitated and turned back. I found Noel packing. He got up as I came in. We were both embarrassed. I held out my hand.

'Good-bye and good luck,' I said.

'Good-bye, Dick,' he said. 'We've drifted rather a long way apart lately. I'm sorry. Don't let's either of us drift up to Heaven. That's all.'

While he was speaking Peter Howes had come in to say good-bye too. 'You two needn't worry,' he said. 'You both have the luck of the devil. If the long-haired boys are to be broken up, I have a hunch that I'll be the first to go.' We both told him not to be a fool and agreed to meet, all three of us, in three months' time in London.

They came out to the car.

'Take care of yourself,' said Peter Howes.

'Your courage amazes me,' said Noel. 'Going back to that bloody awful country, and voluntarily!'

I waved and then Peter Pease and I were round the corner and on our way. I sat silent most of the way to London, confused by a number of disturbing emotions.

Missing

HERBERT CORBY

They told me, when they cut the ready wheat
the hares are suddenly homeless and afraid,
and aimlessly run the stubble with scared feet
finding no homes in sunlight or in shade.
– It's morning, and the Hampdens have returned,
the crews are home, have stretched and laughed and gone:
whence the planes came and the bright neon burned
the sun has ridden the sky and made the dawn.
He walks distraught, circling the landing ground,
waiting the last one in that won't come back,
and like those hares, he wanders round and round,
lost and desolate on the close-cropped track.

The Tattie Dressers

FRED URQUHART

THEY were going to dress Gladstones at the pit near the old sand-stone quarry. It was just after seven o'clock on a bleak, cold April morning. While the men were taking the Potato Sorter off the lorry, the women and the loon started to tirr the pit which stretched uphill over the brow of the field like a furrow thrown over by a giant plough. Maggie Jane straddled on the top and shovelled down the earth, uncovering the straw. She was wearing a crimson waterproof pixie-cap which was almost the same colour as her pretty, round face. It was so cold that even she was silent for once. But as she got warmer she began to speak about how much syrup she had got from the Co-Operative van the day before. 'A pund, Mrs Strachan! Hoo long dae they think that's goin' to last me and the loon?' she cried, her dark eyes flashing vivaciously. 'The vanman said I widna get ony mair till the fourth o' May.'

Mrs Strachan said, 'Ay, ay,' every now and then and went on unhapping the pit. She was a thin, wiry woman with a brown face and grey hair pulled tightly under an old black felt hat. She shovelled the dirt briskly; always three jumps ahead of Maggie Jane. The loon worked steadily, not listening to his mother's chatter. He was a sturdy boy of fourteen with fine eyes like his mother's.

After the men had got the Potato Dresser into place, they set to tirring the pit, too. In no time they had done more than the women and the loon. When they had taken off the first half dozen yards of earth, old Ake said they had better begin to take off the straw. Young Dod and Chae were forking it off at one side when they heard Maggie Jane exclaim from the other: 'My Christ, look at this! Come on awa' hame!'

'What's adae wi' ye, wifie?' Chae called.

She was standing with her graip in one hand, staring down at the potatoes she had uncovered. 'Goad Almichty!' she said slowly.

The two young men grinned at each other. Dod pushed back his cap and scratched his short curly fair hair. 'Dinna stand lookin' at them, wifie!' he said. 'Bend yer back! Or can ye nae bend for yer stays?'

'She hasna got stays on by the look o' her,' Chae grinned.

'But I have sut,' Maggie Jane said with a perky toss of her pixie-cap.

'Ye have nut!' Chae imitated her high-pitched voice.

'I have sut,' she said. 'Would ye like to see?'

'No, we'll leave that to Ake!' Chae winked at Dod and spat on his hands before forking off another bunch of straw.

Mrs Strachan and Maggie Jane stood and shook their heads. The potatoes were so badly frosted that they were welded together in a black pulp, smooth and mottled as a snake's skin. They were like prunes that had been dipped in syrup. Many of them had white and yellow fungus-spots on them. The stench was appalling. Maggie Jane held her nose as she bent down and began to pick gingerly at them. 'Ye'd need yer gas-mask on for this job, Mrs Strachan!'

'Ay, they're gey lads, thae,' old Ake said, bending down and digging his hands into the black morass. 'They need a blitz!'

'Oh, we'll gi'e them that a' richt,' said Maggie Jane.

'Ay, we'll just ha'e to dae oor best to get rid o' them. They're only fit for swine to work amongst. But farm servants are just swine, onywye,' Ake added, grinning maliciously. 'They're awfa fine fowk the now, but just wait till the war's ower!'

'That'll dae ye noo!' Maggie Jane laughed.

'Ay, ay,' Mrs Strachan said. 'Ye've been a farm servant long enough yersel'.'

'Forty years.' Ake shook his head mournfully. 'I was nae as auld as the loon here when I started.'

When they had picked off the worst of the frosted potatoes they wiped their mucky hands on the straw and sacks. 'Eh, but it's richt cauld on the fingers,' Maggie Jane said.

'Ay, ay,' Mrs Strachan said, stepping on the flat box beside the elevator of the Potato Sorter. Maggie Jane stood beside her and they stamped their feet on the box, waiting for young Dod to start scooping the potatoes into the machine. Ake put on sacks for the Seed, and Chae threaded a long needle with binder's twine. The loon put down wicker sculls for the Brock and got the bags ready for the Ware.

'Are ye ready, Dod?' Ake started the engine, and when it was going steadily Mrs Strachan pushed over the handle. There was a rattle as Dod scooped in the first lot of potatoes.

Ake leaned on the end of the machine and watched the potatoes sliding up the elevator towards him. 'Ay, they're gey lads, thae,' he said, watching the women's hands dart out and in, picking out the frosted ones and throwing them away. 'Dae ye ken fut they mind me on?' He deftly unhooked the first sack to be filled and dumped it on the weighing-machine. 'It minds me on yon movin' staircase in London. Eh, ye never saw such a thing! Ye just need to stand ontil't and it moves up, takin' ye along wi' it. Thae tatties are gey like the fowk ye see standin' on the staircase. They're a gey mixed breed.'

'Ay, ay,' Mrs Strachan said, without looking up from the potatoes. They were all used to Ake's reminiscences about London which he had visited once for a Cup Final years before.

'Here, here, wifie, dae ye see that!' Chae took a frosted potato out of the bag he was sewing and held it up in front of Maggie Jane's nose.

'Ay, I see it,' she said. 'I thocht I'd let ye ha'e it.'

Ake frowned as he saw what was coming up the elevator. 'Here's a lot o' gey bubbly-nosed lads!'

'Ay, put it off, put it off!' Maggie Jane cried frantically, her blue-fingered mittened hands lost amongst the rotten tatties piling up in front of her.

Mrs Strachan pushed back the handle and the elevator stopped. And for two or three minutes the women picked out the rotten potatoes, making exclamations of disgust as they squashed to pulp in their fingers.

'A' richt noo?' Ake said, and Mrs Strachan said 'Ay, ay,' and started the elevator again. 'Nae sae fast, Dod!' she called.

'They're gettin' better,' she said after a while. 'They're nae sae weet noo.'

'It's nae afore time,' Maggie Jane said. 'Ma bloody hands are freezin'.'

Occasionally the men swung their arms, slapping their thighs and shoulders to get some heat into their cold fingers. But the women contented themselves with stamping their feet on the box.

'I wish the sun would come oot,' Maggie Jane said.

'It would just bring ower the Jerries,' Ake said. 'It's better to stay cloudy.'

'I wonder where they were last night?' Mrs Strachan said.

'Ye dinna need to worry yersel',' Ake said. 'I dinna think they'll bother themsels payin' a veesit to the Howe o' the Mearns.'

'Begod they'd better nae!' Maggie Jane said.

'Fut would ye dae noo, wifie, if they did?' Ake asked, throwing away a frosted potato that the women had let past them.

'Christ, I'd just dive right under the dresser,' Maggie Jane grinned. 'I'd even dive under the frosted tatties!'

After Dod had been scooping for half-an-hour there was such a big space between the dresser and the pit that he cried: 'We'll ha'e to shift the cuddy!' So Chae scooped out the dirt and potatoes that had accumulated under it, and then they all pushed. The machine moved slowly up the slope. It would not sit evenly, so they had to put sacks under the wheels. 'Are ye ready, you wifies?' Ake shouted to the women who were kneeling beside the two back wheels with folded sacks in their hands. 'Noo, lift!' And the men strained, waiting for the women to put in the cleek-brakes in the holes in the wheels. 'Come on, wifie!' Chae called to Maggie Jane. 'Can ye nae find the hole?' And he muttered something to Ake that made the old man guffaw ribaldly.

'Fut was that?' Maggie Jane cried, dusting the earth from her knees.

But Chae merely grinned and said to Dod: 'It's ma turn for the scoop.'

'What aboot gi'en us a shottie?' Maggie Jane asked. 'We're that cauld standin' here.'

'Ay, ay,' Mrs Strachan said. But Chae grinned and flung a scoopful of potatoes into the dresser. And the women, after running to fling their scullfulls of Brock on the Brock pile, went back to their box.

'Hoo are ye gettin' on wi' the Ware, loon?' Ake asked, threading the needle. 'Are ye managin' to get them into the wagon?'

'Nae bad,' the loon said.

'There was a whilie there when I thocht ye looked real trauchled,' Ake said. 'The wagon's gey heich for ye. Maybe Dod would take a shottie o' it for a while and ye can shoo the bags.'

Another half-hour passed. It still remained dull and the wind blew the dust off the potatoes into their faces. About half-past eight it began to rain. The wind drove it into the women's backs, and they huddled their heads into their collars. 'It winna last long,' Mrs Strachan said. 'It's just an April shower.'

But the rain fell heavier and heavier. Their clothes began to stick to their shoulders and arms. 'The joys o' bein' a farm servant!' Ake said, brushing the raindrops off his lean brown face.

'April showers bring forth May flowers!' Maggie Jane laughed.

'Ay, we'll get flowers quick enough if this rain lasts,' Dod said. 'On our graves!'

They all laughed and repeated this, and Chae stopped scooping to ask what they were laughing at. He came up beside the elevator and looked down at the potatoes. 'Dae ye see that, Mrs wifie!' He held a potato that Maggie Jane had missed in front of her nose. 'Dae ye see that? Fut dae ye think the mannie would say if he'd gotten that among his Seed?'

'Go to hell!' Maggie Jane said in exasperation.

'Go to hell yersel'!'

'I'll gang soon enough,' she said, laughing. And she leaned on the edge of the elevator and said: 'Did ye hear the bar aboot Hitler?'

They all listened, but the machine was making so much noise and she laughed and giggled so much, running her words together, that they couldn't make out what she was saying. 'Put it off, Mrs Strachan,' Ake said.

'Well, it was like this,' said Maggie Jane. 'Hitler and Churchill and Mussolini a' died and went to Hell. The Devil asked them hoo many lies they had tellt, so Churchill tellt him and the Devil said he was to run aince roond Hell. Then Mussolini tellt him and the Devil said he was to run three times roond Hell. Then he turned to ask Hitler hoo mony lies he had tellt. But Hitler was awa' for his bicycle!'

When they had stopped laughing and repeating the joke, Chae began to chaff Maggie Jane about how often she would need to run round Hell. 'Ye'll need new tyres for yer bike afore ye're half feenished,' he said.

'I will nut,' she said.

'Ye will sut!' he said, leaning forward and grinning mischievously in her face. 'Ye're a gey lass!'

'Ye're a gey lad yersel',' she said. 'I doot a bike'll be nae guid for ye.'

'No, I'll need a motor-car!'

'I'll sell ye mine!'

'It's a car I want,' he said. 'Nae a bloody go-car!'

And he laughed and went back to scooping. Ake looked round to see how the loon was getting on with the sewing of the sacks of Seed. 'Eh, John, but I doot we'll ha'e to gi'e somebody else that job,' he said. 'Ye're nae managin' weel ana. Can ony o' you wifies shoo bags?'

'Ay, I'll take a shottie,' Maggie Jane said.

'Dinna let her dae it,' Chae roared. 'She tried it the other day and she sewed hersel' to the bag!'

'I did nut,' Maggie Jane said with dignity, stepping off the box and taking the needle from the loon.

'Ye did sut!' Chae called.

She sewed industriously, frowning as she pushed the long thick needle through the sacking. 'Hurry up, wifie!' Ake said with a laugh as he put another sackful on the machine. 'Ye're fa'in' ahint!'

And when he dumped the next sackful on the weighing-machine he grinned when he saw that Maggie Jane was still frowning over the first bag. 'It's a guid job that this is nae piece-work,' he said. 'Or ye widna ha'e much in yer envelope at the end o' the week.'

He leaned on the end of the dresser and watched Mrs Strachan picking the potatoes. Occasionally he put out his hand and picked one that she had missed. But it was seldom that he needed to do this; she was an expert, her arms flying out and in like pistons, throwing the potatoes on the ground on the other side of the dresser or into the sculls. Dod picked the Ware opposite her and whenever his sacks were full he unhooked them and carried them on his back, emptying them into the wagon. The loon emptied the sculls of

Brock and attended to the Chats which came out of a hole at the side of the potato sorter.

'Is it nae near piece time?' Mrs Strachan asked without looking up from the potatoes rolling upward in front of her.

Ake took a metal watch with a dingy yellowish glass out of his trousers-pocket and scanned it. 'It wants five meenits to nine,' he said.

'Well, we'll ha'e oor piece when we've feenished this bit,' Mrs Strachan said. 'While you lads are shiftin' the dresser.'

'Ah, but that'll nae dae,' Dod said. 'Ye'll ha'e to shove wi' the rest o' us.'

'I ken somebody that's fairly shovin' the noo.' Ake looked round and grinned at Maggie Jane who was struggling to keep in time with him. Three bags were standing beside the weighing-machine waiting to be sewed. 'It's nae the bags she's shooin' – it's the arse o' ma breeks!'

'Well, ye should keep yer big dock oot o' the way!' Maggie Jane retorted. 'And, onywye, ma hands are that cauld they can hardly haud the needle.'

'Never mind, Maggie Jane,' said Mrs Strachan. 'Here's the sun comin' oot.'

The women huddled in the lee of the Ware wagon and ate their piece while the men shifted the dresser. By the time they had finished, the sun was shining quite brightly. Maggie Jane lifted her skirts and gave a few skips as she came back to her place on the box. 'Oh, the nightingale sang in Berkeley Square!' she skirled.

'It's nae a nightingale that's singin' at the Barns o' Dallow, ony-wye,' Chae grinned. 'It's a gey auld hen.'

'And here's a worm for ye!' he cried, throwing it at her.

Maggie Jane wriggled her shoulders with disgust. 'Eh, Chae, ye dirty devil!' And she aimed a kick at him with her wellington boot. He jouked round her and skelped her playfully on the bottom. She chased him round the dresser, but she turned and ran in the opposite direction when he picked up the worm again and held it in front of her. He smacked his lips and said: 'This would gang fine wi' thae frosted tatties!'

'Feech!' Maggie Jane made her eyes cross with disgust.

'We'll maybe ha'e to eat waur yet,' Ake said. 'Ye never ken. They had to eat dogs in Germany in the last war.'

'Well, I nivir!' Maggie Jane exclaimed.

'There's some fowk eatin' dogs the now,' Chae said. 'They tell me that the Polish sodgers at Auchencairn ha'e eaten a wifie's dog.'

Maggie Jane and Mrs Strachan would not believe this, but Chae swore that it was true. 'The doggie's disappeared,' he said. 'Ay,' and he grinned and winked to Ake, 'and it's nae only doggies the Poles are eatin'! Ane o' them bit a woman doon by Stonehaven!'

'Well, I nivir!' cried Maggie Jane. Then she looked at Chae and said: 'Ach, he did nut.'

'He did sut!'

'Ye're a richt leear, Chae,' Mrs Strachan said, without looking up. 'It's richt, isn't it, Ake?'

'Ay, it's richt,' Ake said, leaning on the edge of the sorter and spitting into a bag. 'The Pole took a richt lump oot o' her. He was walkin' her oot and they had a row, so he ups and bites her. There's to be a coort case ower the head o' it.'

'Well, a' I can say is that it serves the bitch bloody well right,' Maggie Jane said decisively. 'She's got nae mair than she deserved for goin' oot wi' ane o' thae bloody foreigners.'

'Ye'll ha'e to watch yersel' the next time ye gang to the pictures,' Chae said. 'See and nae sit doon aside a Pole. Ye never ken fut he might dae in the dark.'

'No, for he'd ha'e a lot o' territory to work on!' Ake said.

'There's nae danger,' Maggie Jane tossed her head. 'I'm havin' nothin' to dae wi' ony bloody Pole.'

They were almost ready to shift the dresser again when they heard a sound above the rattle of the engine. Three aeroplanes were zooming across the sky towards the coast. 'Spitfires!' said Ake.

'They're nae,' Chae said. 'They're Blenheims.'

'Nae, they're Hurricanes,' said Dod.

Mrs Strachan was the only one who did not look up. She went on picking. Maggie Jane craned her neck until the planes were out of sight. 'It's a guid job they're nae Jerries, onywye,' she said, turning her attention to the potatoes.

'They micht be for a' ye ken,' Ake said.

'No, they're Hurricanes,' Dod said.

'Listen!'

Mrs Strachan stopped picking. 'Listen!' she cried again.

There it was unmistakably: the wail of the siren in Auchencairn. 'Goad Almichty!' Maggie Jane said. 'That's surely somebody wi' an awfa sair guts after their breakfast!'

They worked on steadily. One or two aeroplanes flew high overhead, but they knew by the sounds that they were British machines. Suddenly there was a rattle like machine-gun fire. 'Maircy on us!' cried Maggie Jane. 'Fut was that?'

'A stane's got caught in the elevator,' Ake said. 'Put it off, Mrs Strachan.'

They all peered under the rollers, looking for the stone. Mrs Strachan seized the opportunity to get down on her knees and pick up some of the Brock that hadn't gone into the sculls.

'There it is,' Maggie Jane cried. 'See, doon there!'

'Ay, she kent where it was a' the time,' Chae grinned. 'For it was her that did it! She's been workin' for that a' mornin'. Sabotage!'

'I did nut,' Maggie Jane cried indignantly.

'But ye did sut!' he grinned and slapped her on the bottom.

Maggie Jane picked up a frosted potato and threw it at him. But he ducked and the potato went into the Ware wagon. 'Bullseye!' he cried.

Mrs Strachan laughed and began to sing: 'He gets the bullseye! Oh, what a clever young man! He gets the highest score out of a possible eighty-four! Because I love him!'

'He simply is divine!' Ake joined in, driving the needle through the sack in time. 'And I'm going to marry the man who gets a bullseye every time!'

'Ay, I doot that dates us, Mrs Strachan,' he said. 'They hinna got sangs like that nooadays.'

'No, there's a lot o' blethers o' sangs nooadays,' she said. 'Such daft-like words they've got and a' this shakin' their shoothers and a'.'

'Ach away!' Chae said. 'There was nae guid sangs when you were young.'

'That's right, Charles,' said Maggie Jane in a very polite accent.

'Maircy on us! Fut was that?' she cried suddenly, lapsing again into broad Mearns speech.

They all stood and listened to the echo of the crash. A flock of crows flew upwards, startled, from a clump of fir-trees. The whirring of their wings continued the sound for a few seconds, then there was silence. Mrs Strachan had put off the machine to listen.

'That's either a bomb,' Ake said. 'Or a plane down.'

'I thocht for a meenit it was Maggie Jane fa'in' intil a bag,' Mrs Strachan said. 'I looked up expectin' to see her heels stickin' oot o' the bag.'

'I wonder what it could be?' Maggie Jane said.

'Ach, we'll soon find oot,' Ake said. 'Put it on again, Mrs Strachan. We maun get thae Seed dressed, war or nae war.'

*

In the afternoon they heard that it was a German plane that had been brought down three miles on the other side of Auchencairn. The pilot, a loon of nineteen, had been killed instantly.

'Puir bastard!' old Ake said, throwing aside a frosted potato. 'He was somebody's bairn.'

Ode in Fear

C. DAY LEWIS

The lustrous bowl of the sky
Sounds and sustains
A throbbing cello-drone of planes.
Entombed beneath this caving liberty,
We note how doom endorses
Our devious fraud and folly where skeins
Of wild geese flew direct on visionary courses.

Now Fear has come again
To live with us
In poisoned intimacy like pus,
Hourly extending the area of our pain,
It seems I must make the most
Of fever's pulsing dreams and thus
Live to allay this evil or dying lay its ghost.

Fear has so many symptoms –
Planes throbbing above
Like headache, rumours that glibly move
Along the bloodstream, sleep's prophetic phantoms
Condemning what we have built,
Heartburn anxiety for those we love –
And all, yes all, are proof of an endemic guilt.

The bones, the stalwart spine,
The legs like bastions,
The nerves, the heart's natural combustions,
The head that hives our active thoughts – all pine,
Are quenched or paralysed
When fear puts unexpected questions
And makes the heroic body freeze like a beast surprised.

The sap will rise anew in
Both man and brute:
Wild virtues even now can shoot
From the reviled interstices of ruin.
But oh, what drug, what knife
Can wither up our guilt at the root,
Cure our discoloured days and cleanse the blood of life?

Today, I can but record
In truth and patience
This high delirium of nations,
And hold to it the reflecting, fragile word.
Come to my heart then, Fear,
With all your linked humiliations,
As wild geese flight and settle on a submissive mere.

Squadron Move

JOHN SOMMERFIELD

THEY said that the squadron was going to move, any day now; it was a known thing in the conversations at the morning tea break, and Harry the Dripper had got all the details from his hare-lipped friend at Wing. They knew where we were going, too, and the exact dates. A lot of them said it was Ceylon, for strategic reasons not apparent to the uninformed, while others were equally certain that we'd be going back to the Valley. The rumours went on for a fortnight, getting better all the time, and then we were told officially and it was the Valley after all, farther forward than last time, the most advanced landing-strip on the front. Of course they all said they had been right in the first place.

It was raining the day we left. We packed into our three-ton lorry just after sunrise and drove off to the landing-strip, where we waited for an hour and three-quarters while the rain leaked in on to us and our kit. Then we drove back to the camp again and waited about some more. This surprised no one – we had done plenty of moves before: ours was a mobile squadron. The convoy eventually left at ten, after they had packed three more people into our lorry, which was practically impossible.

Jammed wetly against the others, bumped and joggled by kitbags and rifles and waterbottles and haversacks, I suffered against the hard edge of the tailboard as we tore along through slashing rain that drummed on the leaky canvas and hissed under the wheels, and sprayed back from the road and the wheels into the rear of the lorry, making us wetter all the time and distilling a warm, damp smell from our own damp clothes and sweat-wet bodies, while flat miles of flooded rice-fields and rich wet-green countryside went sliding by. And we all began to sing, one song after another, about Love, and Holding you in my arms, and Dreaming of you, and so on, the songs that smell of Saturday night dance-halls and holding hands in the cinema dark and milk bars and gramophones on the river.

Those in front of the lorry couldn't see when we reached the outskirts of the town, but they could tell by the stink. It had stopped raining now and everything was emitting a warm, invisible steam – the filthy little shops, the pavements fouled with blood-coloured splashes of betel-spit, the mounds of rubbish festering in the gutter, the endless ant swarm of brown bodies draped with dirty white dhotis, and the rickshaws, and the emaciated cattle browsing amongst the traffic. Above, the vultures wheeled, and the kites; from somewhere came a continuous tin-can rattling of temple bells.

The traffic jammed and our lorry stopped. In the road the skin and bones of a black dog, covered with sores, scabs and bald patches, lay kicking in the mechanical spasms of its death throes. No one took any notice. It was quite ordinary, like the naked, starving children, rickety and pot-bellied, with old men's faces, the beggars rotting beside the rubbish heaps, the deformed and leprous, the mad, the cripples, the syphilitics. We went on singing Thanks for that lovely week-end.

The station is a sort of railway slum, positively swimming with the sweat of a multitude of travel-harassed troops. Indians seethe madly around, tangled up with umbrellas and complicated luggage wrapped in bits of bedding. The air is full of quarrelling and bullying and ordering about, and the cries of hawkers and the smells of the sticky, aromatic, dangerous-looking foodstuffs that they are selling.

Into this loud and odorous confusion our convoy spews itself and its plentiful baggage. There are stacks of kitbags, piles of tool-boxes, mounds of crates, there are our bed-rolls, our weapons, our hurricane lamps, there's all the cook's apparatus and stores, there are boxes of aircraft spares, drums of lubricating oil and dope, the officers' large tin trunks, Mr Partington's little black puppy, and a great number of miscellaneous objects, mostly very heavy and awkward to handle, all of which have to be unloaded from the lorries, carried through the station (in a temperature of over a hundred in the shade and the humidity of a steam laundry), and somehow fitted into an already overfull train. And we have to wedge ourselves in too.

It's a troop train – bare wooden compartments painted the colour of bed bugs, shiny-slimy with an unspeakable patina of greasy filth, the horrible floor soaked with the spittle of ten thousand coolies, and an indescribable lavatory wafting a stench of warm, sour urine everywhere.

When we take possession our compartment immediately becomes a little colony; kit is unpacked, boots taken off, private stores of food produced; it looks as if we've lived in it for weeks and not cared where we put our rubbish.

Slush spits orange pips out of the window; Ginger Martin, who has taken off his shirt, wipes abundant sweat from his bright pink torso with an old towel; Harry the Dripper and Chalky White argue monotonously about the names of railway stations and the times taken by trains to reach them. Me, I light a pipe, lean back, and try to reconcile myself to the prospect of an unknown number of days of travel misery.

An hour or so passes and then the train unexpectedly glides out of the station, past sidings strung with shabby trucks where emaciated old women and starved children scrabble for bits of coal amongst the sooty stones, and then there's the familiar monsoon landscape again, a green flatness of flooded paddy-fields and growing crops, palm fronds and bamboo sprays trembling in the rain, and now and then the thatched roofs of a village in the midst of banana palms and mango trees; on the telegraph wires perch blue jays, kingfishers, bee-eaters, king crows; cattle egrets stand surprised-looking in the fields; flights of paddy birds flash whitely against dark clouds, and always there are kites and vultures patrolling the rainy sky.

It's the same country in the evening and when the train runs on into darkness, rain still falling, the steamy air still sticky-hot as ever. There are no lights on the train; only the weak yellow glow of our hurricane lamps shuts out the night and its alien sounds and smells. But if you listen you can hear, above the clatter of the wheels, an immense and sonorous croaking of bull-frogs mingled with machinery uproar of millions of crickets.

There's not enough room to stretch out; some try to curl up and sleep on the hard, narrow benches in foetus-like attitudes; some lean back and close their eyes hopefully; others resign themselves to wait until sleep overcomes them of its own accord. Slush reminisced tenderly about the time he was stationed in the Hebrides, his words evoking the unbelievable ghosts of black rocks, icy seas, and northern water. Degenerate Douglas, who was in the same unit with him, explains in great detail the complexities of getting there from London, and how you have sometimes to wait for days for a boat at the little mainland port. The two of them have a few memories together about the local pubs.

'There's a place where you can get bed and breakfast,' says Douglas. 'A wizard place – and you can sleep with the landlady if she likes you. Her husband's in the Navy, and he's always away.'

'Convenient,' says Chalky. 'What was the breakfast like?'

'Wizard breakfast. Porridge, you know, and bacon and eggs – real thick rashers. She's got a son in the Navy as well.'

'Was he away, too?'

'Well, not exactly. He was home on leave. Didn't make no difference though. They're a funny crowd. She was a bit pregnant at the time.'

'Don't suppose that made any difference either,' says Ginger.

'No,' says Douglas. 'You can't afford to be fussy in war-time.'

'*Degenerate* Douglas,' says Slush. 'Debauched, disgusting, dissipated, *degenerate* Douglas.'

The hot night and the train roar and the hysteria of bullfrogs seem to go on for ever. We doze fitfully and fitfully awake with cramped limbs, flesh itchy with dried sweat, and a horrible taste in the mouth.

The train arrived in a grey dawn. It was the end of the line, a flat mistiness, coarse grass trampled into mud, and a few tin-roofed shacks. When we got out immediately ahead was the river, the great river that had flowed three thousand miles, immensely broad, muddy rain-swollen, and swift running, the far bank dimly visible as a horizoning strip of green.

Sullenly we began to unload the baggage. There seemed to be a lot more of it than before, and we had to carry it down to the river's edge – the track continued right to the bank, but the inscrutable powers that pushed us about the map and manipulated our destinies with office machinery had caused the train to stop a hundred yards from the finish of the line.

The invisible sun rose higher; the clouds could not abate its heat, but lay heavy on the humid air, like blankets, and the wet ground steamed. Stumbling along the track or slipping on the muddy grass, we cursed the heat, the loads we bore, and the fate that had plucked us from our homes and set us down in this unfriendly land.

One asked: What's the name of this place? But no one knew or seemed to care; the stupor of travel had descended upon us. All that morning we sprawled on the ground in the shadow of a bamboo shelter and talked at ease. Already the place we had left behind was far away and long ago, and our destination lay in an unpredictable future; there was only now, the irresponsible moment in which we belonged to nowhere. This we did not explain to ourselves, but experienced it as a sort of gaiety and a feeling of friendliness for one another. We hated the country and the way we had to live; as for our sense of comradeship, it was hard to say how deep it went; but at moments like this we could be happy in a special way because we were together and quite separate from anything around us.

We talked of places where the squadron had been, of characters no longer with us whose exploits and peculiarities were remembered through a distorting mist that made all things past seem pleasant. Then we talked of places known before the war, of walking down rows of houses on Sunday mornings and smelling cooking dinners, of the streets and pubs of our home districts. Most of us were Londoners and discussing L.P.T.B. bus routes we were drawn more closely together; the names of roads and stopping places were like poetry and sweet with home-sickness. In the stunning mid-afternoon heat we tasted our native rain, the smells of public bars and fried fish shops; the iron clang of tramcars, the flaring market lights and voices, the milkman's morning cry and the cry of the evening paper-sellers, dwelt in the steamy alien air.

'The Old Kent Road,' said Slush dreamily. 'Where we used to play when we was kids.'

'Remember,' said Ginger. 'Remember the old geezer that kept the lino shop. Russian he was, with millions of whiskers. Remember how he used to juggle with billiard balls and do sword-swallowing.'

'Best sword-swallower I ever saw,' said Slush. 'He used to do an act at the Bedford, you know, before he took up the lino business.

Can't remember his name now, one of those *Russian* names it was.'

'The kids used to call him Old Whiskers,' said Ginger. 'Wish I could remember it. Sounded something *rude* it did.'

It took them a long time to decide that they had forgotten it beyond recall, and then we had to prepare to move off again.

When we returned to the river bank some kind of vessel was moored there, a vast, shabby floating structure, architecturally a cross between a Noah's Ark and a Victorian railway station. Above its huge superstructure protruded a long, thin smoke-stack and it was propelled by a single stern paddle-wheel as big as a house.

We stood, eyeing the waiting mound of our baggage. 'This is where we came in,' said Slush. 'Glad you joined, Ging,' he said. 'Me,' said Ginger, staggering along the gang-plank with a large tool-box on his shoulder, his amiable, humorous, slightly lunatic face scarlet and contorted with exertion. 'Wish I was twins,' he said. 'I'd have me bruvver doing all this.'

Behind him came Harry the Dripper, bent and groaning under the weight of an old tin trunk (that, I happened to know, contained the Armament Warrant Officer's private stocks of cornflakes and cocoa), and muttering something about white coolies and he was a flight mech., not a professional weight-lifter.

The gang-plank led into the boat's gloomy iron bowels. Waiting for us were an army officer and two N.C.O.'s, wearing white armlets with MOVEMENT CONTROL stencilled on them. As we stood bowed under our loads, sweating and uncertain, they issued curt, mutually contradictory orders about where to stack what and which part of the boat we were allotted to. No one took much notice of them.

Later, worn out, we settled down on the upper deck and began to unroll our bedding. Upon us advanced a haggard lance-corporal waving an official-looking piece of paper. We had to move to another and much more crowded part of the deck. 'Movement control,' said Slush. 'You can't beat movement control. There's *nothing* they can't disorganize.'

Members of the crew began to walk about hawking rolls, tiny bananas and hard-boiled eggs the size of marbles at even more than usually exorbitant prices. To our insulting refusals they were impervious, knowing that we were hungry and would be much hungrier before any food was issued to us. The idea was just to get us used to what we would have to pay later.

On the river bank a mob of Indian troops was struggling to embark, complete with kit, small arms, clay water-pots, little tin trunks with flowers painted on them, and some domestic goats.

'Shortly,' I said, 'we are about to witness some rather splendid scenes of indescribable confusion.'

From the lower deck came an uproar of voices mingled with the bleating of goats; soon harassed-looking men with packs and bedding balanced on their heads began to appear at the top of our companion-way, where they jammed, abashed, urged forward by the steadily increasing pressure below and held back by fear of intruding upon our domain, by a long-instilled sense of inferiority in the presence of white sahibs – even ones as scruffy looking as us. But the physical pressure broke down the psychological barrier. Amidst yells of abuse and threats of violence in pidgin Hindustani they overflowed on to the deck, where the above-mentioned scenes of confusion were enacted with considerable gusto.

Eventually those of us on the port side were shifted and we all huddled together on the starboard deck, an invisible line down the centre dividing the close-packed bodies. The ill-feeling was stupendous.

In the midst of the quarrelling and scuffling and settling down the boat had moved off. We leaned against the rail watching the low green banks sliding by and talking of the unattainable delights of a good meal, while a vast and threatening sunset burned in the sky.

Soon it was night. The oil lamps' wan glow lost itself in the wide darkness. A hoarse roar of conversations blended with the rumble of the engines, and from the huddled obscurity below came the sound of a flute – slow, melancholy notes dripping in a silvery sequence, monotonous, timeless, and pastoral. Slush and Ginger were discussing their early sex life in and around the Old Kent Road.

After the second night on the river time loses itself. The place from which we came belongs to a past in which all happenings are equally remote, and it is impossible to think of any ending to our journey's lazy, eventless transience. The waters slide by and it is always the same, the huge muddy river, the flat green banks, the flat green land always stretching to an ever-receding horizon, a land without roads or towns, planted with unnumbered little villages that drowse in rural squalor amidst trees that know no winter.

On deck the bodies lie close-packed, some talking, some reading or playing cards or writing letters, some simply drowsing thoughtlessly in time's slow flow – on one side the brown bodies, on one side the white, mutually exclusive, together and living and thinking in different worlds. Sometimes our pilots' portable gramophone is brought out and played, its music flattened and faded by the horizon's spaciousness, the dance tunes floating over the water like the ghosts of long dead Saturday afternoons, and sometimes from below drifts the sad, bodiless music of the flute. At night a great searchlight in the bows slices across the darkness and the waters, and in the morning it is the same as the other mornings, as if we had not moved and time had circled back again.

Then, towards the evening of the fourth day, distant hills begin to loom, misty and purple, and the river changes, broadens out to include sandbanks and tear-shaped swampy islands. The muddy water is transformed into a dark-gleaming mirror for the green, the livid orange and crimson interfused with indigo of an angry sunset. High up against the sky's sullen dome a flock of river terns moves whitely: the white square sail of a little boat is vivid in the distance; and sail and birds, so small against the dark waters and darker sky, illuminate the gloom like flashes of lightning. The dawn is all ruined clouds, the wreckage of a thunder-storm that woke and wet us in the night. The boat runs close to the eastern bank; there's a fishing village by the water's edge, people washing in the river and tending their boats, and for a few minutes their lives and ours run side by side, as close as opposite rows of houses, yet unmingling, worlds apart. Ahead are rounded hills whose densely wooded tops are cloudy and remote with mist. But the sky is clearing, the sun sucks up night's vapours, and round the next bend lies our destination. It's time we began to pack.

Between the boat and the shore stretched thirty yards of an eighteen-inch wide gang-plank, supported high above water and the mud on tottering bamboo stilts. 'Bloody tight-rope walkers now,' said Harry, getting into gear for a vocal attack of the miseries. 'Me,' said Slush, 'I'm not crossing that with a hundredweight of rubbish on my back without they give me a roll of drums.' And Ginger, ruffling his orange curls, nodding his head from side to side, and blowing out his cheeks so that he looked even more like Harpo Marx than usual, obliged with a loud and rapid performance upon an invisible trumpet of 'The March of the Gladiators'.

Disembarkation was laborious, confused, and unpleasant. There was no feeling of having arrived at a new and significant stage of our journey when we set foot upon the eastern bank. Yet 'east of the river' had a special significance for us: it was one of those geographical phrases coined by the war and used amongst troops as a sort of shorthand symbol for a whole range of unpleasant experiences shared by them alone. East of the river meant the war zone. We were still far from the front, but already the war was here, in a confusion of mudstained troops and tanks and armoured cars and field guns. This place was the bottleneck through which everything and everybody bound for the front had to pass. Troops were British, American, African, Indian, and all day, travel weary, heavy with kit and weapons, they marched from the landing stages in long, slow files through the mud between railway sidings and troop trains and the long files of goods trucks laden with war materials.

The first train had been beastly, but, in comparison with the vile little narrow-gauge wagons into which we had to pack ourselves now, it seemed almost luxurious.

'The thing about this trip,' said Douglas, 'is that it doesn't matter how bloody stinking horrible it is, you can always cheer yourself up to remember that the next bit's going to be a whole lot horribler.'

'You wouldn't nob it,' said Chalky. 'There's the rest camp next – little Dachau we used to call it way back in '42.'

'And then there's the road,' said Slush. 'Fourteen hours jammed in a three-tonner, with a lunatic Wog driver skidding round precipices and you praying for a quick death – and nothing to eat either.'

Crowded together in the brutal afternoon heat, tired, dirty, hungry, itching with sweat rash, feeling like the human cargo battened below deck in a slave ship, we waited wearily and without any hope for food and the train to start.

After about an hour some army biscuits and hunks of brownish bully beef dissolving in its own melting fat were passed round. We were so hungry that we even ate the biscuits, which were hard and brittle, like gramophone records, and tasted of compressed cardboard.

For the next hour, while the train still waited and the heat increased and our clothes gradually became soaked with sweat and the lavatory stink grew even stronger, and more and more flies crowded in and crawled over our exacerbated flesh, we talked about food, recalling pre-war meals with lustful nostalgia.

'. . . a steak,' Ginger was saying. 'About a yard of steak, with chips and green peas.'

'Mushrooms,' said Curly. 'I want mushrooms, too.'

'But I don't *like* mushrooms,' said Ginger.

'Well, – your horrible luck then, chum,' said Curly. 'I'll have your share.'

'What about the afters?' said Chalky. 'Don't forget the afters.'

'Blackberry and apple pie, with lots of cream,' said Slush.

'Cor,' said Ginger. 'Give me plain and syrup. A *bloody* great slab of plain with lashings of syrup.'

We tantalized ourselves with luscious visions of delicacies whose taste we had almost forgotten, spoke with voluptuous tenderness of kippers, of the different ways of cooking ham, of strawberries and cream, of apple pie, pork chops, trifle made with sherry, and the little sandwiches you get at parties. There was a fierce argument about spinach and another about the best way of preparing toasted cheese.

'It's wonderful when you come to think of it,' said Chalky. 'There's so *many* different kinds of lovely things to eat.'

'But none of them's round here,' said Douglas, and suddenly we were all gloomy again.

The train started. It was an immensely long train, very slow, and it kept stopping for no apparent reason. The single track was so hemmed in by jungle that it didn't feel as if we were travelling by train at all, but drifting uneasily through a sea of vegetation. There were frequent islands of dark water, still black pools upon which floated lilies, lotuses, and reflections of the waxen flowers that gleamed above in a green twilight of tall trees and creepers and palm fronds. When the train stopped a rank steamy smell drifted in through the glassless windows, and we felt a stillness, the uneasy quiet of the vegetable world, whose silence conceals a slow, murderous, unceasing struggle.

It was soon dark, and in the stillness were faint animal noises, creakings and grunts and rustlings. Thousands of mosquitoes swarmed into the carriage; they were a particularly unpleasant sort, large, black, equipped with powerful hypodermics that could pierce through our clothes. We sat in the hot, thick blackness, too tired and bad-tempered to talk, not being able to sleep, itching, and feeling hostile towards mosquitoes, while outside, in the jungle sea, tigers, leopards, deer, elephants, and wild pigs rustled and breathed and carried on with their private lives. And the train started again, the engine groaning and puffing, throwing out sparks, its great headlight shooting up the wild darkness, in its wake a long trail of wooden cages crammed with bodies – fifty or sixty tons of living flesh divided into individuals living, thinking, feeling, remembering, in each one's head a whole world with an illusion of separateness from everyone else's world, and all of them incalculably apart from the remote surrounding night.

In the early morning mist we heard the sound of engines shunting, saw trucks, a water tank, signals, mounds of coal. It seemed that out of sight, hidden in the mist, must be a town with streets, houses, shops, and people living town lives. But when the mist cleared there were only tall silent trees hemming us in.

This was the end of the line, the railhead that fed the war. Ahead lay hundreds of miles of unpeopled forest, mountain, and jungle valley. And the next railway, the next town, the next settled and populous country, lay hundreds of miles in the rear of the enemy.

We unloaded our baggage, piled it up neatly in front of the R.T.O.'s office, sat down, and waited for something to happen, preferably breakfast. Our cigarettes were nearly done, and a lot of brisk cadging took place. We looked up hopefully at the sight of a languid, cod-faced young lieutenant approaching. He regarded us and our possessions with repulsion. 'I can't have that,' he said in what he thought was an Oxford accent, pointing to the luggage. 'It won't do there, you know. You'll have to put it somewhere else.'

'I could suggest a place,' said Douglas out of the corner of his mouth.

'When he comes round our house in peace-time peddling vacuum cleaners,' said Slush, 'I'll slam the door in his face.'

We moved the kit. 'Get fell in,' someone said, and we marched off, at a slow shamble. 'Have you ever seen such a dead loss mob in all your life?' said Curly. 'We look like we'd been on the booze and the batter for a week and finished up with a night in the gutter.'

'I feel I had too,' said Ginger. 'Only worse, on account of we didn't have any lovely time to start off with.'

We went about two miles, through a squalid, overgrown village of tin-roofed shanties and miserable little shops stocking mainly flyblown bananas and betel-nut, and out on to the other side into the jungle again. A steady stream of army trucks, mostly empty and mostly bound in the same direction as us, kept going by, splashing us with copious black mud. Then there was a turning off the road marked REST CAMP ('It ought to be "Abandon hope all ye who enter here",' said Douglas), and we went in.

Immediately we were lost in a maze of half-built paths that wound amongst rotting tents under great swamp trees. The bubbling black mud and the sour black soil gave out an insidious smell, musty, mouldy, mildewy, a decaying churchyard smell mingled with the stink of stagnant water.

No one took any notice of our arrival. Our C.O. had gone to see if he could find somebody who could tell him something about what was to happen to us. In the meantime, like a flock of exasperated sheep, we wandered hungrily bleating for breakfast. There were different theories about the location of the airmen's mess, and we split into small parties, straying down the long, dim vistas that opened on every hand, following quaggy tracks that gradually petered out or twisted and turned back on themselves, so that we seemed to be moving in aimless baffled circles. We must have passed the cookhouse several times before we noticed it – a dilapidated mud and straw basha surrounded by trampled mud. Inside were greasy forms and tables, and a smell of old meals. We sat down hopefully, disturbing several hundred thousand large blue flies. On the walls was a gallery of typewritten notices dating from last week back to the beginning of the war, saying troops must not, and disciplinary action will be taken against, and on no account will. When we had finished reading and commenting upon them, we began to bang on the tables with our tin mugs.

A cook, tall, cadaverous, wearing once-white overalls, shambled in with an air of hangdog truculence. Silence. 'Can't help it,' he said, speaking from the side of his mouth. 'Camp orders. No use going on. No breakfast after o-eight hundred hours. 'S camp orders.'

He went away when we started to bang on the tables again, but came back after the shouting had started, this time in the rear of a brisk little sergeant radiating self-confidence and authority, who began to make a powerful speech about why no breakfast, and informed us that there was a canteen up the road where we could get something to eat – a more unfortunate remark than which he couldn't have made, as we hadn't been paid for three weeks and bore considerable ill-will about it, which we explained to him rather loudly. He left with not quite so much vacuum salesman bounce as he had come in with.

Our group pooled their cash and there was enough for a visit to the canteen, where we queued up for half an hour for the same food out of the same tins that we would have had if we'd eaten in the cookhouse. Here we met some of the advance party from the squadron that we were relieving, who encouraged us with stories about the strip being under shell fire and Jap patrols sneaking in at night and tossing grenades about. 'The grub's not too bad when the road's open,' they said. 'Course, you go on half rations now and then when Nip cuts the road.'

'Probably a lot of guff,' said Chalky, as we walked back. 'You know how chaps shoot a line when they're coming down from the Valley.'

But no one felt very happy. And the struggle to find a place to sleep further depressed us. We staggered from tent to tent, sweating under our kit, getting more and more tired and muddy and unhappy. Eventually we were installed in a sort of marquee made of decaying tarpaulins propped up on bamboo poles. The sticky-damp floor was the same stinking mud as outside, and sprouted a crop of horrible pallid toadstools that also oozed from the tarpaulins themselves. 'The men's morale,' said Slush, laying out his ground-sheet, 'is distinctly poor.'

'Wait until you've had some of the grub here,' said Ginger. 'You don't know what the horrors of modern warfare are until you've had a meal in this cookhouse.'

In one corner was a huge net-like web at whose centre crouched a livid green and black spider, big as a young crab. A shrill, excruciating monotony of crying insects bored at our ears. As the heat of the day increased the smell of stagnant water and corruption grew stronger. 'Roll on that boat,' said Douglas. 'Roll on a bloody long time.'

Despite a grisly 5 a.m. breakfast, despite the hanging around and lorry-loading and the normal unpleasantnesses and frustrations accompanying the start of a road convoy everyone was cheerful and inclined to sing the morning we left camp.

Almost at once the road started to climb, gently at first, then more and more steeply, swerving and doubling back on itself so that the direction of our travel was impossible to guess. But, whichever way we headed, before us was always range upon range of hills and clouds. The heavy jungle air was left below; here it was cool, fresh, smelling of emptiness, but though we had left its air behind the jungle still marched with us, still the banana palms hung out their tattered silky fronds, the bamboos still bowed and shivered as we went by, and an unceasing wave of foliage broke and foamed against the road's precipitous sides.

There were few humans to be seen, and those were a little strange and wild, hill tribes, head-hunters, small, sturdy men with gaily-striped loin cloths and blankets, coils of wire round their muscular legs and hung with tinsel jewellery; each carried a large knife and an umbrella; some also had rain capes made of straw, so that from a distance they looked like little travelling houses. As the convoy passed they waved and smiled, gay, innocent smiles, and wrinkled their slanting eyes at our dust. They were not like any people I had seen before: their innocence, their childlike charm, strangely mingled with something that was savage and murderous without being the least repellent. It was impossible to know how we seemed to them, but after being used to fear, suspicion or veiled dislike from every native stranger, after always being treated as members of a hostile occupying army, or as suckers to be swindled, these smiles that asked for nothing in return for their friendliness were heartening.

Then the clouds were all below and ahead the highest ridge of all. The trees silhouetted against pale sky were bare and blackened, bleak shapes of northern winter, belonging to a landscape washed by cold rains, wind-blown and frost-bound, violently incongruous in this winterless land whose seasons all were evergreen. The ridge had been the extreme point of the Japanese advance; they had not been able to cross it, mown down by those metallic gales that had blasted the trees, stripped leaves and branches and blackened the wounded wood. Here, lower down, the earth's skin was scarred with trenches, fox-holes, and shell craters. At the road's edge, tumbled amidst broken trees and down steep green slopes, were charred, mangled remains of tanks, bren carriers, jeeps, and lorries. Tin cans, petrol drums, piles of shell-cases, broken boxes, burst sandbags, bully beef tins, crumpled and bullet-holed sheets of corrugated iron, all the scorched and rusty rubbish that makes the scene of a battle look like a muncipal refuse dump, lay strewn about. The little town was in ruins, the huts burnt out, roofless, or altogether destroyed. The dead had been tidied away out of sight; a few pale crosses thrusting themselves up from fresh-broken ground remained as evidence of the terrors, agonies, and exhaustion of battle – only these and the sordid litter that befouled a little corner of the land's untouched spaciousness.

When we crossed the ridge and began to descend it was into a different country, dry and windy-looking, a country of low scrub, thorny bushes, gnarled trees, and tall tasselled grasses, inhabited by warblers and finches, flocks of little thick-billed seed eaters, larks and shrikes, the homely birds of a more friendly climate. It was an empty land though, without a sign of human habitation; only the tortuous road was alive, its busyness that of any military highway anywhere, with control points, filling stations, even traffic blocks, irrelevant and foolish amongst the endless silent solitary hills. It was uncomfortable to think of all that emptiness unrolling behind us, with only the slender, vulnerable road linking our destination and the whole front with the far-off sources of supply.

The sun began to decline; purplish shadows welled out of the earth's creases and sketched hollows in the flanks of hills. We lay tangled together in an uncomfortable torpor, numbed, dusty, hungry, stupefied with excess of air, our gaze weary with vast expanses, no longer noticing. We had not noticed that for some time the road neither climbed nor descended, but ran straight and level. It was the sight of a little deserted village, burnt out and bullet-riddled, that reminded us of where we were. 'The Valley!' said Douglas. 'It's the Valley,' and at once we woke out of our travel stupor and began to talk, to reminisce of last year, of the other village by the airstrip and the village women with flowers in their hair, who did our washing and brought it back with gifts of jasmine blossom, of air raids, crashes, and dead pilots, the hens we used to keep and frying food at night and going for swims in the river. 'Remember,' said Slush. 'Remember that time Puddled Percy shot a cow. . . .' We had been happy there, with a good and friendly feeling between us and the local people.

The Valley was narrow, and now the sun was low over the hills. A dusty, shining haze hung above the road, that ran between tidy little rice fields, bamboo clumps, and neat huts surrounded by flowering shrubs. We kept passing strolling groups of the Valley people, small and gentle looking, with broad faces and slanting eyes, their spotless clothes extraordinarily gay with skilful dissonances of acid green, lemon yellow, and magenta; the women had a plumpish elegance of carriage, and set off the sleekness of their glossy black hair by little waxy flowers. As we went by they smiled and waved to us, and in the luminous dusty sunset haze the whole village scene had a holiday air; it was like something out of a traveller's idyll of long ago; the war was near, just over the hills, but it seemed far off, in another time.

We drove on, into darkness and then a thin rain. The tyres hissed on wet road. Nothing could be seen but silvery threads of rain slanting across the dimmed headlamps' narrow beams. We belonged to nowhere, had nothing but the memories in our heads and consciousness of movement through darkness. When the lorry stopped the silence and the stillness were overwhelming.

We began stiffly to disentangle ourselves and our belongings. I jumped from the tailboard and landed in soft mud. Torchlights wavered around and there were confused sounds of voices and movement. We stood in the fine rain, stretching ourselves, smelling strangeness, waiting for what was to happen next. In the strange darkness our travel groups had dissolved, we were alone and tired.

A drifting movement began; I followed, blindly trustful, and found myself scrambling up a steep, slippery path. It was hard to tell how far we had climbed when level ground was reached. On a shelf cut in the hillside were some tents that looked out on to a gulf of darkness. People were milling around, falling over guy-ropes, and shouting for their friends. I heard Slush calling my name, and found that the others had already occupied a tent and were unrolling their bedding by the light of a very dim electric torch.

I woke to bright sunshine, lifted the tent flap, and saw below, spread out like a map, a chess board of dilapidated rice-fields sliced by the road's straightness and the geometry of the landing strip that ran parallel with it. Ahead and on either side were new and higher hills, smoking with mist, their tops breathing clouds. The air was cool and fresh, a pleasure to breathe.

A convoy of tanks was clanking along the road, like a row of beetles, and there was an angry noise of aircraft engines running up. Two fighter-bombers roared hungrily down the strip, and another two and another, until twelve of them were airborne and they made off in battle formation towards the hills, from behind which came, like the sound of great doors being slammed, an intermittent roar of artillery fire that soon was augmented by the remote thudding of falling bombs.

It was early. No one was up yet. I stood gazing at the hills for a long time, thinking of the jungle valleys beyond, the mountains and the wild country and then the far fertile plain where once again was a land of roads and towns.

We had come a long way, but longer, harder, and more unpleasant journeys lay ahead.

Flare

(Homs-Tripoli road)

TERENCE TILLER

SUDDENLY the flare dropped. The buxom hills
curved over backwards, fell open like a book,
swam up to meet it. The white roadside walls
sharp as a denture, bars and masses of black
    behind the vast hard light, the vaster ring
    of blindness, lay steely in the frightening
silence of a picture or a clock.

Clear as if airless, a moon-landscape; only
no saintly idiotic planet's face,
earthlight; but hot and horrible and lonely
that flower-sailing eye in menacing glass.
    Beneath it, the earth stirring without lamps:
    the awful breathing of a thousand camps;
the probing gun; animal watchfulness.

Death's haunted stables and the gunner's star:
oh Bethlehem again – *and what rough beast!*
in a night wearing ceremonies of war
hid like a guilt? No singing on this coast;
    no mercy in the impersonal honest sand
    whose (the flare vanished) briefly open hand
shut suddenly to darkness like a fist.

The Sea

Sailor's Song

JAMES HANLEY

'COVER MY FACE,' he said.

'Take it easy,' one said.

'Cover it up.'

'Cool man, cool,' another said.

'Cover my face up, I said. I said cover my face up. Don't want to see any more sea.'

They looked at him, they said nothing, they went their ways.

He looked up at deck-head, counted a thousand rivets, felt weight of steel.

One felt her lurch, one clutched at wood, stroked this, like it were a sudden friend to him, warmth rising out of it, one counted some minutes by his watch. A shout, then many fragments of the same shout, like these were scattering frenzies.

'Going down, she's going down.'

'Cover my face,' he said, 'don't want to see any more sea.'

'She's going –'

'Down!'

Ship heaved and sea heaved, and there were sounds in the heaves.

Sing a song, ship cried, sing a song, sailor, cried sea.

Sing as I go down, sing as I heave up.

One watched this sailor toss, one heard creak of wire, one thought, 'Oh, the sea will cover his face.'

One journey was ended, now begin another. Each heave of the sea cried this, each lurch of ship, each long, more dreadful lurch.

'Cover my face, please,' he said, breathed fetid air.

One went out.

'Cover it up,' he shouted, blood spurting then.

Another went by.

'You'll go with us,' the last one said.

He stood there, he meant to stay, to watch, to take this sailor out.

End one journey, then begin another. Remember one, think of another.

Watching this sailor toss his face was sad, sad as he remembered.

The blow was hard, struck hard, quicker than lightning flash.

Lashed to bars and rope this journey begins. Step by step grope, through maze and mesh, air deluged by ash, steam tearing up, scalding, tearing up, through mesh of steel, all that power was, and all that power proclaimed, struck down at a blow, jungle where order was, crazy gestures of steel.

Bring him through this, across a floor moving, alive and moving, moves with the sea's heave. And then to a ladder.

Think of a man lashed, by bar and by rope, ease him up sure, gently, and still sure, way out at the top. Grope step by step, men turned to bats.

The strain on muscle told, hold hard for breath.

Climbing, still climbing, up, up. From darkness to light, up to a world, oh, breathe that air in, breathe horror out. Slow and yet sure, groping and groping again.

Careful one says. Easy now one says. He got it bad, one says.

Think of light, think only of light.

Spirally this ladder went, crazily high, rest on steel-landings, then climb again. Look back below, all ended below. Step by step up, moan climb on moan. Bear up Jack, one says, steady another cries, nearly there, the third said.

Listen now, one says, I heard, another said, almost there cried the third.

Listened to the sea roar, wind wild around it.

Smelt air come down, lungs opened wide, breathe it all in, breathe horror out. Climb and yet climb.

'Can't hear nothing 'cept sea,' one cried, 'nor can I,' said another.

'What *will* we hear?' said the third, so saying this he took added weight, knew the others were strained.

Many men's voices can be drowned by a sea.

He tossed and stretched there, iron bunk creaking.

Felt weight of steel, counting rivets by thousands, stared up at deck-head.

'Cover my face,' he said, 'want to see no more sea.'

The third man went out. Voices came in on the heel of wind.

He heard a word, 'Go!' he heard a word, 'Raft.'

They came in to the foc'sle then, he watched and counted as they came.

Three men and known, every inch of the way known, through nerve and bone, tested by days and tested by seas, all sailors three.

'One journey ended, another begins,' one said.

One behind him was silent, but thought, 'now where will it end?'

The third one came up, his face bore resolve.

'Pick him up gently,' he cried, against incoming wind, loud sound of seas.

This ship was no man's ship, this ship was sea's ship.

Leave her now. Leave her, oh leave a ship that belongs to a sea.

They bore him up, from creaking bunk, they trod clumsily out.

Eyes met hard light, many a league of sea. They moved slow towards her rail.

'Cover my face,' he said, 'want to see no more sea.'

'Struck hard and quick,' one said, and one was silent, but the third said, 'who struck hard and quick would strike in hell.'

Ship heaved hard over, sea was a hill, high hill, and racing, they held on hard.

'Are you going to cover my face? I tell you I don't want to see any more sea.'

Not one would speak, they were watching this sea.

'Never lower in this,' one said, another nodded his head.

'I'll shut my eyes when we throw,' the third said, looking at this one bound, lashed by bar and rope, 'God forsaken that throw might be.'

All three were strained, they lifted him up, they watched the horizon line.

'Cover my face I tell you. I want no more sea,' they heard him say.

Their answer was silence, they raised him yet higher, then they closed eyes, then they hurled him into a sea. Sea closed him in, one journey was ended, begin another, and this began. Down far, then up again, tossing in this sea.

'O.K.' cried one, jumped clean from her rail.

'Hold hard to him,' cried another, jumped down to a sea.

'Coming,' the third said, leapt clear of her rail.

Each swam towards this man, in the heaving sea, they were bearing him up.

'Raft!'

'There!'

'Where?'

'Swim to it.'

'O.K. by me. You follow.'

One swam towards this raft, then clutched, held. He paused for wind, he climbed aboard. He watched for the others, and struggling they came.

Struggling drew nearer, struggling they got him on, painfully followed, stood but a moment, not a word spoken, all three fell flat. They lay, still.

The bound one still cried out against sight of sea, cried for the cloth to cover his face, but none could hear, and none moved. They lay, motionless, only a sea could move.

The heaving mass, where could it bear them?

A roar roused them up, a roar made them move.

They struggled up, they saw, they watched her go, no man's ship, they watched her go down.

'She's gone!'

'Gone!'

One song was ended, begin another. Sing sailor, cried sea, sing a song, sailor, sing a song.

'I'm gone,' cried the ship, 'I'm yet here,' cried a sea. 'Sing a song, sailor, sing a song.'

Washed over one bound, washed over those three, flat on their backs.

Let sky yawn down, and let the sea heave, let that one cry out against it, and against sight of it, no man could move. One journey ended, one begun.

'Sing a song, sailor.'

'Flat on our backs?' cried one.

'Sing a song flat on your backs,' cried the sea, 'sing sailor, sing.'

Washing over them, washing under them, pressing ship down, pressing men down.

The bound one was still, brain rivet-filled, eye refusing that sky, saw nothing but steel, felt the weight of it, felt the heat of it, somewhere below, far down below, in a big shell, in a steel shell, mouth gobbling ash.

He closed eyes as they looked down at him. Nothing you could do. You could lie still, you could think, you could say things, but when you looked at him, hard bound and fast, by bar and rope, you knew there was nothing you could do but watch a sea.

'Won't last long.'

'Tough!'

'S-sh! He can hear you.'

'Cover my bloody face, mate. I want no more sea,' crying out bound, this one was lost.

'I want to laugh, but I won't,' one said, 'that man never saw no sea. Who sees a sea far down below? I could laugh, but I won't,' saying this he pressed a hand flat over his mouth.

'End one journey, begin another, oh where do we go from here?'

'Where?'

'He's moving, look!'

They crawled, they dragged over to him, first looked to see lashings fast, then looked hard at him.

'Cover my face right up,' he cried at them.

'Dreamin',' one said.

'I can't sing,' the lashed one said.

'Never asked you to sing, no man asked you to sing.'

'Who did?'

'God knows, I don't.'

'He's still dreamin'.'

Sing a song, sailor, cried sea, sing a song.

'There! Hear that?'

'Heard nothing.'

'Neither did I.'

'Listen then,' he cried, rivets dancing in his brain, 'listen then.'

'We're listenin', and we hear nothing.'

'Then cover me up.'

'Can't.'

'Leave him alone, he's just dreamin'.'

Raft heaved and sea heaved, they left him then.

Sing a song, sailor, sing a song.

'Listen,' one said, 'there,' cried another, 'ah, he's dreamin',' said the third.

And then they were listening.

Sing a song, sailor, oh sing a song. And then they were watching him.

'Delirious,' one said.

'One a them voices inside him,' said another.

'Hell! Let him sing, then,' shouted the third, curled up like a cat.

II

O.K. by me, sirs, I'll sing a song. A long one or a short one, a thin one or a fat one, a loud one or a soft one, I can sing a song, sirs, O.K. by me.

Then sing a song, sailor, cried sea, then sing a song.

O.K. by me, sirs, I'll sing a song.

I know a river, know a sea, know where oceans are. Knew this before eye saw them, in the bone, sirs, felt it in the bone. Nine at the time, smelt it off my father. Hear him come along, I'd hear him come along, sprawling walk he had, wasn't a tread, never a tread to that man, sirs, no sailor can tread. Sea sees to that, what makes a sea wild sees to that, and the heave and ho of any ship.

Look out of a window now, and there he is, smell sea everytime he comes home. Dream about whales while he's home, read Moby Dick, nine years I was. At ten I saw a sea.

Watched her from a window, flat and sly today, like a lake is, cunning like that, watched that sea, thought of whales, fumed against a high hill, I wanted to go. Go to a sea. Eleven I was then. Saw my father go, watched hard, thought again of whales, waited, he never came back.

Grew to twelve, thirteen, still watched that sea. Knew her, every move of her, every nerve, wasn't always flat, wasn't always sly, lovely some days, you'd fling yourself at her, that lovely she was.

Went on watching. Went on feeling in a bone, couldn't take my eyes off that sea, sirs.

And while I was watching her, my mother watched me.

Yes sirs, watched hard, watched close and constant, see her eyes now, big and sad eyes, wonder in pools there, watching me. Felt a strain coming on me, it was her strain, deep down, feel it all, every bit of it.

Then sudden there came another one, knew what this was. She was pulling, pulling, God she was pulling with a world's weight this sea was. I watched, and I went on watching.

Never grew too big, never remained too small, and then I got it quick, and then I had it. Got it off my father, his smell all over me. Held me in, hung on hard, my father's smell, sea breathing all over me.

Looked harder at that sea, knew her every inch, I'll sail over that sea, I said, she knew I'd go, she watched it come, not sudden, not overwhelming, just slow, grown sure like that, oh more sure than that again.

She knew, oh, that strain on me, pulling, pulling, and all her strain against mine. How silent she could be, like silence was key turned and door closed fast, like hands folded in a lap.

Said never a word, just went on watching me, never saw her once, not once, my eyes were too full of sea. My eyes were drunk with a sea. Saw a line of ships go by, thought which one shall be mine, which ship shall I sail? Sea knew before I did. One more pull and I'm away, one more pull and I was gone, and still she said nothing.

Knew a sea like I did, and like my father did, said so-long and went. O the cries in my ears then.

'Can you lash and make fast?'

'I can lash and make fast.'

'Can you cry heave and heavo?'

'I can cry heave and heavo.'

'Can you splice and rig up?'

'I can splice and rig up.'

'A pull on a rope and a hold on a mast?'

'Pull on any rope, I'll hold on any mast.'

'There she is then, rides high by that quay.'

I went along then, and then I saw her, how high and proud she rode at a quay.

O the cries in my ears.

'Stand fast there!'

I stood fast as this one cried to me.

'Can you reave and bend, take a weight and hold her?'

'I can reave and bend, I can take a weight and hold her.'

'Stand four-square and take knocks?'

'I can stand four-square and take knocks.'

'Hold hard! Can you stand straight in a crooked world?'

'Not tall, yet not small, that's how I am, and broad in the shoulder, hold anything up.'

'Set to then. This man's ship knows the way she goes.'

I went up then. Got the height of her, got the weight of her, got the feel of her. I knew she knew the way she was going, her nose towards a sea.

Along an iron deck, smelt rope and yarn there, see her tall masts. O the sounds in my ears as I come by her foc's'le.

Then I went in, there were many men there.

The cries in my ears now.

'Take knocks and say nothing,' one said.

'I'll take knocks and say nothing.'

'Know a raw deal if you saw one?'

'I'll learn by and by.'

'Love a ship and hate her?'

'I'll learn by and by.'

'Grow strong on hopes, shake hands with the devil?'

'I'll learn by and by,' I said, looked at one, I looked at them all. Tall and fine they were, one short like me, how he could spit.

'Know the way you go then, learn to step fast. How then d'you feel?'

'Feel it coming up, right inside me now,' I said, 'know I'll love a ship when I get to know her,' said this, then heard them all laugh.

'Then measure it well, for this tide we go. Once gone you're all gone, all gone to a sea. No road this way and no road that, once done, you're done, once in you're fast, once down, you're down. Measure these things well.'

'I'll measure them well,' I said, how they watched me then, had a feeling coming up, I'm nearer to them, I'll be as them soon.

Their smoking choked me, they laughed at that.

Tall not at all, but I wasn't too small, a good shoulder to me, knew I'd hold myself up.

One caught my hair, one held my arm, one lifted me up. My heart cried, 'hold hard,' my heart cried, 'be still,' and I said nothing, and I was quite still. Lifted me clear of her deck they did, then set me down.

'Could be knocked down by spindrift,' one said.

'Could be blown off a rigging.'

'Get under a winch then, then get down to a scupper.'

There came cries to our ears, 'all hands to her deck.'

Oh, how she blew then, the power in her blow. They pushed me out and I sprawled to her deck.

One caught my arm, his face was like fire.

'Get aft there,' he shouted, 'watch how they work. Unship and make fast, heave haul and ply, she's sailing now,' the fire in his face grown ruddier still.

I made my way aft, I did as I was bid. I had my father's smell, had the breath of the sea.

'How old?' said one, and I told him then.

'Hard work,' he said, 'and harder than that again,' he said. 'That's how it is. Not too cruel, not too kind, and it never thinks. Wet if you fall in, deep if you drown.'

Laughing away he said this, then cried, 'haul away on that rope.'

And then I was hauling, hauling with men. Watched her veer away, her nose to a sea. Thought of another sea I'd seen, out of my window. Remembered about whales, could see my mother's look, as I was hauling, could feel the strain in her, as I hauled on that rope.

'Good-bye,' my mind cried, 'good-bye to you. Once done you're done, once away you're away fast, and no turn back.'

I thought of all this as I watched her go. We sailed at ten.

'Make way there!' she cried, strong out of her horn, 'make way, make way.'

While I heard this I got the touch of her, I felt a heave of that sea.

'Hold hard,' one cried, they held, I got my breath back as I, too, held.

'Here it is, the sea, you wanted it, you got it, you're away, you're fast done and done again,' I thought.

Then we were hauling again, as she slipped out, by quay and basin, by dock and lock, out towards a river, then on to a sea, beyond that another one, then oceans, and again oceans, how fine she blew that day I went away to a sea I dreamed of, my father's breath in it, my father's bones.

'All hands stand by for'ard,' her bosun cried.

That night I was on the sea, and in the sea, and of the sea. Hard fast, hard fast.

Take one iron bunk, take one mattress of straw, donkey's breakfast, old timers would say. Take one tin cup and one tin plate, knife, fork, and spoon. Take these and keep your mouth shut if you would be wise. Watch bugs come up, watch rats move, take your share of them, keep your mouth shut. Sleep well while you can, ships' clocks race fast. Stand to at the cry, Out!, stand to no matter where, whereever that cry comes from, even from hell. And at the word Go! you go.

Take a look at what you wanted, all this sea, how far she stretches, far as eye can reach, beyond that again, mind's eye sees further. There it is, you wanted it, have it, all of it, every little bit, by drop and drop measure it, by wave and wave, by a heaving and flatness, by a rainbow's colours in it. Look at it, you're on it, you're in it. Break anything, break steel, anything harder than steel, break bone or heart, you can't break that, the hold there, you can't break that.

Away, away, away, her horn was crying, soon we were sailing fast, by pilot boat, by tug, by lightship and lighthouse, passed these at speed, her great horn blowing, make way, make way. A fresh cry in my ears.

'Hands for'ard, hands for'ard.'

Off I went for'ard with them, I walked just behind them. Thought of my father, I got that smell again, he would bring it home when I was nine.

I turned into my bunk. They let me sleep. I slept, I dreamed about whales. First ache in the bone came, then lightness of air, my head was all buzz. Wakened at twelve, show a leg there, show a leg.

I climbed down from my bunk.

Eyes opened wide on a battered face. This man was speaking.

'Get the measure of things,' this one said, 'you best get the measure of things,' taking my arm, he dragged me after him to a darkened deck.

'Wind's up,' he said, 'get the measure of her.'

I got her measure well and truly, I heard him laughing then as I lay heaped in her port scupper, that wind blew hard.

And then I knew. You got the measure of wind, measure of fog, you got the measure of a rolling sea. Only once my heart cried for a single sight of that window, often I'd looked out of it, at that flat, cunning sea.

'Hands aft.'

I heard that cry, the bosun's mate was behind me.

'Hands aft there,' he bawled, 'hands aft there,' just like it was thunder.

I followed after them, and then I got the measure of my mates. At first I walked on air, at first I stumbled forward, then I got the measure of this deck, rolling sea under her.

Grew tall and more broad, my mind emptied fast. Mother out of it, father out of it, all the thoughts round them, emptying fast.

'You're alone on this sea,' a voice said, and I said under my breath, 'you're alone on this sea.'

I went away a moment, when those others weren't looking, I went right past her poop, I stood where her log was, saw that serpent's line spin out and wondered where, wondered how deep, she was. Saw that water thresh, I heard the sounds of her screws. Then I looked out, far out, beyond where that white log-line could end, and then I felt something, didn't know why it came, didn't know what it was, just went on looking, and sudden I knew. Oh the vastness I saw.

'The great, tumbling, roaring vastness of this,' I cried in my mind.

My ear sang from a blow. That moment I was held fast.

'Goddam! Goddam you!' and I was dragged away to where

those others were working. I started working with them, and then I forgot what I had been thinking.

'Get her fine and shipshape,' I heard.

'Get her gear fast away.'

'Tarpaulins down, lashed fast to coamings, those wedges snug home.'

'Those derricks shipped and tidy.'

I was with them, I was one of them, I felt pride then.

One morning and galesome that ship was mine.

Yes sirs, one morning and windy she was mine. I stood alone on her deck, my heart was full. Men passed me by, one winked at me, but no man spoke.

They went by. That ship was mine. Then when they were gone for'ard I look high and low, about and around, and not a soul in sight, only that eye high up, peering over her strong dodger.

'One fine day I'll make a dodger,' I thought.

How clear and shipshape, how high and splendid she rode, how I looked at her, all the whole length of this wondrous ship.

'Which way do you go?'

I cried this out against wind, as though she had mouth and lips, as though she could speak to me.

'Which way do you go?'

My! How she rode as I stood and watched her, the feel of her strong then.

By the East and the North, by the South and the West, chase sun and moon, hold stars in a grasp. Through this sea and through that, this ocean and that one, and all the time watching, watching you.

Freeze your hair today, sweat out your soul tomorrow. Get the measure of all seas, the sure line on oceans, yet hold you hard down.

Throw you up and down, toss you round and about, make you like blue today, gold the next day, then sudden one craven day, make you hate grey. Get the feel of your bone, touch your nerve-centre, make you writhe, make you mad, touch softness and all trust in you, make you all out and gallant, gird you with a faith, make you cry out against me, make you wince at a rawness, make you easy in your mind.

By the East and West, by the North and South I go, always going, always getting somewhere, ploughing through the middle of no-where. Eye for eye, bone for bone, heart for heart. All the things are known, all the things are measured.

I stood quite still there, I listened, and then I knew that all the things were known and all the things were measured.

Sacred Elegy

GEORGE BARKER

FROM this window where the North Atlantic
Takes the crow in my mind home in a short line
Over the kissing fish in the wave, and the mine
Where the sailor clasps his death as mermaid like
Sex of a knife in the depth, from this window
Watching I see the farewelling seasons fall
Ever between us like rain. And the lachrymal
Memory, trailing its skirts, walks like a widow
Across those seas looking for home. O my Dido
Heart! Sail, sail the ships ever away from us all.

Then at this midnight as instant as the bell
That bangs the sailor from his bed to Europe,
I see tomorrow grow in a tree of hope
Outside the window where, like a branch with a ball,
Your face of kisses hangs in my love
Shattered and happy. The sixteen winds that blow
The small seeds into each other's arms below,
The birds to their boughs above, the sad and evil
Everywhere, shall bring to you, if nothing else avail,
The love that, never coming, always goes.

To cross the divide and desert of this distance
Only a hand is enough. Like the seamew sweeping
The wave with a wing to rise up weeping
The parted heart shall with a bird's persistence
Cross seven oceans to its proper home. The pigeon
With a hundred hieroglyphics at its claw
Less laden drops down with what's waited for
Than the sea-weary heart returning. O let love imagine
Meetings of the long parted at the door
Of expectation with happiness in the margin.

Lovers for whom the world is always absent
Move in their lonely union like twin stars
Twining bright destinies around their cause:
They dazzle to shadow with a meridian present
The wallflower world. Redundant it shall resent
The kiss that annihilates it and the gaze that razes.
O from their grasp a new astronomy rises
Where, morning and evening, the dominant Venus
Dismisses all sad worlds that turn between us
And we shall kiss behind our mask of faces.

Convoy Job

JOHN PUDNEY

CONVOY the dead:
Those humble men who drown,
Dreaming of narrow streets, of alleys snug
In lamplight, love in a furrowed bed,
Pints in a Rose and Crown.

Escort the brave
Whose hearts, unsatisfied
With the kind stairs and tender hearths of love,
Are loyal to the cunning of the wave,
The sparse rule of the tide.

Fly over these,
Humble and brave, who sail
And trim the ships with very life; whose lives
Delineate the seas.
Patrol their deathless trail.

Chief Petty Officer

CHARLES CAUSLEY

He is older than the naval side of British history,
And sits
More permanent than the spider in the enormous wall.
His barefoot, coal-burning soul
Expands, puffs like a toad, in the convict air
Of the Royal Naval Barracks at Devonport.

Here, in depôt, in his stone Nirvana:
More real than the opium-pipes,
The uninteresting relics of his Edwardian foreign-commission.
And, from his thick stone box,
He surveys with a prehistoric eye the hostilities-only ratings.
He has the face of the dinosaur
That sometimes stares from old Victorian naval photographs:
That of some elderly lieutenant
With boots and a celluloid Crippen-collar,
Brass buttons and cruel ambitious eyes of almond.

He was probably made a Freemason in Hong Kong.
He has a son (on War Work) in the Dockyard,
And an appalling daughter
In the W.R.N.S.
He writes on your draft-chit
Tobacco-permit or request-form
In a huge antique Borstal hand,
And pins notices on the board in the Chiefs' Mess
Requesting his messmates not to
Lay on the billiard table.
He is an anti-Semite, and has somewhat reactionary views,
And reads the pictures in the daily news.

And when you return from the nervous Pacific
Where the seas
Shift like sheets of plate-glass in the dazzling morning;
Or when you return
Browner than Alexander, from Malta,
Where you have leaned over the side, in harbour,
And seen in the clear water
The salmon-tins, wrecks and tiny explosions of crystal fish,
A whole war later
He will still be sitting under a pussar's clock
Waiting for tot-time,
His narrow forehead ruffled by the Jutland wind.

The Middle of a War

ROY FULLER

My photograph already looks historic.
The promising youthful face, the matelot's collar,
Say, 'This one is remembered for a lyric.
His place and period – nothing could be duller.'

Its position is already indicated –
The son or brother in the album; pained
The expressions and the garments dated,
His fate so obviously preordained.

The original turns away: as horrible thoughts
Loud fluttering aircraft slope above his head
At dusk. The ridiculous empires break like biscuits –
Ah, life has been abandoned by the boats –
Only the trodden island and the dead
Remain, and the once inestimable caskets.

One Transport Lost

ROY CAMPBELL

WHERE, packed as tight as space can fit them
The soldiers retch, and snore, and stink,
It was no bunch of flowers that hit them
And woke them up, that night, to drink.

Dashing the bulkheads red with slaughter,
In the steep wash that swept the hold,
Men, corpses, kitbags, blood, and water,
Colliding and commingling rolled.

Some clung, like flies, in fear and wonder,
Clutched to the crossbeams, out of reach,
Till sprayed from thence by jets of thunder
That spouted rumbling from the breach.

In this new world of blast and suction,
The bulkhead tilted to a roof;
Friend aided friend – but to destruction,
And valour seemed its own reproof.

Forced by the pent explosive airs
In the huge death-gasp of its shell,
Or sucked, like Jonah, by their prayers
From forth that spiracle of Hell –

The ones that catapulted from it
Saw the whole hull reverse its dome,
Then ram the depths, like some huge comet,
Flood-lit with phosphorus and foam.

The shark and grampus might reprieve,
After their jaunt upon a raft,

The few that got Survivor's Leave –
But those who perished would have laughed!

Their fiercest thirst they've quenched and cupped,
And smashed the glass (this life of slaves!);
No hectoring Redcaps interrupt
Their fornication with the waves.

For us this world of Joad and Julian,
The dithering of abortive schemes;
For them, the infinite, cerulean
Suspension of desires and dreams.

So save your Bait, you Bards and Thinkers!
For us who daren't refuse to chew
Hook, line, and swivel, trace and sinkers,
And rod and all, and like it too!

For them, the wave, the melancholy
Chant of the wind that tells no lies;
The breakers roll their funeral volley
To which the thundering cliff replies.

The black cape-hens in decent crêpe
Will mourn them to the Last Event;
The roaring headlands of the Cape
Are lions on their monument.

Song

ALUN LEWIS

(On seeing dead bodies floating off the Cape)

THE first month of his absence
I was numb and sick
And where he'd left his promise
Life did not return or kick.
The seed, the seed of love was sick.

The second month my eyes were sunk
In the darkness of despair,
And my bed was like a grave
And his ghost was lying there.
And my heart was sick with care.

The third month of his going
I thought I heard him say
'Our course deflected slightly
On the thirty-second day – '
The tempest blew his words away.

And he was lost among the waves,
His ship rolled helpless in the sea,
The fourth month of his voyage
He shouted grievously
'Beloved, do not think of me.'

The flying fish like kingfishers
Skin the sea's bewildered crests,
The whales blow steaming fountains,
The seagulls have no nests
Where my lover sways and rests.

We never thought to buy and sell
This life that blooms or withers in the leaf,
And I'll not stir, so he sleeps well,
Though cell by cell the coral reef
Builds an eternity of grief.

But oh! the drag and dullness of my Self;
The turning seasons wither in my head;
All this slowness, all this hardness,
The nearness that is waiting in my bed,
The gradual self-effacement of the dead.

Words and Ideas

W. J. TURNER

WITH words not ideas is poetry made,
But what is a word? say the word, sword?
It is not the sound, it is not the look,
It is not even the image of the keen bright blade
Of the hero who from the fairyland page of a book
Shook dew-shattered sleep from the Princess found.

Is sleep just a word? Come charmèd Sleep
That rocks the ship-boy on the giddy mast
And smoothes the waves to lulling melodies
Too fast! Too fast! we rush to lilts not ours
For sleep's a too melodious hive of honey
Pillow to Paradise stuffed with singing powers.

Is 'Paradise' – yes, is it not a word?
Only a word? Or pure idea by life unparallel'd?
'Meet me in Paradise.' Is it an Inn
In Greenwich Village, providing bed-and-board?
And 'board', so bed-and-breakfasted –
Surely in Paradise no one has ever dwelled?

All hands aboard! What magic changed that word?
Sea-faring men are naïve and full of hope:
Poor Tom Australia-bound for stealing sheep;
Nothing of him by relatives was heard,
He dropped one night unnoticed overboard
By starlight, crossing the Great Australian Bight.

From the high Southern Cross there hangs a rope,
Pricked on a sailor's back in brightest blue,
Up which imagination climbing the globe

Remembers Palinurus, oarsman too,
Who dropped, in Virgil, also in starlight deep,
And, like poor Tom, unnoticed by the crew.

Is Landfall near? The famed Hesperides —
How far are they? How soft the Western breeze!
Too soft, too mild, too rain-bedewed; let's flit
Like screaming gull to sulphur-cindered Aetna
Not let, in night's dark rags, lightning-tattered roll
Into the shore one single rock-cracked skull.

Only the babe can tell, flesh smooth as peach
Surf-softer flowers, insidious-soft as lies,
Dissolving ocean-murmurs, not the hard wave
And splintered keel of skeletoned mariners
Who bite, flesh gone, the beach salt-bitter stone,
Socket and teeth sunk to their pebbled grave.

Wordless and riddle-hard the skull of man,
It will not wash away, it tells us nothing,
Nothing at all. How soft the pelt of pard
By the warm fireside — panther or spotted leopard,
The fur-like purring fire, friendly, soothing,
Soft, soothing words in their nothingness consuming.

Landfall now here! Here where a Spirit sitting
Takes up its skull, looks at its smitten teeth,
Its bearest meaning, here is poetry
Here where there are no words, wash of flesh-confusion,
Only the ultimate It, result of the Spirit's smiting
Man-anvil, at last motionless, shell-like and without breath.

Declarations

Awake!

W. R. RODGERS

WIND that speeds the bee and plucks the bee-line
Into bows and bends, that clips the spoken word
From the open lips, that claps and batters
The bent-backed and running roaring waters,
That squats and squints and squeals evilly in trees,
That follows and faces the fleeing leaves,
That with hag hands hugs the hooked hawk down,
That hammers like rams' heads the humped body,
And that stamps flat like stallions the shaking
Flaking acres of grass – wind nine times named,
And by these wordy welts nine times inflamed
In mind – O mount now and mightily suck
Up all rooted breath out of the rotted mouth
Of man, collapse his plots and exploits, pluck
Every gut taut with terror, like weed
Tugged tight in withdrawing wave, and heedless
In high hangars hoard one blast, pack one breath.
Then fall, walled wind, all welded and one, clap
Wieldy water, scap, and valley gap
Together, and detach man from his map;
O wind have no pity on the city
With buttery motto and lean dole-line
Like old tapeworm in its intestined street,
Or on the foreign laughter of those who boot
Through orchard pasted under foot with fruit,
Seek, suck, sack such, in each socket set tooth,
High over hoardings hurl, and all ways spill,
Hug the elbowing horde, hard under hill
Huddle hare and hound, let lion and lamb
Lump panic-struck, yoke in one choking hold
Victor and victim, rock trigger and target.

And O, halt our hates, file flat our flights,
With stiff pointed finger stuff and stifle
Every gaping gun and pouting rifle;
Pour over our floors and frontiers and leave
Pavement and field clean and ceiling clear,
And man, like Noah afloat in his ark
On an only sea, looking for landmark,
His heart's scope not yet shrunken into
Private and poisonous pools of feeling.

Alas! Æolus will not listen to
Our lot. No upright God angry and stiff
Will suddenly come turning somersaults
Of mercy and cartwheels of leniency
Toward us Noahs. Nor will words rock or wring,
Or invocation sting. At our appeal
No pulse will leap up like a bell-clapper
Proclaiming peace. To us no Nereus will
Rise from the ring of the sea like a rod,
His hair set and salty as dulse, bringing
Succour and promise. So spare your protests.
There are no interlopers in our fate.
Be sure of this, that in peace or war, we
Are where we are because of what we are:
No censor can excerpt, or scissor-snip
Excise this salient sentence from our lives.
O easy and peaceful were those days when
Our hopes bowled on before us like hoops,
And our biddable purposes pedalled
Slowly on rolling gradients of reason
And reform. Fools! in our stinking ditches
War was born, and grew gigantic legs that
Suddenly kicked the ground away like a frog
From under us all. For that is how
The world moves, not with meant and maintained pace
Toward some hill-horizon or held mood
But in great jags and jerks, probed and prodded

From point to point of anger, exploded
By each new and opposed touch. So War came,
The late and urgent agent of Change, not
Of Chance. So it will always come to wake
The deep sleepers. See how its sudden hands
Now garter and grow round us like quicksands
Here in these islands. O awake! awake!
And let us like the trapped intrepid man
Who on prairie hears the holocaust roar
And sees his horizons running to meet him
In mutinous flames, while the still grasses fill
With rills of refugees, let us calmly
Stand now to windward, and here at our feet
Stooping, light fires of foresight that will clean
And clear the careless ground before us
Of all the dry and tindery increment
Of privilege. So will that other Fate
Arriving find no hold within our state,
And we on ringed ground its roar will wait
Freely. Awake! before it is too late.

Where are the War Poets?

C. DAY LEWIS

THEY who in folly or mere greed
Enslaved religion, markets, laws,
Borrow our language now and bid
Us to speak up in freedom's cause.

It is the logic of our times,
No subject for immortal verse,
That we who lived by honest dreams
Defend the bad against the worse.

War Poet

SIDNEY KEYES

I AM the man who looked for peace and found
My own eyes barbed.
I am the man who groped for words and found
An arrow in my hand.
I am the builder whose firm walls surround
A slipping land.
When I grow sick or mad
Mock me not nor chain me:
When I reach for the wind
Cast me not down:
Though my face is a burnt book
And a wasted town.

March, 1942

Cervières

SIDNEY KEYES

Look, Aimée, and you, Victor, look –
The birds have taken all our cherries –
Down in the brown-walled orchard on the hillside
The cherry-trees are weeping for their fruit;
Only the clusters of green stalks
Remain; the stones are scattered on the grass.
There will be no more cherries, not this summer
Nor next, if we get another. God!
It's beyond bearing that they eat our cherries
And fly away and leave the trees in mourning.
Soon an invader will be taking more than cherries:
They'll be stealing our dreams or breaking up
Our history for firewood.
                                    Children, see
The avenues of cherry-trees are broken
And trampled boughs crawl in the dust. See, Victor,
How the sun bouncing off the mountain strikes
Christ's wooden throat above the cemetery:
Flesh broken like our cherry-trees and ravished.
The path runs open and smiling down the hill;
It leaps the walls and hides behind the ruins.

Now take this moment and create its image
Impregnable to time or trespasser,
And turn your mind to realize your loss.
The cherry-trees are broken and their fruit
Sown on the indecipherable mountains.
Realize your loss and take it in your hands
And turn it like a pebble. You perceive
It has a stone's dumb smell; its patterns
Plot some forgotten map. Regard your loss.

Planting this lump of pain, perhaps a flower
Might burst from it; perhaps a cherry-tree,
Perhaps a world or a new race of men.
Regard your loss. The blossoms of the cherry
Are rotten now; the branch is violated;
The fruit is stolen and our dreams have failed.
Yet somewhere – O beyond what bitter ranges? –
A seed drops from the sky and like a bomb
Explodes into our orchard's progeny,
And so our care may colonize a desert.
They cannot break our trees or waste our dreams,
For their despoiling is a kind of sowing.

Aimée and Victor, stop crying. Can't you understand
They cannot steal our cherries or our joy?
Let them take what they want, even our dreams.
Somewhere our loss will plant a better orchard.

September, 1940

The Persian Version

ROBERT GRAVES

TRUTH-LOVING Persians do not dwell upon
The trivial skirmish fought near Marathon.
As for the Greek theatrical tradition
Which represents that summer's expedition
Not as a mere reconnaissance in force
By three brigades of foot and one of horse
(Their left flank covered by some obsolete
Light craft detached from the main Persian fleet)
But as a grandiose, ill-starred attempt
To conquer Greece – they treat it with contempt;
And only incidentally refute
Major Greek claims, by stressing what repute
The Persian monarch and the Persian nation
Won by this salutary demonstration:
Despite a strong defence and adverse weather
All arms combined magnificently together.

In Defence of P. G. Wodehouse

GEORGE ORWELL

WHEN the Germans made their rapid advance through Belgium in
the early summer of 1940, they captured, among other things, Mr
P. G. Wodehouse, who had been living throughout the early part
of the war in his villa at Le Touquet, and seems not to have realized
until the last moment that he was in any danger. As he was led away
into captivity, he is said to have remarked, 'Perhaps after this I shall
write a serious book'. He was placed for the time being under house
arrest and from his subsequent statements it appears that he was
treated in a fairly friendly way. German officers in the neighbour-
hood frequently 'dropping in for a bath or a party'.

Over a year later, on 25 June 1941, the news came that Wodehouse
had been released from internment and was living at the Adlon
Hotel in Berlin. On the following day the public was astonished to
learn that he had agreed to do some broadcasts of a 'non-political'
nature over the German radio. The full texts of these broadcasts
are not easy to obtain at this date, but Wodehouse seems to have
done five of them between 26 June and 2 July, when the Germans
took him off the air again. The first broadcast, on 26 June, was not
made on the Nazi radio but took the form of an interview with Harry
Flannery, the representative of the Columbia Broadcasting System,
which still had its correspondents in Berlin. Wodehouse also published in the *Saturday Evening Post* an article which he had written
while still in the internment camp.

The article and the broadcasts dealt mainly with Wodehouse's
experiences in internment, but they did include a very few comments
on the war. The following are fair samples:

'I never was interested in politics. I'm quite unable to work up any
kind of belligerent feeling. Just as I'm about to feel belligerent about
some country I meet a decent sort of chap. We go out together and
lose any fighting thoughts or feelings.'

'A short time ago they had a look at me on parade and got the right idea; at least they sent us to the local lunatic asylum. And I have been there forty-two weeks. There is a good deal to be said for internment. It keeps you out of the saloon and helps you to keep up with your reading. The chief trouble is that it means you are away from home for a long time. When I join my wife I had better take along a letter of introduction to be on the safe side.'

'In the days before the war I had always been modestly proud of being an Englishman, but now that I have been some months resident in this bin or repository of Englishmen I am not so sure. . . . The only concession I want from Germany is that she gives me a loaf of bread, tells the gentlemen with muskets at the main gate to look the other way, and leave the rest to me. In return I am prepared to hand over India, an autographed set of my books, and to reveal the secret process of cooking sliced potatoes on a radiator. This offer holds good till Wednesday week.'

The first extract quoted above caused great offence. Wodehouse was also censured for using (in the interview with Flannery) the phrase 'whether Britain wins the war or not', and he did not make things better by describing in another broadcast the filthy habits of some Belgian prisoners among whom he was interned. The Germans recorded this broadcast and repeated it a number of times. They seem to have supervised his talks very lightly, and they allowed him not only to be funny about the discomforts of internment but to remark that 'the internees at Trost camp all fervently believe that Britain will eventually win'. The general upshot of the talks, however, was that he had not been ill-treated and bore no malice.

These broadcasts caused an immediate uproar in England. There were questions in Parliament, angry editorial comments in the Press, and a stream of letters from fellow-authors, nearly all of them disapproving, though one or two suggested that it would be better to suspend judgement, and several pleaded that Wodehouse probably did not realize what he was doing. On 15 July, the Home Service of the B.B.C. carried an extremely violent Postscript by 'Cassandra' of the *Daily Mirror*, accusing Wodehouse of 'selling his country'. This postscript made free use of such expressions as

'Quisling' and 'worshipping the Führer'. The main charge was that Wodehouse had agreed to do German propaganda as a way of buying himself out of the internment camp.

'Cassandra's' Postscript caused a certain amount of protest, but on the whole it seems to have intensified popular feeling against Wodehouse. One result of it was that numerous lending libraries withdrew Wodehouse's books from circulation. Here is a typical news item:

'Within twenty-four hours of listening to the broadcast of Cassandra, the *Daily Mirror* columnist, Portadown (North Ireland) Urban District Council banned P. G. Wodehouse's books from their public library. Mr Edward McCann said that Cassandra's broadcast had clinched the matter. Wodehouse was funny no longer.' (*Daily Mirror*.)

In addition the B.B.C. banned Wodehouse's lyrics from the air and was still doing so a couple of years later. As late as December 1944 there were demands in Parliament that Wodehouse should be put on trial as a traitor. There is an old saying that if you throw enough mud some of it will stick, and the mud has stuck to Wodehouse in a rather peculiar way. An impression has been left behind that Wodehouse's talks (not that anyone remembers what he said in them) showed him up not merely as a traitor but as an ideological sympathizer with Fascism. Even at the time several letters to the Press claimed that 'fascist tendencies' could be detected in his books, and the charge has been repeated since. I shall try to analyse the mental atmosphere of those books in a moment, but it is important to realize that the events of 1941 do not convict Wodehouse of anything worse than stupidity. The really interesting question is how and why he could be so stupid. When Flannery met Wodehouse (released, but still under guard) at the Adlon Hotel in June 1941, he saw at once that he was dealing with a political innocent, and when preparing him for their broadcast interview he had to warn him against making some exceedingly unfortunate remarks, one of which was by implication slightly anti-Russian. As it was, the phrase 'whether England wins or not' did get through. Soon after the interview Wodehouse told him that he was also going to broadcast on the Nazi radio, apparently not realizing that this action had any special significance. Flannery comments:*

'By this time the Wodehouse plot was evident. It was one of the best Nazi publicity stunts of the war, the first with a human angle. . . . Plack (Goebbels's assistant) had gone to the camp near Gleiwitz to see Wodehouse, found that the author was completely without political sense, and had an idea. He suggested to Wodehouse that in return for being released from the prison camp he write a series of broadcasts about his experiences; there would be no censorship and he would put them on the air himself. In making that proposal Plack showed that he knew his man. He knew that Wodehouse made fun of the English in all his stories and that he seldom wrote in any other way, that he was still living in the period about which he wrote and had no conception of Nazism and all it meant. Wodehouse was his own Bertie Wooster.'

The striking of an actual bargain between Wodehouse and Plack seems to be merely Flannery's own interpretation. The arrangement may have been of a much less definite kind, and to judge from the broadcasts themselves, Wodehouse's main idea in making them was to keep in touch with his public and – the comedian's ruling passion – to get a laugh. Obviously they are not the utterances of a Quisling of the type of Ezra Pound or John Amery, nor, probably, of a person capable of understanding the nature of Quislingism. Flannery seems to have warned Wodehouse that it would be unwise to broadcast, but not very forcibly. He adds that Wodehouse (though in one broadcast he refers to himself as an Englishman) seemed to regard himself as an American citizen. He had contemplated naturalization, but had never filled in the necessary papers. He even used, to Flannery, the phrase, 'We're not at war with Germany'.

I have before me a bibliography of P. G. Wodehouse's works. It names round about fifty books, but is certainly incomplete. It is as well to be honest, and I ought to start by admitting that there are many books by Wodehouse – perhaps a quarter or a third of the total – which I have not read. It is not, indeed, easy to read the whole output of a popular writer who is normally published in cheap

* *Assignment in Berlin*, Harry W. Flannery. (Michael Joseph, 1942.)

editions. But I have followed his work fairly closely since 1911, when I was eight years old, and am well acquainted with its peculiar mental atmosphere – an atmosphere which has not, of course, remained completely unchanged, but shows little alteration since about 1925. In the passage from Flannery's book which I quoted above there are two remarks which would immediately strike any attentive reader of Wodehouse. One is to the effect that Wodehouse 'was still living in the period about which he wrote', and the other that the Nazi Propaganda Ministry made use of him because he 'made fun of the English'. The second statement is based on a misconception to which I will return presently. But Flannery's other comment is quite true and contains in it part of the clue to Wodehouse's behaviour.

A thing that people often forget about P. G. Wodehouse's novels is how long ago the better-known of them were written. We think of him as in some sense typifying the silliness of the nineteen-twenties and nineteen-thirties, but in fact the scenes and characters by which he is best remembered had all made their appearance before 1925. Psmith first appeared in 1909, having been foreshadowed by other characters in earlier school-stories. Blandings Castle, with Baxter and the Earl of Emsworth both in residence, was introduced in 1915. The Jeeves-Wooster cycle began in 1919, both Jeeves and Wooster having made brief appearances earlier. Ukridge appeared in 1924. When one looks through the list of Wodehouse's books from 1902 onwards, one can observe three fairly well-marked periods. The first is the school-story period. It includes such books as *The Gold Bat*, *The Pothunters*, etc., and has its high spot in *Mike* (1909). *Psmith in the City*, published in the following year, belongs in this category, though it is not directly concerned with school life. The next is the American period. Wodehouse seems to have lived in the United States from about 1913 to 1920, and for a while showed signs of becoming Americanized in idiom and outlook. Some of the stories in *The Man with Two Left Feet* (1917) appear to have been influenced by O. Henry, and other books written about this time contain Americanisms (*e.g.* 'highball' for 'whisky and soda') which an Englishman would not normally use *in propria persona*. Nevertheless, almost all the books of this period – *Psmith, Journalist*; *The Little Nugget*; *The Indiscretions of Archie*; *Piccadilly Jim* and various others – depend for their effect on the *contrast* between English and American manners. English characters appear in an American setting, or *vice versa*; there is a certain number of purely English stories, but hardly any American ones. The third period might fitly be called the country-house period. By the early nineteen-twenties Wodehouse must have been making a very large income, and the social status of his characters moved upwards accordingly, though the Ukridge stories form a partial exception. The typical setting is now a country mansion, a luxurious bachelor flat or an expensive golf club. The schoolboy athleticism of the earlier books fades out, cricket and football giving way to golf, and the element of farce and burlesque becomes more marked. No doubt many of the later books, such as *Summer Lightning*, are light comedy rather than pure farce, but the occasional attempts at moral earnestness which can be found in *Psmith, Journalist*; *The Little Nugget*; *The Coming of Bill*; *The Man with Two Left Feet* and some of the school stories, no longer appear. Mike Jackson has turned into Bertie Wooster. That, however, is not a very startling metamorphosis, and one of the most noticeable things about Wodehouse is his *lack* of development. Books like *The Gold Bat* and *Tales of St Austin's*, written in the opening years of this century, already have the familiar atmosphere. How much of a formula the writing of his later books had become one can see from the fact that he continued to write stories of English life although throughout the sixteen years before his internment he was living at Hollywood and Le Touquet.

Mike, which is now a difficult book to obtain in an unabridged form, must be one of the best 'light' school stories in English. But though its incidents are largely farcical, it is by no means a satire on the public-school system, and *The Gold Bat*, *The Pothunters*, etc., are even less so. Wodehouse was educated at Dulwich, and then worked in a bank and graduated into novel-writing by way of very cheap journalism. It is clear that for many years he remained 'fixated' on his old school and loathed the unromantic job and the lower middle-class-surroundings in which he found himself. In the early stories the 'glamour' of public-school life (house matches, fagging, teas round the study fire, etc.) is laid on fairly thick, and the 'play the game' code of morals is accepted with not many reservations.

Wrykyn, Wodehouse's imaginary public school, is a school of a more fashionable type than Dulwich, and one gets the impression that between *The Gold Bat* (1904) and *Mike* (1909) Wrykyn itself has become more expensive and moved farther from London. Psychologically the most revealing book of Wodehouse's early period is *Psmith in the City*. Mike Jackson's father has suddenly lost his money, and Mike, like Wodehouse himself, is thrust at the age of about eighteen into an ill-paid subordinate job in a bank. Psmith is similarly employed, though not from financial necessity. Both this book and *Psmith, Journalist* (1915) are unusual in that they display a certain amount of political consciousness. Psmith at this stage chooses to call himself a Socialist – in his mind, and no doubt in Wodehouse's, this means no more than ignoring class distinctions – and on one occasion the two boys attend an open-air meeting on Clapham Common and go home to tea with an elderly Socialist orator, whose shabby-genteel home is described with some accuracy. But the most striking feature of the book is Mike's inability to wean himself from the atmosphere of school. He enters upon his job without any pretence of enthusiasm, and his main desire is not, as one might expect, to find a more interesting and useful job, but simply to be playing cricket. When he has to find himself lodgings he chooses to settle at Dulwich, because there he will be near a school and will be able to hear the agreeable sound of the ball striking against the bat. The climax of the book comes when Mike gets the chance to play in a county match and simply walks out of his job in order to do so. The point is that Wodehouse here sympathizes with Mike: indeed he identifies himself with him, for it is clear enough that Mike bears the same relation to Wodehouse as Julian Sorel to Stendhal. But he created many other heroes essentially similar. Through the books of this and the next period there passes a whole series of young men to whom playing games and 'keeping fit' are a sufficient life-work. Wodehouse is almost incapable of imagining a desirable job. The great thing is to have money of your own, or, failing that, to find a sinecure. The hero of *Something Fresh* (1915) escapes from low-class journalism by becoming physical-training instructor to a dyspeptic millionaire: this is regarded as a step up, morally as well as financially.

In the books of the third period there is no narcissism and no serious interludes, but the implied moral and social background has changed much less than might appear at first sight. If one compares Bertie Wooster with Mike, or even with the rugger-playing prefects of the earliest school stories, one sees that the only real difference between them is that Bertie is richer and lazier. His ideals would be almost the same as theirs, but he fails to live up to them. Archie Moffam, in *The Indiscretions of Archie* (1921), is a type intermediate between Bertie and the earlier heroes: he is an ass, but he is also honest, kind-hearted, athletic and courageous. From first to last Wodehouse takes the public-school code of behaviour for granted, with the difference that in his later, more sophisticated period he prefers to show his characters violating it or living up to it against their will:

'Bertie! You wouldn't let down a pal?'
'Yes, I would.'
'But we were at school together, Bertie.'
'I don't care.'
'The old school, Bertie, the old school!'
'Oh, well – dash it!'

Bertie, a sluggish Don Quixote, has no wish to tilt at windmills, but he would hardly think of refusing to do so when honour calls. Most of the people whom Wodehouse intends as sympathetic characters are parasites, and some of them are plain imbeciles, but very few of them could be described as immoral. Even Ukridge is a visionary rather than a plain crook. The most immoral, or rather unmoral, of Wodehouse's characters is Jeeves, who acts as a foil to Bertie Wooster's comparative high-mindedness and perhaps symbolizes the widespread English belief that intelligence and unscrupulousness are much the same thing. How closely Wodehouse sticks to conventional morality can be seen from the fact that nowhere in his books is there anything in the nature of a sex joke. This is an enormous sacrifice for a farcical writer to make. Not only are there no dirty jokes, but there are hardly any compromising situations: the horns-on-the-forehead motif is almost completely avoided. Most of the full-length books, of course, contain a 'love interest', but it is always at the light-comedy level: the love affair, with its complications and its idyllic scenes, goes on and on, but, as the saying goes, 'nothing happens'. It is significant that Wodehouse, by nature a writer of farces, was able to collaborate more than once with Ian Hay, a serio-comic writer and an exponent (vide *Pip*, etc.) of the 'clean-living Englishman' tradition at its silliest.

In *Something Fresh* Wodehouse had discovered the comic possibilities of the English aristocracy, and a succession of ridiculous but, save in a very few instances, not actually contemptible barons, earls and what-not followed accordingly. This had the rather curious effect of causing Wodehouse to be regarded, outside England, as a penetrating satirist of English society. Hence Flannery's statement that Wodehouse 'made fun of the English', which is the impression he would probably make on a German or even an American reader. Some time after the broadcasts from Berlin I was discussing them with a young Indian Nationalist who defended Wodehouse warmly. He took it for granted that Wodehouse *had* gone over to the enemy, which from his own point of view was the right thing to do. But what interested me was to find that he regarded Wodehouse as an anti-British writer who had done useful work by showing up the British aristocracy in their true colours. This is a mistake that it would be very difficult for an English person to make, and is a good instance of the way in which books, especially humorous books, lose their finer nuances when they reach a foreign audience. For it is clear enough that Wodehouse is *not* anti-British, and not anti-upper class either. On the contrary, a harmless old-fashioned snobbishness is perceptible all through his work. Just as an intelligent Catholic is able to see that the blasphemies of Baudelaire or James Joyce are not seriously damaging to the Catholic faith, so an English reader can see that in creating such characters as Hildebrand Spencer Poyns de Burgh John Hanneyside Coombe-Crombie, 12th Earl of Dreever, Wodehouse is not really attacking the social hierarchy. Indeed, no one who genuinely despised titles would write of them so much. Wodehouse's attitude towards the English social system is the same as his attitude towards the public-school moral code – a mild facetiousness covering an unthinking acceptance. The Earl of

Emsworth is funny because an earl ought to have more dignity, and Bertie Wooster's helpless dependence on Jeeves is funny partly because the servant ought not to be superior to the master. An American reader can mistake these two, and others like them, for hostile caricatures, because he is inclined to be Anglophobe already and they correspond to his preconceived ideas about a decadent aristocracy. Bertie Wooster, with his spats and his cane, is the traditional stage Englishman. But, as any English reader would see, Wodehouse intends him as a sympathetic figure, and Wodehouse's real sin has been to present the English upper classes as much nicer people than they are. All through his books certain problems are consistently avoided. Almost without exception his moneyed young men are unassuming, good mixers, not avaricious: their tone is set for them by Psmith, who retains his own upper-class exterior but bridges the social gap by addressing everyone as 'Comrade'.

But there is another important point about Bertie Wooster: his out-of-dateness. Conceived in 1917 or thereabouts, Bertie really belongs to an epoch earlier than that. He is the 'knut' of the pre-1914 period, celebrated in such songs as 'Gilbert the Filbert' or 'Reckless Reggie of the Regent's Palace'. The kind of life that Wodehouse writes about by preference, the life of the 'clubman' or 'man about town', the elegant young man who lounges all the morning in Piccadilly with a cane under his arm and a carnation in his button-hole, barely survived into the nineteen-twenties. It is significant that Wodehouse could publish in 1936 a book entitled *Young Men in Spats*. For who was wearing spats at that date? They had gone out of fashion quite ten years earlier. But the traditional 'knut', the 'Piccadilly Johnny', *ought* to wear spats, just as the pantomime Chinese ought to wear a pigtail. A humorous writer is not obliged to keep up to date, and having struck one or two good veins, Wodehouse continued to exploit them with a regularity that was no doubt all the easier because he did not set foot in England during the sixteen years that preceded his internment. His picture of English society had been formed before 1914, and it was a naïve, traditional and, at bottom, admiring picture. Nor did he ever become genuinely Americanized. As I have pointed out, spontaneous Americanisms do occur in the books of the middle period, but Wodehouse remained

English enough to find American slang an amusing and slightly shocking novelty. He loves to thrust a slang phrase or a crude fact in among Wardour Street English ('With a hollow groan Ukridge borrowed five shillings from me and went out into the night'), and expressions like 'a piece of cheese' or 'bust him on the noggin' lend themselves to this purpose. But the trick had been developed before he made any American contacts, and his use of garbled quotations is a common device of English writers running back to Fielding. As Mr John Hayward has pointed out,* Wodehouse owes a great deal to his knowledge of English literature and especially of Shakespeare. His books are aimed, not, obviously, at a highbrow audience but at an audience educated along traditional lines. When, for instance, he describes somebody as heaving 'the kind of sigh that Prometheus might have heaved when the vulture dropped in for its lunch', he is assuming that his readers will know something of Greek mythology. In his early days the writers he admired were probably Barry Pain, Jerome K. Jerome, W. W. Jacobs, Kipling and F. Anstey, and he has remained closer to them than to the quick-moving American comic writers such as Ring Lardner or Damon Runyon. In his radio interview with Flannery, Wodehouse wondered whether 'the kind of people and the kind of England I write about will live after the war', not realizing that they were ghosts already. 'He was still living in the period about which he wrote,' says Flannery, meaning, probably, the nineteen-twenties. But the period was really the Edwardian age, and Bertie Wooster, if he ever existed, was killed round about 1915.

If my analysis of Wodehouse's mentality is accepted, the idea that in 1941 he consciously aided the Nazi propaganda machine becomes untenable and even ridiculous. He *may* have been induced to broadcast by the promise of an earlier release (he was due for release a few months later, on reaching his sixtieth birthday), but he cannot have realized that what he did would be damaging to British interests. As I have tried to show, his moral outlook has remained that of a public-school boy, and according to the public-school code, treachery in time of war is the most unforgivable of all the sins. But how could he fail to grasp that what he did would be a big

*P. G. *Wodehouse*, by John Hayward. (*The Saturday Book*, 1942.)

propaganda score for the Germans and would bring down a torrent of disapproval on his own head? To answer this one must take two things into consideration. First, Wodehouse's complete lack – so far as one can judge from his printed works – of political awareness. It is nonsense to talk of 'Fascist tendencies' in his books. There are no post-1918 tendencies at all. Throughout his work there is a certain uneasy awareness of the problem of class distinctions, and scattered through it at various dates there are ignorant though not unfriendly references to Socialism. In *The Heart of a Goof* (1926) there is a rather silly story about a Russian novelist, which seems to have been inspired by the factional struggle then raging in the U.S.S.R. But the references in it to the Soviet system are entirely frivolous and, considering the date, not markedly hostile. That is about the extent of Wodehouse's political consciousness, so far as it is discoverable from his writings. Nowhere, so far as I know, does he so much as use the words 'Fascism' or 'Nazism'. In left-wing circles, indeed in 'enlightened' circles of any kind, to broadcast on the Nazi radio, to have any truck with the Nazis whatever, would have seemed just as shocking an action before the war as during it. But that is a habit of mind that had been developed during nearly a decade of ideological struggle against Fascism. The bulk of the British people, one ought to remember, remained anaesthetic to that struggle until late into 1940. Abyssinia, Spain, China, Austria, Czechoslovakia – the long series of crimes and aggressions had simply slid past their consciousness or were dimly noted as quarrels occurring among foreigners and 'not our business'. One can gauge the general ignorance from the fact that the ordinary Englishman thought of 'Fascism' as an exclusively Italian thing and was bewildered when the same word was applied to Germany. And there is nothing in Wodehouse's writings to suggest that he was better informed, or more interested in politics, than the general run of his readers.

The other thing one must remember is that Wodehouse happened to be taken prisoner at just the moment when the war reached its desperate phase. We forget these things now, but until that time feelings about the war had been noticeably tepid. There was hardly any fighting, the Chamberlain Government was unpopular, eminent publicists were hinting that we should make a compromise peace as quickly as possible, trade union and Labour Party branches all over the country were passing anti-war resolutions. Afterwards, of course things changed. The Army was with difficulty extricated from Dunkirk, France collapsed, Britain was alone, the bombs rained on London, Goebbels announced that Britain was to be 'reduced to degradation and poverty'. By the middle of 1941 the British people knew what they were up against and feelings against the enemy were far fiercer than before. But Wodehouse had spent the intervening year in internment, and his captors seem to have treated him reasonably well. He had missed the turning-point of the war, and in 1941 he was still reacting in terms of 1939. He was not alone in this. On several occasions about this time the Germans brought captured British soldiers to the microphone, and some of them made remarks at least as tactless as Wodehouse's. They attracted no attention, however. And even an outright Quisling like John Amery was afterwards to arouse much less indignation than Wodehouse had done.

But why? Why should a few rather silly but harmless remarks by an elderly novelist have provoked such an outcry? One has to look for the probable answer amid the dirty requirements of propaganda warfare.

There is one point about the Wodehouse broadcasts that is almost certainly significant – the date. Wodehouse was released two or three days before the invasion of the U.S.S.R., and at a time when the higher ranks of the Nazi Party must have known that the invasion was imminent. It was vitally necessary to keep America out of the war as long as possible, and in fact, about this time the German attitude towards the U.S.A. did become more conciliatory than it had been before. The Germans could hardly hope to defeat Russia, Britain and the U.S.A. in combination, but if they could polish off Russia quickly – and presumably they expected to do so – the Americans might never intervene. The release of Wodehouse was only a minor move, but it was not a bad sop to throw to the American isolationists. He was well known in the United States, and he was – or so the Germans calculated – popular with the Anglophobe public as a caricaturist who had made fun of the silly-ass Englishman with his spats and his monocle. At the microphone he could be trusted to damage British prestige in one way or another, while his release would demonstrate that the Germans were good fellows and knew how to treat their enemies chivalrously. That presumably was the calculation, though the fact that Wodehouse was only broadcasting for about a week suggests that he did not come up to expectations.

But on the British side similar though opposite calculations were at work. For the two years following Dunkirk, British morale depended largely upon the feeling that this was not only a war for democracy but a war which the common people had to win by their own efforts. The upper classes were discredited by their appeasement policy and by the disasters of 1940, and a social levelling process appeared to be taking place. Patriotism and left-wing sentiments were associated in the popular mind, and numerous able journalists were at work to tie the association tighter. Priestley's 1940 broadcasts, and 'Cassandra's' articles in the *Daily Mirror*, were good examples of the demagogic propaganda flourishing at that time. In this atmosphere, Wodehouse made an ideal whipping-boy. For it was generally felt that the rich were treacherous, and Wodehouse – as 'Cassandra' vigorously pointed out in his broadcast – was a rich man. But he was the kind of rich man who could be attacked with impunity and without risking any damage to the structure of society. To denounce Wodehouse was not like denouncing, say, Beaverbrook. A mere novelist, however large his earnings may happen to be, is not of the possessing class. Even if his income touches £50,000 a year he has only the outward semblance of a millionaire. He is a lucky outsider who has fluked into a fortune – usually a very temporary fortune – like the winner of the Calcutta Derby Sweep. Consequently, Wodehouse's indiscretion gave a good propaganda opening. It was a chance to 'expose' a wealthy parasite without drawing attention to any of the parasites who really mattered.

In the desperate circumstances of the time, it was excusable to be angry at what Wodehouse did, but to go on denouncing him three or four years later – and more, to let an impression remain that he acted with conscious treachery – is not excusable. Few things in this war have been more morally disgusting than the present hunt after traitors and Quislings. At best it is largely the punishment of the guilty by the guilty. In France, all kinds of petty rats – police officials, penny-a-lining journalists, women who have slept with German soldiers – are hunted down while almost without exception the big rats escape. In England the fiercest tirades against Quislings are uttered by Conservatives who were practising appeasement in 1938 and Communists who were advocating it in 1940. I have striven to show how the wretched Wodehouse – just because success and expatriation had allowed him to remain mentally in the Edwardian age – became the *corpus vile* in a propaganda experiment, and I suggest that it is now time to regard the incident as closed. If Ezra Pound is caught and shot by the American authorities, it will have the effect of establishing his reputation as a poet for hundreds of years; and even in the case of Wodehouse, if we drive him to retire to the United States and renounce his British citizenship, we shall end by being horribly ashamed of ourselves. Meanwhile, if we really want to punish the people who weakened national morale at critical moments there are other culprits who are nearer home and better worth chasing.

The Patient Khaki Beast

Instead of a Carol

RAYNER HEPPENSTALL

THE winter hardens. Every night, I hear
The patient, khaki beast grieve in his stall,
His eyes behind the hard fingers soft as wool.
His cheerful morning face puts me in mind
Of certain things were rumoured far and near
To hearts wherein there fretted and repined
A world that came to its last dated year.

December, 1940

Alamein

KEITH DOUGLAS

I AM not writing about these battles as a soldier, nor trying to discuss them as military operations. I am thinking of them – selfishly, but as I shall always think of them – as my first experience of fighting: that is how I shall write of them. To say I thought of the battle of Alamein as an ordeal sounds pompous: but I did think of it as an important test, which I was interested in passing. I observed these battles partly as an exhibition – that is to say that I went through them a little like a visitor from the country going to a great show, or like a child in a factory – a child sees the brightness and efficiency of steel machines and endless belts slapping round and round, without caring or knowing what it is all there for. When I could order my thoughts I looked for more significant things than appearances; I still looked – I cannot avoid it – for something decorative, poetic or dramatic.

The geography of the country in which I spent those few months is already as vague to me as if I had learnt it from an atlas much longer ago. The dates have slipped away, the tactical lessons have been learnt by someone else. But what remains in my mind – a flurry of violent impressions – is vivid enough. Against a background of indeterminate landscapes of moods and smells, dance the black and bright incidents.

I had to wait until 1942 to go into action. I enlisted in September 1939, and during two years or so of hanging about I never lost the certainty that the experience of battle was something I must have. Whatever changes in the nature of warfare, the battlefield is the simple, central stage of the war: it is there that the interesting things happen. We talk in the evening, after fighting, about the great and rich men who cause and conduct wars. They have so many reasons of their own that they can afford to lend us some of them. There is nothing odd about their attitude. They are out for something they want, or their Governments want, and they are using us to get it for them. Anyone can understand that: there is nothing unusual or humanly exciting at that end of the war. I mean there may be things to excite financiers and parliamentarians – but not to excite a poet or a painter or a doctor.

But it is exciting and amazing to see thousands of men, very few of whom have much idea why they are fighting, all enduring hardships, living in an unnatural, dangerous, but not wholly terrible world, having to kill and to be killed, and yet at intervals moved by a feeling of comradeship with the men who kill them and whom they kill, because they are enduring and experiencing the same things. It is tremendously illogical – to read about it cannot convey the impression of having walked through the looking-glass which touches a man entering a battle.

I had arrived in the Middle East in August, 1941. As a result of passing a course on which I was sent by accident, I found myself posted away from my regiment to a Divisional staff. I still wanted to get into action, and probably looked impatiently at my colleagues and superiors on this staff. For eight months I honestly tried hard to make sense of the job I was given – in other words to persuade the staff colonel and major to whose department I was attached to give me some work to do. The situation emerged clearly and simply as the months passed. My job was to give camouflage training. The Staff officers of G staff, under the General, arranged training programmes: they invariably forgot to include camouflage. At first they airily agreed to my humble reminders with a wealth of condescending language – the General alone refrained from calling me 'old boy' although he said good morning, good morning as civilly as Siegfried Sassoon's General.

After eight months of relative inaction, not being at any time a patient person, and having a hatred for wasted time, I tried to get back to my regiment. I could not be released: with the charm and politeness with which everyone on a staff always speaks to everyone else, I was told I was indispensable. Any disclaimer of this, any statement that I was doing nothing but waste Government petrol and money, appeared to strike them as a conventionally modest reply, equivalent to saying 'I'm only doing my job, old boy'. The offensive loomed very large in rumour, among so many officers living more or less inside the horse's mouth. I decided, if there were no other means of going into action with my regiment, to run away from divisional headquarters in my truck, and report to my Colonel. I thought vaguely that this might be straightened out later. To plan this was the natural result of having the sort of little-boy mentality I still have. A little earlier, I might have wanted to run away and be a pirate. But it is surprising how easily the plan was realized and justified. For eight months I had done no mechanized training, my regiment was equipped with tanks, guns and wireless sets which I had never handled, scarcely seen, in my life; and it seemed possible, and even likely, that my Colonel who had applied for me before the battle, would not want an untrained officer to join him during action and endanger everyone's life while learning his job. If he refused me I was determined not to come back to Division but to drive away down the coast road to Alexandria, and from there through Cairo and Ismailia and across the Sinai desert to Palestine, to amuse myself until I was caught and court-martialled.

The battle of Alamein began on the 23 October 1942. Six days afterwards I set out in direct disobedience of orders to rejoin my regiment. My batman was delighted with this manoeuvre. 'I like you, sir,' he said. 'You're shit or bust, you are.' This praise gratified me a lot . . .

*

We began our approach march for the last advance on Tripoli at night, in brilliant moonlight, an interminable column of three files in which every vehicle in the Brigade was moving. These were the most physically miserable and painful hours I ever spent. The dust was like a blanket, and made breathing continually difficult, at times scarcely to be attempted. My left eye and forehead had swelled up inexplicably, the skin smarting and my head and eye aching dully, an ache as sensitive to sudden movements as an alcoholic headache. One of my eyes was covered with an eyepatch. The other had to be strained through the dust, which was a cloud before the moon and plunged us into a grey, almost complete opacity. I had one leg swollen with a big desert sore and bandaged until it looked more like a pudding than a leg. By the second night of the advance, having had very little sleep during the day, I was very sleepy. Only the bitter night cold of the beginning of January kept me awake. I had to ensure, hour after hour, that I kept my tank opposite the tank of my troop in the next file. Sometimes this was very difficult, because one file would halt and the others continue moving on. The track was marked by shaded red lights, some of which had inevitably been run over and smashed by tanks or vehicles ahead. After a few hours' sleep, in the early hours of the second morning, we began our advance on Tripoli – our orders, which I had noted down on a scrap of paper in Greek characters, with a vague idea of security in my mind, gave the regiment a line of advance which ended astride the road twenty miles on the far side of Tripoli. For all our new pennons, we were not to enter the city.

Anyone who takes part in a modern battle in a tank, which is equipped with a wireless, has an advantage over the infantrymen, and over all the soldiers and generals of earlier wars. Before his mind's eye the panorama of the battle is kept, more vividly even than before the general of other times who watched his soldiers from a vantage point, or was kept posted by telephones and runners. Suppose a tank officer in the Crusader squadron of an armoured regimental group (for he is the best informed of all, more instantly and clearly aware of each event of the battle in his area even than his senior commanders). During the day or two before going into action he has listened to the scheme of orders for the whole army. He knows or has had represented to him by a coloured diagram on a map (the main outline of which is soon fixed by the skill of habit in his mind) the position, the route, the objectives of each Division and Brigade. In his own Brigade he knows where his own and other regiments are going, he knows where the squadrons, the supply vehicles, the guns and infantry of his regimental group are, and their radio code names. Within his squadron – let us suppose him a troop leader – he knows the positions of the other troops and of his squadron leader, and finally of the tanks of his troop. As he moves forward, the coloured lines advance across the map of his mind. He may or may not have an actual map in front of him: if he is a junior officer, it will probably be stowed, in battle. The earphones of his wireless set hang round his neck, or at noisier moments over his ears, as they are usually depicted. He hears a continuous account of the battle through these earphones. The idioms are as stereotyped as in the most ceremonial exchange of courtesies. There are things which are not said; awkward silences, epigrams, jokes: even an occasional outburst of emotion is confined by conventional phrases. The conversation follows the course of the battle with the most vivid, inimitable running commentary in the world.

The idiom of our wireless traffic, the mysterious symbolic language in some ways like that of a wildly experimental school of poets; or unemotional, dull, and thus humorous like the conversation of the two Englishmen in *The Lady Vanishes*, came from two sources. A wireless code and procedure had been laid down by someone who had vague ideas of security and no idea of the mentality of mechanized (or unmechanized) cavalrymen. For I think to a greater extent than the Royal Tank battalions, the Yeomanry found the official vocabulary unenterprising and a nuisance to learn, and supplemented it with 'veiled talk' of their own – code names and allusions as local as possible, and as typically English as possible, by which it was hoped enemy listening posts would be deceived. Unfortunately, the lack of method on the side of the speakers and the amazing deductive ability of the other side made this sort of talk quite insecure. But I can still best conjure up for myself the actual atmosphere of battle by repeating these phrases, and indeed the most officially approved wireless conversations are no more mysterious and dramatic to an ordinary listener, so that a little of this battle conversation may give a nearer impression than my adjectives and descriptions. This, then, is how the battle goes.

Each speaker has his own code name, shortened, after the initial netting calls, to a letter and a number, or simply a letter in the case of a control station. We are quite inconsistent: some of these letters change daily, some never change. Some are codes, some simply initials or Christian and nicknames (which gave us away to the enemy more than anything else). All these disguises are used and interchanged according to whim. The enemy, who wants to find out what kind of formation we are, and if he has seen us before, and a great many smaller details, is not much deceived by our mysterious asides – but this we are not to find out until later.

Piccadilly Jim (the Colonel) is accustomed to say – and in san-
guine moments we believe him – that we have a good wireless
discipline. This should mean that no one interrupts or speaks at un-
necessary length, and that every vital message gets through in one.
In fact, it means that we keep off the air when Piccadilly Jim is
speaking, while he interrupts, dilates, or ignores messages entirely.
No one ever interrupts or ignores him. For this offence, no stress of
battle, except death, is an excuse. The result of this is clearly that,
whatever happens, Piccadilly Jim retains absolute control of the air,
and, therefore, of the regimental group. It may mean that he misses
important information. There are painful moments, when a somewhat facetious conversation of Jim's: 'Oh, there you are, Nuts
Orange. That's just where I want you. I'm very pleased to see you
. . . Look, I'm waving to you . . . I'm taking off my hat to you . . .
I'm blowing you a kiss . . . er . . . Over,' and the required polite
reply, 'Nuts Orange . . . er . . . O.K. . . . off,' drowns an anxious
message . . . 'King 2 Ack, six enemy tanks advancing towards me on
my right. They are out of my range. Could George have a go at
them? Over.' But in general Piccadilly Jim is given a good idea of
anything which is happening outside his own vision, by the
Crusader squadron.

From the first appearance of the enemy, a Crusader troop leader,
well out in front of the regiment, sees and hears the whole action,
almost as if it were a pageant prepared for his entertainment: for
hours on end it may continue to be exciting in quite an impersonal
way. He sees a suspicious blob on the horizon; halts his squat turret
almost level with a ridge and scrutinizes the blob through his glasses.
Pressing the switch of his microphone, releasing it a moment to see
if someone else is talking, and pressing it again, he says: 'King 2.
Something that looks like a tank to my front, about three miles, I'm
on your right. Over.' 'King 2. O.K. off to you. King, did you hear
King 2's message?' 'King, yes. Let him keep bumming on. But be
cautious.' 'Off,' says Piccadilly Jim to Edward. 'King 1,' says Edward, calling the squadron, 'slow down a bit and have a good look
from hull down before you go swanning over ridges. Over.' '2 O.K.
off, 3 O.K. off. 4 O.K. off.' 'King 2, 3, 4, O.K. off to you. King 5,
did you get my last message?' 'King 5. Yes. Over.' 'King 5, well

bloody well wake up and acknowledge. Off' caps the rebuke, like a telephone receiver being hung up. We have two main sources of allusion, horses and cricket. 'Uncle Tom, what's the going like over this next bit? Can we bring the, er, unshod horses over it?' 'Uncle Tom, I'm *just* going over Beecher's myself, you want to hold 'em in a bit and go carefully, but after that it's good going for the whole field.' 'King 2 Ack,' says someone who has broken a track. 'I shall need the farrier, I've cast a shoe.' Someone else is 'having trouble with my horse's insides. Could I have the Vet?' Metaphor changes 'King 2, someone is throwing stones. I can't see where from yet Over', and a little later Piccadilly Jim asks: 'King 2, now that that chap has retired to the pavilion, how many short of a full team are you?' As the action goes on, metaphors, direct speech, codes, sequences of messages are intermingled, until a good deal of concentration is needed to disentangle them. 'King 2. There are a couple of 88's on that grey ridge to my right. One is near the brew up, and the other is to the left of it, about two degrees. Over.' 'King 2. O.K. off to you. Orange Pip, can you see those 88's of King 2's? Over.' 'George 4, is that a vehicle moving on your right front? Over.' 'Orange Pip, yes. Getting gunfire on now. Over.' 'George 4. Yes I reported it just now. Over.' 'George 4, can you bring fire on to it?' 'King, have you anything to report? Over.' 'George, one of your children came up in the middle of my transmission then, when I was trying to talk to King. It's most difficult and annoying, and I won't have it . . . Tell him to bloody well keep off the air when I am trying to fight a battle. Off . . . er, to you. King, King, have you anything to report? Over.' 'King, King, Signals. Over.' 'King 2 or whoever that is, GET OFF THE BLOODY AIR when I am trying to talk to somebody. Off . . . King, King, signals over.' 'King, strength NINER. I'm sorry, I was talking to my jockey. Could you say again? Over.' And so on.

From the conversation it emerges that the Crusaders are held up, that the regiment on the right is under heavy and destructive fire, that there are some of our own armoured cars working forward on our left, which we mustn't fire at. The heavy tanks are engaging targets on the ridge in front of us, behind which we can see the tops of telegraph poles. Every turn of events is recorded on the air.

Someone asks for 'the little fat man' – this means they are hopelessly broken down and want the technical adjutant, known officially over the wireless as 'Tock Ack', to arrange their recovery. The regiment on our right asks for 'our bald-headed friend' on such occasions. It is these individual peculiarities which an enemy listening officer will note. The armoured cars in front, 'Our red friends on ponies, the Cherry Ps', wheel away towards the regiment on our right – 'Uncle Gordon's boys'. Now and then an awkward, hesitating transmission creates a short silence – 'Nuts three calling. We 'ave, er, 'ad a misfortune. The horse 'as fallen, driver is no more. Can we have Monkey Orange?' The gunner of a tank which has been hit, shaken by the impact of the shell, the sight of one of his friends beheaded, and another bleeding from a great wound, has forgotten his wireless procedure, if he ever knew it. If the M.O. is not already attending to someone, he will try to reach the tank in a scout car. Meanwhile, the gunner must try to get the unconscious corporal out, because the tank is burning, and bandage him roughly, because he is bleeding to death.

LESSONS OF THE WAR

To Alan Michell

Vixi duellis nuper idoneus
Et militavi non sine gloria

1. Naming of Parts

HENRY REED

TO-DAY we have naming of parts. Yesterday,
We had daily cleaning. And to-morrow morning,
We shall have what to do after firing. But to-day,
To-day we have naming of parts. Japonica
Glistens like coral in all of the neighbour gardens,
      And to-day we have naming of parts.

This is the lower sling swivel. And this
Is the upper sling swivel, whose use you will see,
When you are given your slings. And this is the piling swivel,
Which in your case you have not got. The branches
Hold in the gardens their silent, eloquent gestures,
      Which in our case we have not got.

This is the safety-catch, which is always released
With an easy flick of the thumb. And please do not let me
See anyone using his finger. You can do it quite easy
If you have any strength in your thumb. The blossoms
Are fragile and motionless, never letting anyone see
      Any of them using their finger.

And this you can see is the bolt. The purpose of this
Is to open the breech, as you see. We can slide it
Rapidly backwards and forwards: we call this
Easing the spring. And rapidly backwards and forwards
The early bees are assaulting and fumbling the flowers:
      They call it easing the Spring.

They call it easing the Spring: it is perfectly easy
f you have any strength in your thumb: like the bolt,
And the breech, and the cocking-piece, and the point of balance,
Which in our case we have not got; and the almond blossom
ilent in all of the gardens and the bees going backwards and forwards,
　　　For to-day we have naming of parts.

Dam

R. N. CURREY

I FEEL uneasy living beneath this dam.
The walls reach up to hold the infinite sky,
The hidden weight of waters, the poised hills –
And all the unguessed future; fragile walls
Buttressed by relics of a feudal past
And some two centuries' power, a world propped up
By boards that curve and strain; through sizeable cracks
The waters splash and spray along the rim.
O lovely world of morning – plumaged skies
And wide gun-metal waters; teal and snipe –
The whirring fighters and formation flights
Of poised out-reaching bombers; as I lie here,
Under the atlas-shoulders of this dam,
I hear the waters walk above my head!

Dunkirk Pier

ALAN ROOK

DEEPLY across the waves of our darkness fear
like the silent octopus feeling, groping, clear
as a star's reflection, nervous and cold as a bird,
tells us that pain, tells us that death is near.

Why should a woman telling above her fire
incantations of evening, thoughts that are
older and paler than history, why should this lark
exploring extinction and oneness of self and air

remind us that, lonely and lost as flowers in deserted
weed-mastered gardens, each faint face averted
from the inescapable confusion, for each of us slowly
death on his last, most hideous journey has started?

What was our sin? – that heartless to the end
falls now the heavy sickle on the foe, on friend,
and those that we love, value and regret
surrender quickest to death's empty hand.

Failure to suffer? We who in years past
have suffered, yes, in this or that, but in the last
irrevocable act of suffering, as a dog suffers deeply,
blindly, completely, are not versed.

What hope for the future? Can we who see the tide
ebbing along the shore, the greedy, lined
with shadows, dare with puny words support
a future that belongs to others? Dare we build

now, at this last movement of sunshine above
the crests of oncoming events, like waves which move
remorselessly nearer, future generations
with sacrifice? *We* who taught hate, expect them to love?

Desert Flowers

KEITH DOUGLAS

1.

PERCHED on a great fall of air
a pilot or angel looking down
on some eccentric chart, the plain
dotted with the useless furniture
discerns dying on the sand vehicles;
squashed dead or still entire, stunned
like beetles: scattered wingcases and
legs, heads, appear when the dust settles.
But you who like Thomas come
to poke fingers in the wounds
find monuments and metal posies.
On each disordered tomb
the steel is torn into fronds.
by the lunatic explosive.

2.

On sand and scrub the dead men wriggle
in their dowdy clothes. They are mimes
who express silence and futile aims
enacting this prone and motionless struggle
at a queer angle to the scenery,
crawling on the boards of the stage like walls,
deaf to the one who opens his mouth and calls
silently. The decor is a horrible tracery
of iron. The eye and mouth of each figure
bear the cosmetic blood and the hectic
colours death has the only list of.

A yard more, and my little finger
could trace the maquillage of these stony actors:
I am the figure writhing on the backcloth.

3.

Living in a wide landscape are the flowers —
Rosenberg, I only repeat what you were saying —
the shell and the hawk every hour
are slaying men and jerboas, slaying
the mind. But the body can fill
the hungry flowers and the dogs who cry words
at nights, the most hostile things of all.

But that is not new. Each time the night discards
draperies on the eyes and leaves the mind awake
I look each side of the door of sleep
for the little coin it will take
to buy the secret I shall not keep.
I see men as trees suffering
or confound the detail and the horizon.
Lay the coin on my tongue and I will sing
of what the others never set eyes on.

Egypt, 1943

How to Kill

KEITH DOUGLAS

Under the parabola of a ball,
a child turning into a man,
I looked into the air too long.
The ball fell in my hand, it sang
in the closed fist: *Open Open
Behold a gift designed to kill.*

Now in my dial of glass appears
the soldier who is going to die.
He smiles, and moves about in ways
his mother knows, habits of his.
The wires touch his face: I cry
NOW. Death, like a familiar, hears

and look, has made a man of dust
of a man of flesh. This sorcery
I do. Being damned, I am amused
to see the centre of love diffused
and the waves of love travel into vacancy.
How easy it is to make a ghost.

The weightless mosquito touches
her tiny shadow on the stone,
and with how like, how infinite
a lightness, man and shadow meet.
They fuse. A shadow is a man
when the mosquito death approaches.

Tunisia-Cairo, 1943

Aristocrats

'I think I am becoming a God'

KEITH DOUGLAS

THE noble horse with courage in his eye
clean in the bone, looks up at a shellburst.
Away fly the images of the shires
but he puts the pipe back in his mouth.

Peter was unfortunately killed by an 88:
it took his leg away – he died in the ambulance.
When I saw him crawling, he said:
"It's most unfair – they've shot my foot off."

How can I live among this gentle
obsolescent breed of heroes, and not weep?
Unicorns, almost,
for they are fading into two legends
in which their stupidity and chivalry
are celebrated. Each, fool and hero, will be an immortal.

These plains were their cricket pitch
and in the mountains the tremendous drop fences
brought down some of the runners. Here then
under the stones and earth they dispose themselves,
in famous attitudes of unconcern.
It is not gunfire I hear but a hunting horn.

Enfidaville, Tunisia, 1943

All Day It Has Rained . . .

ALUN LEWIS

ALL day it has rained, and we on the edge of the moors
Have sprawled in our bell-tents, moody and dull as boors,
Groundsheets and blankets spread on the muddy ground.
And from the first grey wakening we have found
No refuge from the skirmishing fine rain
And the wind that made the canvas heave and flap
And the taut wet guy-ropes ravel out and snap.
All day the rain has glided, wave and mist and dream,
Drenching the gorse and heather, a gossamer stream
Too light to stir the acorns that suddenly
Snatched from their cups by the wild south-westerly
Pattered against the tent and our upturned dreaming faces.
And we stretched out, unbuttoning our braces,
Smoking a Woodbine, darning dirty socks,
Reading the Sunday papers – I saw a fox
And mentioned it in the note I scribbled home; –
And we talked of girls, and dropping bombs on Rome,
And thought of the quiet dead and the loud celebrities
Exhorting us to slaughter, and the herded refugees;
– Yet thought softly, morosely of them, and as indifferently
As of ourselves or those whom we
For years·have loved, and will again
Tomorrow maybe love; but now it is the rain
Possesses us entirely, the twilight and the rain.

And I can remember nothing dearer or more to my heart
Than the child I watched in the woods on Saturday
Shaking down burning chestnuts for the schoolyard's merry play,
Or the shaggy patient dog who followed me
By Sheet and Steep and up the wooded scree
To the Shoulder o' Mutton where Edward Thomas brooded long
On death and beauty – till a bullet stopped his song.

Dawn on the East Coast

ALUN LEWIS

From Orford Ness to Shingle Street
The grey disturbance spreads uneasily
Washing the icy seas on Deben Head.

Cock pheasants scratch the frozen fields,
Gulls lift thin horny legs and step
Fastidiously among the rusted mines.

The soldier leaning on the sandbagged wall
Hears in the combers' curling rush and crash
His single self-centred monotonous wish;

And Time is a froth of such transparency,
His drowning eyes see what they wish to see,
A girl laying his table with a white cloth.

*

The light assails him from a flank,
Two carbons touching in his brain
Crumple the cellophane lanterns of his dream.

And then the day, grown feminine and kind,
Stoops with the gulfing motion of the tide
And pours his ashes in a tiny urn.

From Orford Ness to Shingle Street
The grey disturbance lifts its head
And one by one, reluctantly,
The living come back slowly from the dead.

Ward 'O' 3 (b)

ALUN LEWIS

I

WARD 'O' 3 (b) was, and doubtless still is, a small room at the end
of the Officers' Convalescent Ward which occupies one wing of the
rectangle of one-storeyed sheds that enclose the 'lily-pond garden' of
No. X British General Hospital, Southern Army, India. The other
three wings contain the administrative offices, the Officers' Surgical
Ward and the Officers' Medical Ward. An outer ring of buildings
consist of the various ancillary institutions, the kitchens, the labora-
tory of tropical diseases, the mortuary, the operating theatres and
the X-ray theatre. They are all connected by roofed passage-ways;
the inner rectangle of wards has a roofed verandah opening on the
garden whose flagstones have a claustral and enduring aura. The
garden is kept in perpetual flower by six black, almost naked
Mahratti gardeners who drench it with water during the dry season
and prune and weed it incessantly during the rains. It has tall flowering jacquarandas, beds of hollyhock and carnation and stock, rose
trellises and sticks swarming with sweet peas; and in the arid months
of burning heat the geraniums bud with fire in red earthenware pots.
It is, by 1943 standards, a good place to be in.

At the time of which I am writing, autumn 1942, Ward 'O' 3 (b),
which has four beds, was occupied by Captain A. G. Brownlow-
Grace, Lieut.-Quartermaster Withers, Lieut. Giles Moncrieff and
Lieut. Anthony Weston. The last-named was an R.A.C. man who
had arrived in India from home four months previously and had been
seriously injured by an anti-tank mine during training. The other
three were infantrymen. Brownlow-Grace had lost an arm in
Burma six months earlier, Moncrieff had multiple leg injuries there
and infantile paralysis as well. 'Dad' Withers was the only man over
twenty-five. He was forty-four, a regular soldier with twenty-five
years in the ranks and three in commission; during this period he
had the distinction of never having been in action. He had spent all
but two years abroad; he had been home five times and had five

children. He was suffering from chronic malaria, sciatica and rheumatism. They were all awaiting a medical board, at which it is decided whether a man should be regraded to a lower medical category, whether he is fit for active or other service, whether he be sent home, or on leave, or discharged the service with a pension. They were the special charge of Sister Normanby, a regular Q.A.I.M.N.S. nurse with a professional impersonality that controlled completely the undoubted flair and 'it' which distinguished her during an evening off at the Turf Club dances. She was the operating theatre sister; the surgeons considered her a perfect assistant. On duty or off everybody was pleased about her and aware of her; even the old matron whose puritan and sexless maturity abhorred prettiness and romantics had actually asked Sister Normanby to go on leave with her, Sister deftly refusing.

II

The floor is red parquet, burnished as a windless lake, the coverlets of the four beds are plum red, the blankets cherry red. Moncrieff hates red, Brownlow-Grace has no emotions about colours, any more than about music or aesthetics; but he hates Moncrieff. This is not unnatural. Moncrieff is a University student, Oxford or some bloody place, as far as Brownlow-Grace knows. He whistles classical music, wears his hair long, which is impermissible in a civilian officer and tolerated only in a cavalry officer with at least five years' service in India behind him. Brownlow-Grace has done eight. Moncrieff says a thing is too wearing, dreadfully tedious, simply marvellous, wizard. He indulges in moods and casts himself on his bed in ecstasies of despair. He sleeps in a gauzy veil, parades the ward in the morning in chaplies and veil, swinging his wasted hips and boil-scarred shoulders from wash-place to bed; and he is vain. He has thirty photographs of himself, mounted enlargements, in S.D. and service cap, which he is sending off gradually to a network of young ladies in Greater London, Cape Town where he stayed on the way out, and the chain of hospitals he passed through on his return from Burma. His sickness has deformed him; that also Brownlow-Grace finds himself unable to stomach.

Moncrieff made several attempts to affiliate himself to Brownlow-Grace; came and looked over his shoulder at his album of photographs the second day they were together, asked him questions about hunting, fishing and shooting on the third day, talked to him about Burma on the third day and asked him if he'd been afraid to die. What a shocker, Brownlow-Grace thought. Now when he saw the man looking at his mounted self-portraits for the umpteenth time he closed his eyes and tried to sleep himself out of it. But his sleep was liverish and full of curses. He wanted to look at his watch but refused to open his eyes because the day was so long and it must be still short of nine. In his enormous tedium he prayed Sister Normanby to come at eleven with a glass of iced nimbo pani for him. He doesn't know how he stands with her; he used to find women easy before Burma, he knew his slim and elegant figure could wear his numerous and expensive uniforms perfectly and he never had to exert himself in a dance or reception from the Savoy in the Strand through Shepheards in Cairo to the Taj in Bombay or the Turf Club in Poona. But now he wasn't sure; he wasn't sure whether his face had sagged and aged, his hair thinned, his decapitated arm in bad taste. He had sent an airgraph to his parents and his fiancée in Shropshire telling them he'd had his arm off. Peggy sounded as if she were thrilled by it in her reply. Maybe she was being kind. He didn't care so much nowadays what she happened to be feeling. Sister Normanby however could excite him obviously. He wanted to ask her to go to a dinner dance with him at the Club as soon as he felt strong enough. But he was feeling lonely; nobody came to see him; how could they, anyway? He was the only officer to come out alive. He felt ashamed of that sometimes. He hadn't thought about getting away until the butchery was over and the Japs were mopping up with the bayonet. He'd tried like the devil then, though; didn't realize he had so much cunning and desperation in him. And that little shocker asking him if he'd been afraid to die. He hadn't given death two thoughts.

There was Mostyn Turner. He used to think about Death a lot. Poor old Mostyn. Maybe it was just fancy but looking at some of Mostyn's photographs in the album, when the pair of them were on shikari tiger-hunting in Belgaum or that fortnight they had together in Kashmir, you could see by his face that he would die. He always attracted the serious type of girl; and like as not he'd take it too far. On the troopship to Rangoon he'd wanted Mostyn to play poker after the bar closed; looked for him everywhere, couldn't find him below-decks, nor in the men's mess deck where he sometimes spent an hour or two yarning; their cabin was empty. He found him on the boat deck eventually, hunched up by a lifeboat under the stars. Something stopped him calling him, or even approaching him; he'd turned away and waited by the rails at the companionway head till Mostyn had finished. Yes, finished crying. Incredible, really. He knew what was coming to him, God knows how; and it wasn't a dry hunch, it was something very moving, meant a lot to him somehow. And by God he'd gone looking for it, Mostyn had. He had his own ideas about fighting. Didn't believe in right and left boundaries, fronts, flanks, rears. He had the guerrilla platoon under his command and they went off into the blue the night before the pukka battle with a roving commission to make a diversion in the Jap rear. That was all. He'd gone off at dusk as casually as if they were on training. No funny business about Death then. He knew it would come, so he wasn't worrying. Life must have been more interesting to Mostyn than it was to himself, being made that way, having these thoughts and things. What he'd seen of Death that day, it was just a bloody beastly filthy horrible business, so forget it.

His hands were as long and thin and elegant as his body and his elongated narrow head with the Roman nose and the eyes whose colour nobody could have stated because nobody could stare back at him. His hands crumpled the pillow he was clutching. He was in a way a very fastidious man. He would have had exquisite taste if he hadn't lacked the faculty of taste.

'Messing up your new sheets again,' Sister Normanby said happily, coming into the room like a drop of Scotch. 'You ought to be playing the piano with those hands of yours, you know.'

He didn't remind her that he only had one left. He was pleased to think she didn't notice it.

'Hallo, Sister,' he said, bucking up at once. 'You're looking very young and fresh considering it was your night out last night.'

'I took it very quietly,' she said. 'Didn't dance much. Sat in the back of a car all the time.'

'For shame, my dear Celia,' Moncrieff butted in. 'Men are deceivers ever was said before the invention of the internal combustion engine and they're much worse in every way since that happened.'

'What is my little monkey jabbering about now,' she replied, offended at his freedom with her Christian name.

'Have you heard of Gipsy Rose Lee?' Moncrieff replied inconsequentially. 'She has a song which says "I can't strip to Brahms!" Can you?'

'Course she can,' said Dad Withers, unobtrusive at the door, a wry old buck, 'so long as she's got a mosquito net, isn't it, Sister?'

'Why do you boys always make me feel I haven't got a skirt on when I come in here?' she said.

'Because you can't marry all of us,' said Dad.

'Deep, isn't he?' she said.

She had a bunch of newly-cut antirrhinums and dahlias, the petals beaded with water, which she put in the bowl, arranging them quietly as she twitted the men. Moncrieff looked at her quizzically as though she had aroused conjecture in the psychoanalytical department of his brain.

'Get on with your letter-writing, Moncrieff,' she said without having looked up. He flushed.

'There's such a thing as knowing too much,' Dad said to her paternally. 'I knew a girl in Singapore once, moved there from Shanghai wiv the regiment, she did. She liked us all, the same as nurses say they do. And when she found she liked one more than all the others put together, it come as a terrible shock to her and she had to start again. Took some doing, it did.'

'Dad, you're crazy,' she said, laughing hard. 'A man with all your complaints ought to be too busy counting them to tell all these stories.' And then, as she was about to go, she turned and dropped the momentous news she'd been holding out on them.

'You're all four having your medical board next Thursday,' she said. 'So you'd better make yourselves ill again if you want to go back home.'

'I don't want to go back "home",' Brownlow-Grace said, laying sardonic stress on the last word.

'I don't know,' Dad said. 'They tell me it's a good country to get into, this 'ere England. Why, I was only reading in the *Bombay Times* this morning there's a man Beaverage or something, made a report, they even give you money to bury yourself with there now. Suits me.'

'You won't die, Dad,' Brownlow-Grace said kindly. 'You'll simply fade away.'

'Well,' said Sister Normanby. 'There are your fresh flowers. I must go and help to remove a clot from a man's brain now. Good-bye.'

'Good-bye,' they all said, following her calves and swift heels as she went.

'I didn't know a dog had sweat glands in his paws before,' Brownlow-Grace said, looking at his copy of *The Field*.

The others didn't answer. They were thinking of their medical board. It was more interesting really than Sister Normanby.

III

Weston preferred to spend the earlier hours in a deck chair in the garden, by the upraised circular stone pool, among the ferns; here he would watch the lizards run like quicksilver and as quickly freeze into an immobility so lifeless as to be macabre, and the striped tree rats playing among the jacquaranda branches; and he would look in vain for the mocking bird whose monotony gave a timeless quality to the place and the mood. He was slow in recovering his strength; his three operations and the sulphanilamide tablets he was taking had exhausted the blood in his veins; most of it was somebody else's blood, anyway, an insipid blood that for two days had dripped from a bottle suspended over his bed, while they waited for him to die. His jaw and shoulderbone had been shattered, a great clod of flesh torn out of his neck and thigh, baring his windpipe and epiglottis and exposing his lung and femoral artery; and although he had recovered very rapidly, his living self seemed overshadowed by the death trauma through which he had passed. There had been an annihilation, a complete obscuring; into which light had gradually dawned. And this light grew unbearably white, the glare of the sun on a vast expanse of snow, and in its unbounded voids he had moved without identity, a pillar of salt in a white desert as pocked and cratered as the dead face of the moon. And then some mutation had taken place and he became aware of pain. A pain that was not pure like the primal purity, but polluted, infected, with racking thirsts and suffocations and writhings, and black eruptions disturbed the whiteness, and coloured dots sifted the intense sun glare, areas of intolerable activities appeared in those passive and limitless oceans. And gradually these manifestations became the simple suppurations of his destroyed inarticulate flesh, and the bandaging and swabbing and probing of his wounds and the grunts of his throat. From it he desired wildly to return to the timeless void where the act of being was no more than a fall of snow or the throw of a rainbow; and these regions became a nostalgia to his pain and soothed his hurt and parched spirit. The two succeeding operations had been conscious experiences, and he had been frightened of them. The preliminaries got on his nerves, the starving, the aperients, the trolley, the prick of morphia, and its false peace. The spotless theatre with its walls of glass and massive lamps of burnished chrome, the anaesthetist who stuttered like a worn gramophone record, Sister Normanby clattering the knives in trays of lysol, the soft irresistible waves of wool that surged up darkly through the interstices of life like water through a boat; and the choking final surrender to the void his heart feared.

And now, two and a half months later, with his wounds mere puckers dribbling the last dregs of pus, his jaw no longer wired up and splinted, his arm no longer inflamed with the jab of the needle, he sat in the garden with his hands idle in a pool of sunlight, fretting and fretting at himself. He was costive, his stockings had holes in the heel that got wider every day and he hadn't the initiative to ask Sister for a needle and wool; his pen had no ink, his razor blade was blunt, he had shaved badly, he hadn't replied to the airmail letter that lay crumpled in his hand. He had carried that letter about with him for four days, everywhere he went, ever since he'd received it.

'You look thrillingly pale and Byronic this morning, Weston,' Moncrieff said, sitting in the deck chair opposite him with his writing pad and a sheaf of received letters tied in silk tape. 'D'you mind me sharing your gloom?'

Weston snorted.

'You can do what you bloody well like,' he said, with suppressed irritation.

'Oh dear, have I gone and hurt you again? I'm always hurting people I like,' Moncrieff said. 'But I can't help it. Honestly I can't. You believe me, Weston, don't you?'

Disturbed by the sudden nakedness of his voice Weston looked up at the waspish intense face, the dark eyebrows and malignant eyes.

'Of course I believe you, monkey,' he said. 'If you say so.'

'It's important that you should believe me,' Moncrieff said moodily. 'I must find somebody who believes me wherever I happen to be. I'm afraid otherwise. It's too lonely. Of course I hurt some people purposely. That dolt Brownlow-Grace for example. I enjoy making him wince. He's been brought up to think life should be considerate to him. His mother, his bank manager, his batman, his bearer – always somebody to mollycoddle him and see to his wants. Christ, the fellow's incapable of wanting anything really. You know, he even resents Sister Normanby having to look after other people beside himself. He only considered the war as an opportunity for promotion; I bet he was delighted when Hitler attacked Poland. And there are other people in this world going about with their brains hanging out, their minds half lynched – a fat lot he understands.' He paused, and seeming to catch himself in the middle of his tirade, he laughed softly. 'I was going to write a letter-card to my wife,' he said. 'Still, I haven't got any news. No new love. Next Thursday we'll have some news for them, won't we? I get terribly worked up about this medical board, I can't sleep. You don't think they'll keep me out in India, Weston, do you? It's so lonely out here. I couldn't stay here any longer. I just couldn't.'

'You are in a state, monkey,' Weston said, perturbed and yet laughing, as one cheers a child badly injured. 'Sit quiet a bit, you're speaking loudly. Brownlow'll hear you if you don't take care.'

'Did he?' Moncrieff said suddenly apprehensive. 'He didn't hear me, did he? I don't want to sound as crude as that, even to him.'

'Oh, I don't know. He's not a bad stick,' Weston said. 'He's very sincere and he takes things in good part, even losing his arm, and his career.'

'Oh, I know you can preach a sermon on him easily. I don't think in terms of sermons, that's all,' Moncrieff said. 'But I've been through Burma the same as he has. Why does he sneer at me?' He was silent. Then he said again, 'It's lonely out here.' He sighed. 'I wish I hadn't come out of Burma. I needn't have, I could have let myself go. One night when my leg was gangrenous, the orderly gave me a shot of morphia and I felt myself nodding and smiling. And there was no more jungle, no Japs, no screams, no difficulties at home, no nothing. The orderly would have given me a second shot if I'd asked him. I don't know why I didn't. It would have finished me off nicely. Say, Weston, have you ever been afraid of Death?'

'I don't think it's as simple as that,' Weston said. 'When I was as good as dead, the first three days here, and for a fortnight afterwards too, I was almost enamoured of death. I'd lost my fear of it. But then I'd lost my will, and my emotions were all dead. I hadn't got any relationships left. It isn't really fair then, is it?'

'I think it's better to fear death,' Moncrieff said slowly. 'Otherwise you grow spiritually proud. With most people it's not so much fear of death as love of life that keeps them sensible. I don't love life, personally. Only I'm a bit of a coward and I don't want to die again. I loathe Burma, I can't tell you how terribly. I hope they send me home. If you go home, you ought to tell them you got wounded in Burma, you know.'

'Good God, no,' Weston said, outraged. 'Why should I lie?'

'That's all they deserve,' Moncrieff said. 'I wonder what they're doing there now? Talking about reconstruction, I suppose. Even the cinemas will have reconstruction films. Well, maybe I'll get a job in some racket or other. Cramming Sandhurst cadets or something. What will you do when you get home?'

'Moncrieff, my good friend,' Weston said. 'We're soldiers, you know. And it isn't etiquette to talk about going home like that. I'm going in where you left off. I want to have a look at Burma. *And I don't want to see England.*'

'Don't you?' Moncrieff said, ignoring the slow emphasis of

Weston's last words and twirling the tassel of his writing-pad slowly. 'Neither do I, very much,' he said with an indifference that ended the conversation.

IV

The sick have their own slightly different world, their jokes are as necessary and peculiar to them as their medicines; they can't afford to be morbid like the healthy, nor to be indifferent to their environment like the Arab. The outside world has been washed out; between them and the encircling mysteries there is only the spotlight of their obsessions holding the small backcloth of ward and garden before them. Anyone appearing before this backcloth has the heightened emphasis and significance of a character upon the stage. The Sikh fortune-tellers who offered them promotion and a fortune and England as sibilantly as panders, the mongoose-fight-snake wallahs with their wailing sweet pipes and devitalized cobras, the little native cobblers and pedlars who had customary right to enter the precincts entered as travellers from an unknown land. So did the visitors from the Anglo-Indian community and brother officers passing on leave. And each visitor was greedily absorbed and examined by every patient, with the intenser acumen of disease.

Brownlow-Grace had a visitor. This increased his prestige, like having a lot of mail. It appeared she had only just discovered he was here, for during the last four days before his medical board she came every day after lunch and stayed sitting on his bed until dusk had conferred upon them an intimacy that evoked in the others a green nostalgia.

She was by any standards a beautiful woman. One afternoon a young unsophisticated English Miss in a fresh little frock and long hair; the next day French and exotic with the pallor of an undertaker's lily and hair like statuary; the third day, exquisitely Japanese, carmined and beringed with huge green amber stones, her hair in a high bun that only a great lover would dare unloose. When she left each evening Sister Normanby came in with a great bustle of fresh air and practicality to tidy his bed and put up his mosquito net. And he seemed equally capable of entertaining and being entertained by both ladies.

On the morning of the medical board Brownlow-Grace came and sat by Anthony among the ferns beside the lily pool; and this being a gesture of unusual amiability in one whom training had made rigid, Weston was unreasonably pleased.

'Well, Weston,' he said. 'Sweating on the top line over this medical board?'

'What d'you mean?' Weston asked.

'Well, d'you think everything's a wangle to get you home or keep you here like that little squirt Moncrieff?'

'I don't think along those lines, personally,' Weston said. He looked at the long languid soldier sprawled in the deck chair. 'The only thing I'm frightened of is that they'll keep me *here*, or give me some horrible office job where I'll never see a Valentine lift her belly over a bund and go grunting like a wild boar at – well, whoever happens to be there. I got used to the idea of the Germans. I suppose the Japs will do.'

'You're like me; no enemy,' Brownlow-Grace said. 'I didn't think twice about it – till it happened. You're lucky, though. You're the only one of us four who'll ever see action. I could kill some more. What do I want to go home for? They hacked my arm off, those bastards; I blew the fellow's guts out that did it, had the muzzle of my Colt rammed into his belly, I could feel his breath, he was like a frog, the swine. You, I suppose you want to go home, haven't been away long, have you?'

'Six months.'

'Six months without a woman, eh?' Brownlow-Grace laughed, yet kindly.

'Yes.'

'I'm the sort who'll take somebody else's,' Brownlow-Grace said. 'I don't harm them.'

Weston didn't reply.

'You've got a hell of a lot on your mind, haven't you, Weston? Any fool can see something's eating you up.' Still no reply. 'Look here, I may be a fool, but come out with me tonight, let's have a party together. Eh?' Surprisingly, Weston wasn't embarrassed at this extreme gesture of kindness. It was so ingenuously made. Instead he felt an enormous relief, and for the first time the capacity to speak.

Not, he told himself, to ask for advice. Brownlow-Grace wasn't a clergyman with a healing gift; but it was possible to tell him the thing simply, to shift the weight of it a bit. 'I'm all tied up,' he said. 'A party wouldn't be any use, nor a woman.'

'Wouldn't it?' Brownlow-Grace said drily, standing up. Weston had a feeling he was about to go. It would have excruciated him. Instead he half turned, as if to disembarrass him, and said, 'The flowers want watering.'

'You know, if you're soldiering, there are some things you've got to put out of bounds to your thoughts,' Weston said. 'Some things you don't let yourself doubt.'

'Your wife, you mean?' Brownlow-Grace said, holding a breath of his cigarette in his lungs and studying the ants on the wall.

'Not only her,' Weston said. 'Look. I didn't start with the same things as you. You had a pram and a private school and you saw the sea, maybe. My father was a collier and he worked in a wet pit. He got rheumatism and nystagmus and then the dole and then parish relief. I'm not telling you a sob story. It's just I was used to different sounds. I used to watch the wheel of the pit spin round year after year, after school and Saturdays and Sundays; and then from 1926 on I watched it not turning round at all, and I can't ever get that wheel out of my mind. It still spins and idles, and there's money and nystagmus coming into the house or no work and worse than nystagmus. I just missed the wheel sucking me down the shaft. I got a scholarship to the county school. I don't know when I started rebelling. Against that wheel in my head. I didn't get along very well. Worked in a grocer's, and a printer's, and no job was good enough for me, I had a bug. Plenty of friends too, plenty of chaps thinking the same as me. Used to read books in those days, get passionate about politics, Russia was like a woman to me. Then I did get a job I wanted, in a bookshop in Holborn. A French woman came in one day. I usually talked to customers, mostly politics; but not to her. She came in several times, once with a trade union man I knew. She was short, she had freckles, a straight nose, chestnut hair, she looked about eighteen; she bought books about Beethoven, Schopenhauer, the Renaissance, biology – I read every book she bought, after she'd gone back to France. I asked this chap about her. He said she was a big name, you know the way revolutionary movements toss up a woman sometimes. She was a Communist, a big speaker in the industrial towns in North France, she'd been to Russia too. And, well, I just wanted her, more and more and more as the months passed. Not her politics, but her fire. If I could hear her addressing a crowd, never mind about wanting her in those dreams you get.

'And then the war came and most of my friends said it was a phoney war, but I was afraid from the beginning that something would happen to France and I wanted to hear her speaking first. I joined up in November and I made myself such a bloody pest that they posted me to France to reinforcements. I got my war all right. And I met her, too. The trade unionist I told you about gave me a letter to introduce myself. She lived in Lille. She knew me as soon as the door opened. And I was just frightened. But after two nights there was no need to be frightened. You get to think for years that life is just a fight, with a flirt thrown in sometimes, a flirt with death or sex or whatever happens to be passing, but mostly a fight all the way along. And then you soften up, you're no use, you haven't got any wheel whirring in your head any more. Only flowers on the table and a piano she plays sometimes, when she wants to, when she wants to love.'

'I've never been to France,' Brownlow-Grace said. 'Hated it at school, French I mean. Communists, of course – I thought they were all Bolshies, you know, won't obey an order. What happened after Dunkirk?'

'It was such burning sunny weather,' Weston said. 'It was funny, having fine weather. I couldn't get her out of my mind. The sun seemed to expand inside the lining of my brain and the whole fortnight after we made that last stand with Martel at Cambrai I didn't know whether I was looking for her or Dunkirk. When I was most exhausted it was worst, she came to me once by the side of the road, there were several dead Belgian women lying there, and she said, "Look, Anthony, I have been raped. They raped me, the Boche." And the world was crashing and whirring, or it was doped, wouldn't lift a finger to stop it, and the Germans crossing the Seine. A year before I'd have said to the world Serve you right. But not now, with Cecile somewhere inside the armies. She'd tried.'

'And that was the end?' Brownlow-Grace said.

'Yes,' said Weston. 'Just about. Only it wasn't a beautiful end, the way it turned out. I had eight months in England, and I never found out a thing. The Free French didn't know. One of them knew her well, knew her as a lover, he told me; boasted about it; I didn't tell him; I wanted to find her, I didn't care about anything else. And then something started in me. I used to mooch about London. A French girl touched me on the street one night. I went with her. I went with a lot of women. Then we embarked for overseas. I had a girl at Durban, and in Bombay; sometimes they were French, if possible they were French. God, it was foul.'

He got up and sat on the edge of the pool; under the green strata of mosses the scaled goldfish moved slowly in their palaces of burning gold. He wiped his face which was sweating.

'Five days ago I got this letter from America,' he said. 'From her.'

Brownlow-Grace said, 'That was a bit of luck.' Weston laughed.

'Yes,' he said. 'Yes. It was nice of her to write. She put it very nicely, too. Would you like to read it?'

'No,' said Brownlow-Grace. 'I don't want to read it.'

'She said it often entered her mind to write to me, because I had been so sweet to her, in Lille, that time. She hoped I was well. To enter America there had been certain formalities, she said; she'd married an American, a country which has all types, she said. There is a Life, she said, but not mine, and a war also, but not mine. Now it is the Japanese. That's all she said.'

'She remembered you,' Brownlow-Grace said.

'Some things stick in a woman's mind,' Weston said. 'She darned my socks for me in bed. Why didn't she say she remembered darning my socks?'

Brownlow-Grace pressed his hand, fingers extended, upon the surface of the water, not breaking its resistance, quite.

'I don't use the word,' he said. 'But I guess it's because she loved you.'

Weston looked up, searching and somehow naïve.

'I don't mind about the Japanese,' he said, 'if that were so.'

V

Dad Withers had his medical board first; he wasn't in the board room long; in fact he was back on the verandah outside 'O' 3 (b) when Weston returned from sending a cable at the camp post office.

'Did it go all right, Dad?' Weston asked.

'Sure, sure,' Dad said, purring as if at his own cleverness. 'Three colonels and two majors there, and the full colonel he said to me, "Well, Withers, what's your trouble? Lieutenant Quartermaster, weren't you?" And I said, "Correct, sir, and now I'm putting my own body in for exchange, sir. It don't keep the rain out no more, sir." So he said, "You're not much use to us, Withers, by the look of you." And I said, "Not a bit of use, sir, sorry to report." And the end of it was they give me a free berth on the next ship home wiv full military honours and a disability pension and all. Good going, isn't it now?'

'Very good, Dad. I'm very pleased.'

'Thank you,' Dad said, his face wrinkled and benign as a tortoise. 'Now go and get your own ticket and don't keep the gentlemen waiting. . . .'

Dad lay half sleeping in the deck chair, thinking that it was all buttoned up now, all laid on, all made good. It had been a long time, a life time, more than twenty hot seasons, more than twenty rains. Not many could say that. Not many had stuck it like him. Five years in Jhansi with his body red as lobster from head to toe with prickly heat, squirting a water pistol down his back for enjoyment and scratching his shoulders with a long fork from the bazaar. Two big wars there'd been, and most of the boys had been glad to go into them, excited to be posted to France, or embark for Egypt. But he'd stuck it out. Still here, still good for a game of nap, and them all dead, the boys that wanted to get away. And now it was finished with him, too.

He didn't know. Maybe he wasn't going home the way he'd figured it out after all. Maybe there was something else, something he hadn't counted on. This tiredness, this emptiness, this grey blank wall of mist, this not caring. What would it be like, in the small Council house with five youngsters and his missus? She'd changed a lot, the last photo she sent she was like his mother, spectacles and fat legs, full of plainness. Maybe the kids would play with him, though, the two young ones?

He pulled himself slowly out of his seat, took out his wallet, counted his money; ninety chips he had. Enough to see India just once again. Poor old India. He dressed hurriedly, combed his thin hair, wiped his spectacles, dusted his shoes, and left before the others came back. He picked up a tonga at the stand outside the main gates of the hospital cantonment, just past the M.D. lines, and named a certain hotel down town. And off he cantered, the skinny old horse clattering and letting off great puffs of bad air under the tongawhalla's whip, and Dad shouting 'Jillo, jillo,' impatient to be drunk.

Brownlow-Grace came in and went straight to the little bed table where he kept his papers in an untidy heap. He went there in a leisurely way, avoiding the inquiring silences of Weston and Moncrieff and Sister Normanby, who were all apparently doing something. He fished out an airgraph form and his fountain-pen and sat quietly on the edge of his bed.

'Oh damn and blast it,' he said angrily. 'My pen's dry.'

Weston gave him an inkbottle.

He sat down again.

'What's the date?' he said after a minute.

'12th,' Moncrieff said.

'What month?' he asked.

'December.'

'Thanks.'

He wrote slowly, laboriously, long pauses between sentences. When he'd finished he put his pen away and looked for a stamp.

'What stamp d'you put on an airgraph?' he said.

'Three annas,' Moncrieff said patiently.

Sister Normanby decided to abolish the embarrassing reticence with which this odd man was concealing his board result. She had no room for broody hens.

'Well,' she said, gently enough. 'What happened at the board?'

He looked up at her and neither smiled nor showed any sign of recognition. Then he stood up, took up his cane and peaked service cap, and brushed a speck of down off his long and well fitting trousers.

'They discharged me,' he said. 'Will you post this airgraph for me, please?'

'Yes,' she said, and for some odd reason she found herself unable to deal with the situation and took it from him and went on with her work.

'I'm going out,' he said.

Weston followed him into the garden and caught him up by the lily-pool.

'Is that invitation still open?' he asked.

'What invitation?' Brownlow-Grace said.

'To go on the spree with you tonight?' Weston said.

Brownlow-Grace looked at him thoughtfully.

'I've changed my mind, Anthony,' he said – Weston was pleasurably aware of this first use of his Christian name – 'I don't think I'd be any use to you tonight. Matter of fact, I phoned Rita just now, you know the woman who comes to see me, and she's calling for me in five minutes.'

'I see,' Weston said. 'O.K. by me.'

'You don't mind, do you?' he said. 'I don't think you need Rita's company, do you? Besides, she usually prefers one man at a time. She's the widow of a friend of mine, Mostyn Turner; he was killed in Burma, too.'

Weston came back into the ward to meet Sister Normanby's white face. 'Where's he gone?' she said.

Weston looked at her, surprised at the emotion and stress this normally imperturbable woman was showing.

He didn't answer her.

'He's gone to that woman,' she said, white and virulent. 'Hasn't he?'

'Yes, he has,' he said quietly.

'She always has them when they're convalescent,' she said, flashing with venom. She picked up her medicine book and the jar with her thermometer in it. 'I have them when they're sick.'

She left the ward, biting her white lips.

'I didn't know she felt that way about him,' Weston said.

'Neither did she,' said Moncrieff. 'She never knows till it's too late. That's the beauty about her. She's virginal.'

'You're very cruel, Moncrieff.'

Moncrieff turned on him like an animal.

'Cruel?' he said. 'Cruel? Well, I don't lick Lazarus's sores, Weston. I take the world the way it is. Nobody cares about you out here. Nobody. What have I done to anybody? Why should they keep me here? What's the use of keeping a man with infantile paralysis and six inches of bone missing from his leg? Why didn't the board let me go home?'

'You'll go home, monkey, you'll go home,' Weston said gently. 'You know the Army. You can help them out here. You're bound to go home, when the war ends.'

'Do you think so?' Moncrieff said. 'Do you?' He thought of this for a minute at least. Then he said, 'No, I shall never go home. I know it.'

'Don't be silly, monkey. You're a bit run down, that's all.' Weston soothed him. 'Let's go and sit by the pool for a while.'

'I like the pool,' Moncrieff said. They strolled out together and sat on the circular ledge. The curving bright branches held their leaves peacefully above the water. Under the mosses they could see the old toad of the pond sleeping, his back rusty with jewels. Weston put his hand in the water; minnows rose in small flocks and nibbled at his fingers. Circles of water lapped softly outwards, outwards, till they touched the edge of the pool, and cast a gentle wetness on the stone, and lapped again inwards, inwards. And as they lapped inwards he felt the ripples surging against the most withdrawn and inmost ledges of his being, like a series of temptations in the wilderness. And he felt glad tonight, feeling some small salient gained when for many reasons the men whom he was with were losing ground along the whole front to the darkness that there is.

'No,' said Moncrieff at last. 'Talking is no good. But perhaps you will write to me sometimes, will you, just to let me know.'

'Yes, I'll write to you, monkey,' Weston said, looking up.

And then he looked away again, not willing to consider those empty inarticulate eyes.

'The mosquitoes are starting to bite,' he said. 'We'd better go now.'

Had Each a Voice,
What Would His Fingers Cry?

MERVYN PEAKE

His fingers that were trained to bind
The shadows of his mind
To paper with slim lead,
Grasp grimmer substance than a pencil's measure.

Not cedar but the trigger's steel
Is what they feel,
And in a long barrel
Lead of as fleet an impulse waits the pressure.

His perjured fingers have no throats;
His wrist no source of sound supports;
His crook'd forefinger
Curls like a tongue, severed and voice-forsaken;

Had each a voice, what would his fingers cry
But 'Treachery'?
Until their shrill pipes echoing up the arms
Should find and force the tyrant brain to hearken.

Conscript

FRANCIS SCARFE

DELICATE ingenuous his quivering blue eye
Miniatures the horizon of the condemned sky
Where burns all history in the bones of children
And fall the tears of remorse and breaks the heart of heaven.

Mothered for pitted dunes and these livid grasses
He stands on the edge of murder motionless
As the green statues that to his fame shall moulder
With love's and death's stone wings touching his shoulder.

While all he meant to live for hides behind
The click of hell released by his unskilled finger,
Index of Europe's hand dyed red with honour
Which wields the boy a puppet of its anger.

Tranquil the thrush sings on the twisted pylon
Its song unwinding the unbearable pattern
Of loss, fear, blood, night's aching empty arms,
Back to the heat of love and the smell of home.

Drill

TIMOTHY CORSELLIS

At the hoary bellow of a single man
The ragged line of desperate identity
Springs to spontaneous activity:
Rhythmic rocking, hobnails knocking,
Bodies to the sacrifice take their advice.
The significant figure is ignorant of importance,
Only a sudden voice roars out a hoarse noise,
Alters the angle.

Forward and backward to the desperate drum
Of the increasing madness
The wheel whirl roll unfurl,
Encroaches on the dead mind in a dying body,
Eats further into the interior.

Heroes

KATHLEEN RAINE

This war's dead heroes, who has seen them?
They rise in smoke above the burning city,
Faint clouds, dissolving into sky.

And who sifting the Libyan sand can find
The tracery of a human hand,
The faint impression of an absent mind,
The fade-out of a soldier's day dream?

You'll know your love no more, nor his sweet kisses —
He's forgotten you, girl, and in the idle sun
In long green grass that the east wind caresses
The seed of man is ravished by the corn.

Soldiers Bathing

F. T. PRINCE

THE sea at evening moves across the sand.
Under a reddening sky I watch the freedom of a band
Of soldiers who belong to me. Stripped bare
For bathing in the sea, they shout and run in the warm air;
Their flesh worn by the trade of war, revives
And my mind towards the meaning of it strives.

All's pathos now. The body that was gross,
Rank, ravenous, disgusting in the act or in repose,
All fever, filth and sweat, its bestial strength
And bestial decay, by pain and labour grows at length
Fragile and luminous. 'Poor bare forked animal,'
Conscious of his desires and needs and flesh that rise and fall,
Stands in the soft air, tasting after toil
The sweetness of his nakedness: letting the sea-waves coil
Their frothy tongues about his feet, forgets
His hatred of the war, its terrible pressure that begets
A machinery of death and slavery,
Each being a slave and making slaves of others: finds that he
Remembers his old freedom in a game
Mocking himself, and comically mimics fear and shame.

He plays with death and animality;
And reading in the shadows of his pallid flesh, I see
The idea of Michelangelo's cartoon
Of soldiers bathing, breaking off before they were half done
At some sortie of the enemy, an episode
Of the Pisan wars with Florence. I remember how he showed
Their muscular limbs that clamber from the water,
And heads that turn across the shoulder, eager for the slaughter,
Forgetful of their bodies that are bare,
And hot to buckle on and use the weapons lying there.
– And I think too of the theme another found

When, shadowing men's bodies on a sinister red ground,
Another Florentine, Pollaiuolo,
Painted a naked battle: warriors, straddled, hacked the foe,
Dug their bare toes into the ground and slew
The brother-naked man who lay between their feet and drew
His lips back from his teeth in a grimace.

They were Italians who knew war's sorrow and disgrace
And showed the thing suspended, stripped: a theme
Born out of the experience of war's horrible extreme
Beneath a sky where even the air flows
With lacrimae Christi. For that rage, that bitterness, those blows,
That hatred of the slain, what could they be
But indirectly or directly a commentary
On the Crucifixion? And the picture burns
With indignation and pity and despair by turns,
Because it is the obverse of the scene
Where Christ hangs murdered, stripped, upon the Cross. I mean,
That is the explanation of its rage.

And we too have our bitterness and pity that engage
Blood, spirit, in this war. But night begins,
Night of the mind: who nowadays is conscious of our sins?
Though every human deed concerns our blood,
And even we must know, what nobody has understood,
That some great love is over all we do,
And that is what has driven us to this fury, for so few
Can suffer all the terror of that love:
The terror of that love has set us spinning in this groove
Greased with our blood.
                          These dry themselves and dress,
Combing their hair, forget the fear and shame of nakedness.
Because to love is frightening we prefer
The freedom of our crimes. Yet, as I drink the dusky air,
I feel a strange delight that fills me full,
Strange gratitude, as if evil itself were beautiful,
And kiss the wound in thought, while in the west
I watch a streak of red that might have issued from Christ's breast.

The Conscript

LOUIS MACNEICE

BEING so young he feels the weight of history
Like clay around his boots; he would, if he could, fly
In search of a future like a sycamore seed
But is prevented by his own Necessity,
His own yet alien, which, whatever he may plead,
To every question gives the same reply.
Choiceless therefore, driven from pillar to post,
Expiating his pedigree, fulfilling
An oracle whose returns grow less and less,
Bandied from camp to camp to practise killing
He fails even so at times to remain engrossed
And is aware, at times, of life's largesse.

From camp to camp, from Eocene to chalk,
He lives a paradox, lives in a groove
That runs dead straight to an ordained disaster
So that in two dimensions he must move
Like an automaton, yet his inward stalk
Vertically aspires and makes him his own master.

Hence, though on the flat his life has no
Promise but of diminishing returns,
By feeling down and upwards he can divine
That dignity which far above him burns
In stars that yet are his and which below
Stands rooted like a dolmen in his spine.

Confessions and Conclusions

Lullaby

W. H. AUDEN

LAY your sleeping head, my love,
Human on my faithless arm;
Time and fevers burn away
Individual beauty from
Thoughtful children, and the grave
Proves the child ephemeral:
But in my arms till break of day
Let the living creature lie,
Mortal, guilty, but to me
The entirely beautiful.

Soul and body have no bounds:
To lovers as they lie upon
Her tolerant enchanted slope
In their ordinary swoon,
Grave the vision Venus sends
Of supernatural sympathy,
Universal love and hope;
While an abstract insight wakes
Among the glaciers and the rocks
The hermit's carnal ecstasy.

Certainty, fidelity
On the stroke of midnight pass
Like vibrations of a bell,
And fashionable madmen raise
Their pedantic boring cry;
Every farthing of the cost,
All the dreaded cards foretell
Shall be paid, but from this night

Not a whisper, not a thought,
Not a kiss nor look be lost.

Beauty, midnight, vision dies:
Let the winds of dawn that blow
Softly round your dreaming head
Such a day of welcome show
Eye and knocking heart may bless,
Find our mortal world enough;
Noons of dryness find you fed
By the involuntary powers,
Nights of insult let you pass
Watched by every human love.

Aubade

WILLIAM EMPSON

HOURS before dawn we were woken by the quake.
My house was on a cliff. The thing could take
Bookloads off shelves, break bottles in a row.
Then the long pause and then the bigger shake.
It seemed the best thing to be up and go.

And far too large for my feet to step by.
I hoped that various buildings were brought low.
The heart of standing is that you cannot fly.

It seemed quite safe until she got up and dressed.
The guarded tourist makes the guide the test.
Then I said The Garden? Laughing she said No.
Taxi for her and for me healthy rest.
It seemed the best thing to be up and go.

The language problem but you have to try.
Some solid ground for lying could she show?
The heart of standing is you cannot fly.

None of these deaths were her point at all.
The thing was that being woken he would bawl
And finding her not in earshot he would know.
I tried saying Half an Hour to pay this call.
It seemed the best thing to be up and go.

I slept, and blank as that I would yet lie.
Till you have seen what a threat holds below,
The heart of standing is you cannot fly.

Tell me again about Europe and her pains,
Who's tortured by the drought, who by the rains.

Glut me with floods where only the swine can row
Who cuts his throat and let him count his gains.
It seemed the best thing to be up and go.

A bedshift flight to a Far Eastern sky.
Only the same war on a stronger toe.
The heart of standing is you cannot fly.

Tell me more quickly what I lost by this,
Or tell me with less drama what they miss
Who call no die a god for a good throw,
Who say after two aliens had one kiss
It seemed the best thing to be up and go.

But as to risings, I can tell you why.
It is on contradiction that they grow.
It seemed the best thing to be up and go.
Up was the heartening and the strong reply.
The heart of standing is we cannot fly.

Sickert at St Peter's

DENTON WELCH

I HAD been in Broadstairs for months, trying to recover some sort of health after a serious road accident.

My doctor, knowing that I was an art student, tried to persuade Sickert to come and see me, but he wouldn't. I was told that he stormed off down the street saying, 'I have no time for district visiting!'

That was while I was still in bed. When at last I got up, someone engineered an invitation to tea on Saturday afternoon. So he did not escape me after all.

Just as I was about to leave the nursing home for St Peter's, Sister sailed into my room closely followed by Gerald, an art school friend. He had evidently come all the way from London to see me.

I controlled my face as best I could and said:

'I'm going to tea with Sickert. What are you going to do? Can you wait here till I get back?'

He gave me one rapid glance and then said firmly:

'I'll come too.'

I was horrified. 'But you haven't been asked!' I burst out.

'That doesn't matter. One more won't make any difference.'

Feeling powerless in my convalescent state against his strength of will, I let him climb up beside me in the aged taxi which bore us swayingly to 'Hauteville'.

Sickert had not lived long in the house and it was still being altered. One entered through what at one time had been the 'cloak-room'. I remember with vividness the slight shock I received on being confronted with a glistening white 'w.c.' as soon as the door was opened.

Mrs Sickert stood beside it, welcoming us charmingly, with great quietness. She led us into what must have been the original hall. It was now a sort of dining-room, furnished with a strange mixture of interesting and commonplace things. An early Georgian mirror with flat bevelling and worn gilt frame hung over the Art Nouveau grate. Seen thus together, each looked somehow startling and new.

We left our coats and passed on into the much loftier and larger drawing-room. The first thing I noticed was that the floor was quite bare, with that stained 'surround' which makes the white boards in the middle look so naked. By the sofa stood a stringy man who was about to go bald. The pale gold hair was still there, but one could tell how thin the crop would be next year. He looked at us with piercing eyes and fidgeted with his teaspoon. Mrs Sickert only had time to tell us that her husband was still resting but that he would be down soon, before this man engaged her again in earnest conversation. She could only show us attention by pouring out cups of tea. My cup was of that white china which is decorated with a gold trefoil in the centre of each piece. Gerald's was quite different. It was acid-blue, I think, with an unpleasant black handle and stripe; but I noted that both our spoons were flimsy and old. I turned mine over and saw, amongst the other hall-marks, the little head of George III winking up at me.

I looked at the other things on the table, at the brown enamel teapot, the familiar red and blue Huntley and Palmer's tin, and at the strange loaf which seemed neither bread nor cake. In spite of myself, I felt that at last I was seeing Bohemian life.

I was glad that the man was keeping Mrs Sickert so busy, for it gave me time to stare at everything in the room. I saw that along most of the walls ran narrow panels, almost in monochrome. They looked like bas-reliefs flattened by a steam-roller. They were most decorative. Mixed with these, but standing on easels or resting on the floor, were some of Sickert's own paintings. Gwen Ffrangçon-Davies dressed in Elizabethan farthingale and ruff, with harsh white light on her face, looked out from a picture mostly green and red.

Toylike, bustled ladies and Derby-hatted men, all in soft greys and pinks, skated on a country pond. Pinned to the canvas was the original *Punch* drawing from which the composition had been taken.

Near the fireplace stood the long, brown haggard picture of the miner with his swinging lamp, just come up from the pit, grasping his wife fiercely and kissing her mouth.

As I was looking at this last picture Sickert appeared in the door. My first sight of him was rather overwhelming. Huge and bearded, he was dressed in rough clothes and from his toes to his thighs reached what I can only describe as sewer-boots.

He had seen me staring at the picture and now said directly to me:

'That picture gives you the right feeling, doesn't it? You'd kiss your wife like that if you'd just come up from the pit, wouldn't you?'

I was appalled by the dreadful heartiness of the question. I found myself blushing, and hated him for making me do so.

Sickert came right up to me and looked me all over.

'Well, you don't look very ill,' he said. 'I thought you'd be a terrible mess. Didn't you fracture your spine or something?'

I nodded my head.

He made an amusing, whining baby's face.

'Look here, I'm very sorry I didn't come and see you, but I can't go round visiting.' He waved his hand round the room. 'You see I have to keep painting all these pictures because I'm so poor.'

He took up a position with his back to the fireplace. Mrs Sickert got up and carried a cup of tea to her husband. The stringy man also rose and floated to the door. He was still talking to Mrs Sickert over his shoulder, and the last words I heard as he left the room were '. . . couldn't pass water for six days!'

This sounded so surprising that for one moment I forgot Sickert. Then I remembered him with a jolt, for he had begun to dance on the hearth in his great sewer-boots. He lifted his cup and, waving it to and fro, burst into a German drinking-song. There was an amazingly theatrical and roguish look on his broad face.

I could not believe that he always drank his tea in this way, and I felt flattered, because he seemed to be doing it especially for us.

I don't know how long the dance or the song would have lasted if the front-door bell had not rung. Sickert suddenly broke off and waited, while Mrs Sickert hurried out of the room.

She returned with a Mr Raven whom I had met once before. After giving him a cup of tea, she left him standing on the hearth beside Sickert. He sipped his tea in silence for a few moments; then he began to feel in his breast-pocket. At last he brought out a rather crumpled shiny object, and I saw that it was a photograph.

'This is my mother,' he said, pushing it under Sickert's nose.

Sickert drew back perceptibly, and gave a grunt which might have meant anything.

Mr Raven continued unruffled. 'Interesting face, isn't it? If you'd like to do a painting of it, I'd be very pleased to lend you the photograph for as long as you liked.'

There was another grunt from Sickert.

When Mr Raven realized that this was the only answer he was going to get, he turned very red and hurriedly thrust the portrait of his mother back into his breast-pocket. He looked just as if he had been caught in the act of displaying an indecent postcard.

Gerald and I exchanged glances. I think we were both sorry for Mr Raven, and yet glad that his efforts towards cheap immortality for his mother had been frustrated.

Sickert, evidently prompted by Mr Raven's action, opened a drawer in a cabinet, and also produced a photograph.

'Isn't she lovely?' he said, holding it out to me.

I took the yellowing little 'carte-de-visite' between my fingers and saw that it was of some young woman of the eighties. She had her back to the camera, so that her face was seen in profile, resting on one shoulder. She appeared to me quite hideous with a costive, pouchy look about the eyes and mouth.

I wondered who she could be. Perhaps she was someone famous; or perhaps she was one of Sickert's past wives or mistresses.

I felt in a very difficult position. Thinking as I did, I hated to be sycophantic and say, 'Yes, she's beautiful.' So I compromised very clumsily by answering:

'The photograph is so tiny that I can't see very much of her; but I love the clothes of that period, don't you?'

Sickert snatched the photograph from me.

'Tiny! What do you mean by tiny?' he roared.

He held the picture up and pointed to it, as if he were demonstrating something on a blackboard; then he shouted out in ringing tones for the whole room to hear:

'Do you realize that I could paint a picture as big as this' (he stretched out his arms like an angler in a comic paper) 'from this "tiny" photograph as you call it?'

Horribly embarrassed and overcome by this outburst, I smiled weakly and cast my eyes down so that they rested on his enormous boots.

I was not thinking of his boots. I was thinking of nothing but the redness of my face. But Sickert evidently thought that I was curious, for the next moment he had opened another attack with:

'Ah, I see that you're staring at my boots! Do you know why I wear them? Well, I'll tell you. Lord Beaverbrook asked me to a party and I was late, so I jumped into a taxi and said: "Drive as fast as you can!" Of course, we had an accident and I was thrown on to my knees and my legs were badly knocked about; so now I wear these as a protection.'

In a dazed way, I wondered if he meant that he wore the boots to protect the still bruised legs, or if he meant that he intended to wear them as a permanent safeguard, in case he should ever again have an accident as he hurried to a party of Lord Beaverbrook's. I thought of the sensation they would create amongst the patent-leather shoes.

By this time I was so exhausted that I was pleased when Sickert turned his attention to Gerald. He started to talk about politicians, and I thought it was clever of him to guess that Gerald had an enormous appetite for tit-bits about the famous.

As I sank down on the sofa beside Mrs Sickert, I heard them begin on Anthony Eden. Sickert was describing his good looks. He must have sensed that I was still listening, for he suddenly turned his face on me, and his eyes were twinkling with fun and malice.

'Ugly ones like us haven't a chance when there's someone like Eden about, have we?' he called out across the room.

I was so surprised at being lumped together with Sickert in ugliness, as opposed to the handsomeness of Anthony Eden (who had never struck me as anything but middle-aged), that I took him quite seriously and could answer nothing.

I hurriedly tried to compensate myself for the humiliation by telling myself that, although it might not be saying very much, I was undoubtedly by far and away the best-looking person in the room, and this in spite of my long illness.

Mrs Sickert saw that I was ruffled, and very kindly started to talk about my career. She asked me if I intended to go back to an art school when I was well enough. We discussed the various objects in the room. She told me that the two glittering monstrances had come from a Russian church. We went up to them and I took one of the sparkling things in my hands. The blue and white paste lustres were backed with tinsel. They were fascinatingly gaudy and I coveted them.

We sat talking together on the sofa for a little longer. Through our words I caught snatches of what Sickert was saying. Gerald evidently had got him on to Degas and anecdotes were streaming out. Gerald was drinking them up thirstily, while Mr Raven hovered rather uncomfortably at the edge of the conversation.

At last he decided to go. Coming forward, he coughed slightly and held out his hand to Mrs Sickert. Then, as he passed Sickert on his way to the door, he felt in his pocket and with almost incredible courage brought out the crumpled little photograph again.

Putting it down on the table, he said simply:

'I'll leave this just in case . . .'

His voice tailed off as he saw the completely blank look on Sickert's face. I knew exactly what was coming and waited for it.

Sickert gave the same enigmatic grunt. It was somehow quite baffling and insulting.

Mr Raven crept unhappily to the door and Mrs Sickert followed swiftly to put salve on his wounds.

Immediately Raven was out of the room Sickert became boisterous. He started to dance again, thumping his great boots on the floor. Gerald and I caught some of his gaiety. We did not mention Raven, but I knew we were all celebrating his defeat. It was pleasant to feel that Sickert treated us as fellow-artists. I wondered how many people each year asked him to paint pictures for love.

As Mrs Sickert did not return, we went into the hall where Sickert dragged on our coats as if he were dressing sacks of turnips. Then dancing and singing in front of us, he led the way through the 'cloak-room' to the front door. I half expected some remark about the shining flush-closet, but none came.

It was dark outside. We walked over the greasy cobbles. Sickert was still leading us. He threw open the creaking stable-yard door and stood there with his hand on the latch. He looked gigantic.

We passed through and started to walk down the road.

'Good-bye, good-bye!' he shouted after us in great good humour. 'Come again when you can't stop quite so long!'

And at these words a strange pang went through me, for it was what my father had always said as he closed the book, when I had finished my bread and butter and milk, and it was time for me to go to bed.

A Shooting Incident

STEVIE SMITH

Man does not live by bread alone
Nor die alone for lack of it
For he may be well fed, and die,
There is a hunger of the heart
Will slay him, though each day he feast
On bread and wine, and go well dresst,
And such a one was Colonel Yeast.
He was a noble simple man
But all within his heart was black
And as he walked the way along
He cried, alas alack,
And cried and sighed and sighed and cried,
I am a long-delayèd suicide.
It was as though a fiend had swung
Him by the toe when he was young
And swung him so
And to and fro
And swore and said he should be most oppressed
When most against a loving friend he pressed.
And now he walks with gun and roar –
He is a colonel in the Indian Army –
Sporting upon a tiger's spoor
And with him goes his faithful escort, Harmi.
Oh Harmi dear I love the sun
And all the crooked jungle path
But most the water holes I love
With creatures peering from above.
Why do I pick the wilder animal?
It is because he is not fanciful.
I had a dog in England once,
I loved him well, his name was Bunce,
And now I think I see him here,

And as I think, the scene grows clear,
An English scene. The colonel sighed.
The misty fells lay open wide
Upon his loving thought,
And dog Bunce ran again to start
The timid hare, and play his part
As he was taught.
Wild creatures' eyes, the colonel said,
Are innocent and fathomless,
And when I look at them I see
That they are not aware of me,
And oh I find and oh I bless
A comfort in this emptiness.
They only see me when they want
To pounce upon me in the hunt.
But in the tame variety
There couches an anxiety
As if they yearned, yet knew not what
They yearned for, nor they yearned for not.
And so my dog would look at me
And it was pitiful to see
Such love and such dependency.
The human heart is not at ease
With animals that look like these.
The colonel paused and wiped his brow,
He felt his words were too dramatic
But as he knew no English they
Were lost upon the Asiatic.
Ah me, the bitter bitter love,
Why must it be so bitter,
Or animal, or man, or tree –
Would not no love be better?
As still in recollection bound
The colonel gazed upon the ground
It seemed his senses in a swound
Had left him quite,
Then turning to his gun again
And stamping on his heavy pain,

He loaded up and in the sight
Beheld a tiger stepping bright.
He steps so brightly in his death,
The colonel shot him through the teeth.
I had a dream I beat dear Bunce,
He said, with many a weal
Until he lay down at my feet
All red from toe to heel
Then in my dream I rose and fled,
Crying, The dog, the dog is dead.
Now, Harmi, mark, when daylight came,
My night and dream to shatter through
My dog came and so looked at me
I said, Why, Bunce, what's the matter with you?
Oh day and night, oh Holy Dove,
We slay the thing we most do love,
And it is pitiful to see
Our friends live but in memory.
But they are safe in memory
And are they not? the colonel said,
He turned and looked at Harmi so
That Harmi dropped his gun and fled.
When he came back again he found
The colonel dying of a wound,
And crying close upon the ground:
Oh bright bright blood that flows so bright
Within the wound myself did make
Oh jungle grass that drinks it up
And with my life thy thirst doth slake
Why has my hand this hour postponed
That sees me now with dust conjoined?
The Indian's tears fell like a blot
Upon the colonel's face
And carefully before he left
He put his hands in place.
Later upon his tomb, now grave now gay,
He daily danced to keep the fiends away.

A Bit of a Smash in Madras

J. MACLAREN-ROSS

ABSOLUTE fact, I knew damn all about it; I'd been on a blind in Fenner's with some of the boys and I was on my way back when a blasted pi dog ran out in the road and I swerved the car a bit to avoid it. I don't remember the crash or anything, I must have hit into them and driven straight on to the bungalow without stopping. I was so damn tight I don't remember anything, but these fellows were coming out of Fenner's, the two of 'em, and they saw it all right and this bastard Krishnaswami recognized me: I'd a big open Vauxhall in those days and I was driving with the hood down.

The night-watchman from Spinner's saw it too and he came across and there were these coolies pretty badly smashed about, one of them had a broken leg and God knows what, and Krishnaswami was shouting that he'd seen me and knew who I was. Mind you, he was properly sewn-up himself, and the other bloke with him was so bad that the station inspector refused to accept his evidence. But Krishnaswami had got the number of my car, so after they'd carted the two coolies off to hospital, the inspector came down to the bungalow to see me.

At that time I shared quarters with a chap called Stanton, he was with the company too, a damn decent chap, and when the peon told him this inspector was out there asking for me, he came into my room and there I was, of course, dead to the world. So Stanton went out and told the inspector I was asleep and could he come back later and the inspector said all right. When he'd gone Stanton woke me up and told me about it. Honest, it came like a bolt from the ruddy blue: I couldn't remember a thing.

'Accident?' I said. 'What the hell are you talking about? I haven't had any accident.'

'One of the coolies may die,' Stanton said.

'But it's nothing to do with me.'

'The inspector says he's got your number.'

'Holy smoke,' I said.

'You'd better snap out of it,' Stanton said. 'He's coming back presently,' so I got up and bawled for the peon to get my bath ready. This was five in the morning, mind you, and I felt foul. I'd an awful head and a mouth like a sewer from smoking. I couldn't understand what it was all about; I thought they'd got me mixed up with someone else.

After my bath I felt better, but I was still pretty bad. I kept drinking socking great cups of black tea, and about seven the inspector came back. He was a native, but quite a nice chap; I've forgotten his name. He brought two other men with him, and these stayed outside taking photographs of my car, which had a mudguard buckled and one of the headlamps knocked back. I'd already had a look at it, and it certainly seemed I had been in a smash, though I still couldn't remember anything.

Of course, directly these fellows started taking photos, I saw the red light, so when the inspector asked me if I'd make a statement, I said no, not without seeing a lawyer first.

'Very well,' the inspector said, 'but I'm afraid I shall have to ask you to accompany me to the station.'

'Is this necessary?' I said.

'I'm afraid so, sir,' he said. 'Purely a matter of form, you know,' so I said all right but could I call at my solicitor's on our way down. The inspector said certainly and who was my solicitor?

'Mr Shankran,' I said.

Of course the inspector knew Shankran: everyone in Chandrapore did. I'd never had to employ him myself, but we'd always been good pals and I knew he'd always be ready to help me out of a hot spot. Besides he was a damn smart lawyer: look what he did for Cornford that time he crashed into a Mohammedan funeral and killed five. Why, Cornford would have got life if it hadn't been for Shankran; as it was he got off with three years, and on top of that Shankran raised such an awful stink everyone was scared stiff of him; he had several officials sacked, two police sergeants reduced to the ranks, and even got the magistrate reprimanded – all through pull. I tell you, if Shankran couldn't get me off, nobody could.

But on the way to the station, I remembered that I didn't know his address, so I asked the inspector to pull up at Fenner's, which he did.

'By God, Adams old boy,' Fenner said when he saw me, 'you're in a mess this time.'

'I seem to be,' I said: luckily the inspector had stayed outside in the car.

'By God you are,' Fenner said. 'I've had the police round wanting to know all about you, what state you were in when you left, if you were sober, and God knows what. Course they got no change out of me.'

'Did they ask to see the bar-chits?'

'Not yet. But you needn't worry: I've fixed those.'

'Thanks, old boy,' I said.

'Anything to oblige,' Fenner said, winking.

'Did you see the accident?' I asked him.

'No, but it sounds pretty serious from what I hear.'

'I'm just off to the station now.'

'Seen a lawyer yet?'

'No, I'm going to get Shankran.'

'Couldn't do better, old boy.'

'Matter of fact, that's what I came to ask you for – his address.'

So Fenner told me and I went back to the inspector and he drove me round to Shankran's bungalow. He was just having *chota hazri* when his boy announced us and he jumped up from the table as we came in, holding out his hand. He was a Brahmin, small and wearing gold-rimmed glasses, and you couldn't tell his age from his looks.

'Hullo, hullo, hullo,' he said. 'Adams, eh? How are you keeping? Sit down, sit down. Boy, bring some gin! Sit down, Adams, don't look so worried!'

He seemed a bit surprised to see the inspector, but he said hullo to him too, and spoke a few words in Tamil, and the inspector smiled.

'Look here, Shankran,' I said, 'I'd like your advice. It seems I had a bit of a smash last night.'

'Oh? Well, well. Not a bad one, I hope? Ah, here's the gin. That's right, put it on the table. Help yourself, Adams. Inspector?'

The inspector said he wouldn't, being on duty. I felt better after I'd swallowed some gin.

'Now tell me all about it,' Shankran said. He spoke to the inspector in Tamil and the inspector went out on the verandah, leaving us together. I told Shankran what I knew, while he walked up and down saying 'Yes. Yes. Yes,' sucking at a cigarette without touching it to his lips, the way Brahmins do.

'Yes. Yes,' he said. 'Of course I'll do my best for you. Trust me. Yes. Inspector!'

The inspector came in.

'How badly are these coolies hurt?' Shankran asked him.

'One of them is not expected to live, sir.'

'H'm. H'm. That's bad, Yes.' Shankran turned to me. 'Pity you couldn't come here at once, directly it happened. There'd have been no case, I would have squashed it from the start. Now, of course – h'm.' He sucked at his cigarette, thinking. Then suddenly he turned to me again, holding out his hand. 'All right,' he said. 'Don't you worry. I'll see you through. Make no statements to any one. Keep mum and meet me in Fenner's tonight, nine o'clock.'

He came to the door with us, telling me again not to worry, and we drove off. He was a damn good scout, Shankran, and except for his skin a good deal whiter than some of those swine that swank about the club thinking they're sahibs. I felt better now the case was in his hands.

We got down at the station and went in and there were a few native police standing about in boots and puttees, but nobody else. The inspector sat down at his desk and was starting to ask me a few questions when suddenly there were voices raised outside and that swine Holt, the Assistant Commissioner, came storming in.

'Arrest that man!' he shouted as soon as he saw me. 'Put him under arrest!'

'But Mr Holt,' I started to say.

'Be silent!' he shouted, and to the inspector: 'Detain him, don't let him get away. He's a dangerous man!'

Of course this was damn ridiculous, and unprecedented to boot, treating a European that way. Truth was, I'd had a bit of trouble with Holt over the licensing of buses: he was Traffic Commissioner as well and he didn't like me. He was only doing this to get his own back.

'Can I have bail, sir?' I said.

'Bail? Yes. A thousand rupees,' and with that he stamped out of the station. Well, of course, the inspector didn't put me in a cell; I was simply shut in a room on my own. I'd just thought I should be phoning the office, when who should roll in but old Major Brant: he'd been with me the night before and had heard about the accident from Fenner.

'Well, Adams, old boy,' he said, 'in a jam again?'

'By God I am. It's that bastard Holt. He put me under arrest.'

'Won't they let you have bail?'

'A thousand chips.'

'That's all right, old boy. I'll fix it for you.'

So he went bail for me and the inspector let us out. We went down to Fenner's and Brant said: 'Boy, bring Master a large brandy.' So I drank three large brandies altogether and Brant said he'd testify I was sober the night before, because a short time before I left I'd been playing the big drum in the dance band and it's difficult to keep time when you're tight – although I had done it apparently. What's more, Brant said, I had been dancing with his wife earlier on, and he certainly wouldn't let his wife dance with a drunken man. He winked at me and I thanked him and got off to the office. When I came in there the secretary had a message the Old Man wanted to see me.

'What's the meaning of all this, Adams?' Sir Alec said.

'Well, sir, I had a bit of a smash last night.'

'So you said last time you drove your car into a tree and smashed it up completely. Were you drunk?'

'No, sir.'

'Why didn't you stop then?'

'I must have lost my nerve.'

'Humph!' Sir Alec said. 'Well, this is Dr Menon, the company solicitor, who will act for you.'

Dr Menon came forward and shook hands. He was a Hindu, Oxford-degree, B.B.C. accent, and all in European dress, even to the green felt hat lying on the desk: people don't wear topees the whole time out East the way you read about in books. I knew Menon slightly: he was a slimy skite and I wouldn't trust him an inch. I didn't let on I'd already been to Shankran.

Menon suggested we should go down to the scene of the accident, and I said all right, without telling him I didn't know where it was. I knew it was somewhere near Fenner's because the inspector had told me so, and we drove down there. Of course all traces had gone by this time, and Menon said he could do nothing more at the moment.

'It all depends on the condition of the coolies,' he said. 'I will inquire at the hospital and let you know later.'

'Righto,' I said.

That night I went into Fenner's to wait for Shankran. I was sitting outside drinking a double scotch when a chap came up to me called Turpin, awful little squirt he was, supposed to be a jockey, though he never seemed to do any riding. Matter of fact, I found out afterwards he'd been warned off.

'Evening, Mr Adams,' this chap said to me.

'Evening,' I said. I'd never spoken to the little bastard before and wondered what in hell he wanted.

'Sorry to hear about your smash last night,' he said. 'It was a bad break.'

'Yes.'

'Nasty thing to happen.'

'Yes.'

'Suppose this coolie croaks. You'll be in the cart.'

'Yes.'

'But maybe I can help.'

'How?' I said.

He looked round to see no one was listening, then leant across the table. I moved back a bit: the little bleeder stank of booze.

'Look here,' he said. 'It happens I know the bloke that's making all the bother. Name of Krishnaswami. He's the bloke you want to look out for.'

'How d'you mean?' I said: I hadn't heard of Krishnaswami until now.

'He's the bloke that saw it all. Took your number. Told the police.'

'I see. I didn't know they had a witness.'

'You bet they have. He's the star turn.'

'Well, what about it?'

'He might be fixed,' Turpin said, looking at me and putting a finger alongside his nose.

'But if he's given his evidence.'

'He could slip out of that easy enough. He's got pull, see? His dad's Trade Commissioner back home. A big bug. He could pull strings.'

'Ah.' I began to see daylight. Turpin and Krishnaswami were in cahoots, and Turpin was the pilot-fish. But I didn't let on I'd spotted their little game, and simply nodded to what he'd said.

'Suppose you talked to Krishnaswami, see? Just a friendly chat. It wouldn't hurt you.'

'Where can I meet him?'

'He'll be here in a tick. He said he was coming at eight.'

'All right.'

'I'll get along then. If Krishnaswami comes in, shall I send him over?'

'Yes, do.'

'Right you are.'

He went out, and I guessed he'd gone to fetch Krishnaswami. Sure enough, in about five minutes, this bloke blew in, complete with white bum-freezer and smoking a cheroot. I'd often seen him about, without knowing who he was. He always seemed to have plenty of cash to sling about. He was a thickset chap with a little moustache and a brown spot on the white of his right eye. He looked sly, and he was, as things turned out.

'Excuse me,' he said, 'but am I addressing Mr Adams?'

'You are.'

'May I sit down?'

'Certainly.'

He gave a little bow and sat down opposite me.

'What'll you have?' I said.

'A brandy, if I may.'

He sat there smiling and looking smug until the boy brought his brandy. Then he said: 'Mr Adams,' and stopped.

'Yes?' I said.

'It seems that my action in giving evidence last night has caused you much inconvenience,' Krishnaswami said. 'I should like to apologize for the trouble to which you have been put.' He spread his hands and smiled. 'Believe me, I am sincerely sorry.'

'That's all right,' I said.

'You are very kind. But perhaps if you will allow me to explain, you will understand the motives actuating my conduct. I feel sure you will understand.'

'Carry on.'

'Mr Adams, I am an Indian! Those coolies whom your car injured are Indians also – my own people. I am an enlightened man, a democrat. I do not believe in the caste system. It is barbarous and should be abolished. To me, all men are brothers. These coolies are human beings like ourselves, are they not?'

'Oh, absolutely,' I said.

'Imagine, then, my feelings when on emerging from Fenner's, I saw these men struck down by your car and left bleeding and mangled in the roadway, while you yourself drove on without heed. Indians, Mr Adams, my own people! Natives, it is true, but not animals, to be slaughtered like cattle. I knelt down beside them, I was bathed in their blood. One had sustained terrible injuries to his head, it seemed as though he might die there in my arms. You can understand my anger, Mr Adams, and why, having noted the number of your car, I immediately denounced you to the police. Also, I must admit, I was at the time slightly intoxicated. Under the influence of liquor. It had gone to my head. Had I but reflected, I should not have taken the course which I did. But I acted on impulse. Upon the spur of the moment. Now I realize that I was wrong, that if you drove on it was from some other reason than callousness, and I am prepared, so far as I am able, to make amends. I cannot, alas, retract my statement to the police, but there are ways and means by which its effect may be softened.' He pulled a handkerchief out of his sleeve and started to mop his forehead. He'd got very heated talking about the coolies. He drank some brandy and went on. 'If for instance you were to offer some compensation to the family of the injured man . . .'

'Would that do any good?'

'In my opinion, yes. It would be a point in your favour when the case is brought to court.'

'How much money should I offer?'

'Something in the nature of five hundred rupees.' He looked at me sideways out of the eye that had the brown spot in it. 'If you were to give some such sum into my hands, I would see that it was distributed to the best advantage and in a manner which would redound to your credit.'

'Oughtn't I to give it them myself?'

'No. I think perhaps it would come better through me – one of their own people, you know. I should of course make it quite clear that you were the donor, and that I was merely acting as intermediary.'

'Well, I tell you what. I'll sleep on it and let you know. How's that?'

'Admirable. I am staying at the Laburnum, just round the corner. Here is my card. You can always get in touch with me there.'

'Right.'

'And with regard to my evidence, I think we might achieve some compromise. My father, as you are doubtless aware, is Trade Commissioner in England at the moment. He would gladly exert his influence on your behalf.'

'Thanks.'

'I am pleased to be of service,' Krishnaswami said. 'Will you join me in a drink?'

'No, I won't have another now, thanks.'

'Just to show there is no ill-feeling.'

'No, really, thanks. Not now.'

'As you wish,' Krishnaswami said. 'But I see you are a good sport, you do not bear malice. And perhaps you are wise not to drink too much. The police have an unworthy suspicion that you are a man of intemperate habits. Mr Holt, the commissioner, is your enemy. Beware of his spies. You are being watched at this very moment!'

'How d'you know all this?'

Krishnaswami smiled, smoking his cheroot. 'We natives have many systems of communication unknown to the European. Besides, news travels fast in the East. If you observe that table behind you, you will see that I am speaking the truth.'

I looked behind me. There was an awful crowd of Mohammedan sods sitting at that table: they looked more like cut-throats than detectives, but they were watching me right enough.

'Agents of Mr Holt,' Krishnaswami said. He got up from the table and bowed. 'Till our next meeting, Mr Adams.'

'So long,' I said, and watched him walk out, strutting, with the cheroot cocked up at a jaunty angle in his mouth. I looked at the card he'd given me, H. B. KRISHNASWAMI, it said, BACHELOR OF ARTS, OXON, and written underneath, 'Laburnum Hotel, Madras'. I took another look at those Mohammedans. Detectives be damned. More likely some of Krishnaswami's pals, keeping an eye on me, It'd take more than them to stop me drinking. 'Boy!' I called, 'Bring another whisky. A large one.'

Soon after this Shankran rolled in, all smiles as usual.

'Well, well, well! How's it going?'

'Not too good,' I told him.

'Now, now, don't get downhearted. Never say die, you know. This case isn't as bad as it seems, I've been making inquiries. It appears the police have a witness. A man called Krishnaswami.'

'I know, I've just been talking to him.'

'What!'

I told him what Krishnaswami had said to me. Shankran listened, holding a cigarette with his hand cupped round it, sucking up smoke from time to time. 'Yes. Yes. Yes,' he said, and when I'd finished: 'It's as you thought. This Krishnaswami is a crook. I have him taped, I've been on his track for some time. That's why I was pleased when I came in just now. If Krishnaswami appears in court I shall unmask him as an impostor. His evidence will be discredited.'

'But isn't he the son of Sir Somebody Krishnaswami then?'

'No, no. That's all bunk. Absolute nonsense. He's an impostor.'

'He said I was being watched by detectives. At the table behind.'

'What? Those ruffians? Bunk, my boy, bunk. Krishnaswami's after your cash.'

'That's what I thought.'

'You were right. But don't worry, we can circumvent him. He

doesn't present a serious obstacle. No. The main thing is that coolie.
If he dies, Holt will make it hot for you.'

'He put me under arrest this morning.'

'I know, I know. And Major Brant bailed you out.'

'News travels fast in the East,' I said.

Shankran said: 'I got it from the inspector. He and I are good
friends. He will keep me posted with all details and developments as
to police-work.' Suddenly he looked very serious. 'But if that
coolie dies . . .' He shook his head.

'What about the other one?' I asked.

'Oh, he's all right. A broken leg, that's all. We needn't worry
about him.' Shankran tapped on the table. 'And listen, on no account give Krishnaswami any money. Stall him, you understand.
Procrastinate. But give him nothing. Take no one's advice but mine.'

'Sir Alec has called in Dr Menon, for the company.'

'Menon? I know him. One of these kid-glove lawyers. No pep.
Not the man for this case. Pay no attention to him.'

'All right.'

'I'll deal with Krishnaswami. For the rest, pray to God that
coolie doesn't die. Pray to God. I will pray for you myself tonight.'
He was very serious.

'Holy smoke!' I said.

'Boy, bring some gin!' Shankran said.

There were two mosquitoes had got in my net that night, and I
couldn't sleep. Every time I dozed off, one of the bastards'd come
singing round and sting me, and at last I had to get up and swat
them. Even so I couldn't sleep for thinking of that coolie. It was
bloody hot and I was sweating and I thought, suppose he does die?
I didn't want to get three years like Cornford. I don't mind telling
you I did pray that night, I was in an awful state. At last I managed
to sleep, and woke late in the morning feeling lousy. I fined the
blasted boy an anna for each of those mosquitoes and got off to the
office. I hadn't been there long before the Old Man sent for me. I
went up and he had Dr Menon with him, who looked serious.

'About this accident of yours, Adams,' Sir Alec said. 'Did you
know the police have a witness?'

'Yes, sir,' I said. 'I've spoken to him.'

'Is it true he is the son of the Trade Commissioner in England?' Dr Menon said.

'He told me he was.'

Menon nodded. I could see he was impressed.

'What did he speak to you about?' Sir Alec said.

'He suggested that I should offer compensation to the injured man's family, sir.'

'Humph! How much?'

'Five hundred chips.'

'Humph! What d'you think, Menon?'

'It wouldn't do any harm to parley with them, sir,' Menon said. 'Have you got his address, Mr Adams?'

'Yes. Here's his card.'

'Well, we might go round there and see him this evening, eh?' He looked at Sir Alec, who grunted 'Good idea', so I agreed.

That evening Menon and I went round to Krishnaswami's hotel back of Mount Road. He was in right enough, very smooth and pleased to see us. It was a bloody sight to see those two, Menon and him, both talking Oxford-English and trying to outdo each other at it. By God, you should have heard them. Krishnaswami let off a little bit about his father and I could see Menon believed him. He swallowed it whole. At last, after a lot of this, we got down to brass tacks. Krishnaswami still stuck out for five hundred chips and Menon seemed to think it would be a good thing if I shelled out.

'But look here,' I said. 'The police are prosecuting me, not this fellow's family at all. How will it help to give them five hundred?'

'It would make a good impression on the court,' Menon said.

'But in any case the sum seems a bit stiff,' I said, and so it was. Why, what the hell, five hundred chips was pretty near a whole month's screw.

'Oh come, Mr Adams,' Krishnaswami said. 'When I think of that poor coolie, with his blood and brains bespattering the roadway, when I think of his poor family, of the terrible worry and uncertainty which they must be undergoing, I sometimes wonder whether any sum of money, however large, could be adjudged sufficient compensation.'

'Well anyhow,' I said, 'he's not dead yet, because I phoned up the hospital this afternoon and they say he's getting along nicely.'

I had been keeping this up my sleeve as a trump card, and I could see it was a set-back for Krishnaswami; he didn't like it at all. Then Menon came in with another one.

'Well,' he said, 'we will consider your proposal, Mr Krishnaswami. I personally am in favour of it. If Mr Adams will appoint some responsible person to distribute this sum among the man's family, I have no doubt that such an action would influence the court favourably.'

Krishnaswami didn't like that either. He'd counted on getting hold of the dough himself. He bowed and showed his teeth, but it wasn't a smile. He said: 'Perhaps Mr Adams would prefer to consult his *other lawyer*, Mr Shankran, before committing himself to any course?'

'Mr Shankran?' Menon said. He frowned.

'I think I am correct, Mr Adams, am I not?' Krishnaswami said. 'Mr Shankran is acting for you also?'

'Yes,' I said.

I wondered for a moment how the hell he knew, and then I remembered those Mohammedans.

'News travels fast in the East,' I said.

Krishnaswami smiled and bowed. He knew I'd caught on, but he didn't care. He saw the game was up. Menon was still frowning. He didn't say any more about Shankran, but he was upset all the same. Going downstairs, I tried to explain to him how it was, but he turned away and said: 'It is most unprofessional having two solicitors. You should have informed me before now.'

In the car he'd evidently thought up something, because he said: 'I wonder if it would be possible to see Mr Shankran this evening. Since this state of affairs has been allowed to transpire, perhaps it can be turned to advantage. Mr Shankran and I should compare notes as soon as possible.'

'We can see if he's in,' I said.

He was. We found him sitting at a table covered with briefs, busy on a big case, he told us.

'Dr Menon and I have just seen Krishnaswami,' I said.

'Oh yes? What happened?'

Menon, still upstage and on his dignity, said: 'Apparently Mr Adams consulted you first, before Sir Alec called me in. I think therefore that we should pool our knowledge and work together as far as possible from now on.'

'Yes, yes. Quite. A pleasure Dr Menon. What did Krishnaswami say?'

Menon told him.

'Are you satisfied that this man has no ulterior motive in suggesting compensation?' Shankran said.

'For my part, I am perfectly satisfied,' Menon said. They argued about it for some time, but Shankran wouldn't agree: he still didn't like the idea. At last Menon got up to go. He'd said good-bye and was at the door, when he turned round again as if he'd remembered something.

'Oh yes. One moment, Mr Shankran.' He turned to me. 'I am sure you will excuse us, Mr Adams. Just a technical point.'

'Sure,' I said, 'don't mind me.' So they went out on the verandah together while I mixed myself another whisky and soda and as I was drinking it I could hear them out there talking away in Tamil. Presently they came back, both smiling, and Menon seemed in a better temper.

'That's settled then,' he said. 'If you should decide in favour of compensation, will you let me know, Mr Shankran?' and Shankran said he would, and Menon went out. He didn't shake hands with me, just said 'Good-bye,' and I think he was still a bit put out. Directly he'd gone, Shankran stopped smiling and turned round on me.

'The dirty bainchut,' he said. 'D'you know what he told me outside?'

'I've no idea.'

'"Don't worry, Shankran," he said. "Get as much out of him as you can. I'm paid by the company, I won't ask you for a cut." You see? The corrupt bainchut. They're all the same out here: squeeze you for your last anna. By God, Adams, you can thank your stars I'm straight!' He tapped on the table again. 'As for Krishnaswami, if he comes near that court I'll smash him. But he won't, depend upon it. Those five hundred rupees, he wants them for his hotel-bill. It's the amount he owes the proprietor!'

'What!' I said. 'How do you know?'

'I found it out,' Shankran said. 'It's my business to find out things. Krishnaswami's up to his nose in debt. He's a twister!'

He took off his glasses and wiped them. He was so furious he started sweating hard, and the sweat ran down his nose on to his glasses so that he couldn't see. He wiped the glasses and said: 'However, he won't appear in court. He knows I'm after him!'

'You don't think Menon's working with Krishnaswami, do you?' I said.

'Menon? Oh no. He's a twister too, but not that kind. Hasn't got the guts.'

'You don't think so?'

'I'm sure of it, my boy, sure of it. No. You needn't worry about that. As for the case, it'll go off all right if that coolie recovers.'

'He's doing well so far. I'm going up to see him at the hospital tomorrow.'

'That's fine,' Shankran said. 'But remember, don't give him any money. I'll tell you when the time comes to pay out.'

'Righto,' I said.

I got up to the hospital the next day and there was this coolie with his head and face bound up in bandages and all his family weeping and wailing round the bedside. The other coolie who had a broken leg was there too, but he didn't seem to have any family, or at least I didn't see them anyway.

The mother of the broken-headed coolie came across and spoke to me. Of course it was all in Tamil and I couldn't understand the half of it, but I told her in English how sorry I was, and I think she understood, because she made a salaam and pointed to her boy and said a piece more, weeping all the time. I felt awful. The old woman didn't sound angry, only very sad, but she couldn't stop crying. I bloody near wept myself, I don't mind telling you. I spoke to the coolie, but he didn't answer: he was lying back with his eyes closed where you could see them through the bandages, and he looked pretty bad to me. I felt terrible. I spoke to the other coolie and he grinned up at me and seemed quite cheerful, so I said a bit more to the old mother, who salaamed again, still sobbing, and the rest of the family crowded round all chattering and some of them salaamed too. They could tell I was sorry. Then I got out and told the matron to give the coolies anything extra they wanted and charge it up to me.

'That's very good of you, Mr Adams,' she said, 'but I think they are quite comfortable. They have all they want.'

'The one with the broken head looks bad. Will he live?'

'Certainly. He's quite out of danger now,' she said, so I thanked her and went out. Driving back to the bungalow I still felt awful about it, though.

A week went by and I heard nothing more, except I had a summons from the police saying I was to appear on various charges in three days' time. Then one morning Sir Alec sent for me.

'Adams,' he said, 'Dr Menon was here yesterday. He says he wants to give up the case as you already have a solicitor acting for you. Is that so?'

'Yes, sir,' I said.

'Who is he? A good man?'

'Yes, sir. Mr Shankran.'

'Humph! I've heard of him. Sails a bit near the wind sometimes, doesn't he?'

'He's a smart lawyer, sir.'

'Humph. Didn't he act for Cornford?'

'Yes, sir.'

'Think he'll get you off?'

'He seems pretty certain of it.'

'I'm glad of that. Sure you don't need Menon then?'

'No, sir.'

'Very well,' Sir Alec said, 'if you're satisfied.'

I couldn't find Shankran anywhere. He'd gone off on a case and nobody seemed to know where he was. I was due to appear next day and didn't know what the hell to do. I sat in Fenner's sopping up straight Scotch and feeling awful. Then suddenly, towards the end of the evening, Shankran came in. By God I was never so glad to see anyone in my life.

'Hullo, hullo, hullo,' he said. 'How are you? I've just come back from the hills. Been chasing a witness. Boy, bring some gin!'

'Listen,' I said. 'My case comes off tomorrow at twelve. Have you got everything fixed?'

'Tomorrow? I can't appear for you tomorrow. I'm up to my eyes. Rape. A very difficult case. I've bribed the chief witness but there are still two I've got to get at. Tomorrow's impossible. I shan't be here.'

'Well, what the hell's going to happen?'

'Don't worry. You won't appear either.'

'But I've had the summons!'

Shankran shook his head. 'You won't appear. You're ill. You can't appear if you're ill.'

'What d'you mean – ill?'

'You're sick. You've got dysentery.'

'I haven't at all.'

'Of course you have. Don't be silly. We'll get the case postponed. Meet me tomorrow morning and I'll fix it for you.'

So I met him next morning and he drove me right down to George Town, through the bazaar and a lot of stinking little streets and stopped at a chemist's shop that had posters up on the walls outside, advertising cures for siph.

'Up here,' Shankran said, so we went up some awful filthy stairs and into a doctor's waiting room full of natives covered in sores. Shankran sent in his card and the doctor saw us straightaway. He was a Hindu with a big black beard.

'Ah, yes. Mr Adams. How do you do? Dysentery, isn't it? I'll make the certificate out at once.'

He sat down and wrote a certificate saying I was suffering from dysentery and we thanked him and went.

'That's settled,' Shankran said. 'Drop me at the court as we go by, I'll just file the certificate. Don't be alarmed if you don't hear from me for a while, I've got to get after those witnesses. Curse the corrupt bainchuts. Baksheesh, that's all they think about in this country.'

Fenner said to me one night: 'Seen Krishnaswami lately?'

'No,' I said.

'Well, you won't, either. He's shot the moon. Blown off to Bangalore.'

'By God. Is that so?'

'It bloody well is. He owes that fellow at the Laburnum five hundred chips.'

'By God. Does he owe you anything?'

'No. But that little blighter Turpin does, and he's gone too. They've done a bunk together.'

'By God,' I said. 'Have another drink?'

Well at last the case came off. I met Shankran the night before and he gave me a whacking great list of answers I had to make in court.

'Better memorize those,' he said. 'Learn them off by heart. You won't have much trouble, I know the magistrate. He's a gentleman. You won't have to go in the box. As for witnesses, Krishnaswami's gone. He got out when I threatened him with exposure. The night-watchman from Spinner's saw the smash, but I've fixed him all right. Major Brant will of course speak for you. The inspector's on our side as well. You'll have to give him three hundred chips by the way, when it's all over.'

'D'you think we'll win?'

'Of course we shall. Without Krishnaswami they've got no case at all. It'll be a walk-over.'

The court was very hot and crowded, with bags of natives sprawling about the corridors, all chattering to beat the band, gobbing and chewing betel-nut, and peons with red sashes and great brass plates on their chests strutting up and down bawling for silence and making more row than all the rest put together.

Inside, some native police were keeping order and it looked pretty much like the American courts on the cinema, with benches all the way down and a high dais for the magistrate to sit at. I saw old Brant and several of the boys, but no sign of Krishnaswami. Holt wasn't there, of course, being commissioner, but all the coolie's family were, and soon after an ambulance rolled up and the coolies themselves were carried in on stretchers.

'Have you got the answers off pat?' Shankran asked me.

'Yes,' I said.

Then the magistrate came in and we all stood up. He was a Mohammedan and Shankran knew him well. He rapped with the gavel and we all sat down again. Mine was the first case called. The inspector gave his evidence first, for the prosecution, then Shankran called Major Brant, for the defence.

After he had spoken, Krishnaswami's name was called. No answer. The usher walked up and down shouting 'Mr Krishnaswami!' but Krishnaswami didn't show up. The inspector was called back to the box. He read out the statement made by Krishnaswami, to the effect that I had caused the accident and furthermore had callously driven on, being at the time under the influence of drink.

Shankran jumped up. He was sweating hard. He wiped his glasses and the back of his neck and shouted: 'Do you deny that this witness was himself intoxicated at the time of giving his evidence, and that moreover one of his companions was in such an unseemly condition that you refused to accept his statement?'

The inspector didn't deny it.

'Therefore the case for the prosecution rests solely upon the evidence of two men who were themselves in a state of intoxication, and who have since left the city?' Shankran said. 'Thank you, that is all.' He sat down again.

'You say these witnesses cannot be found?' the magistrate said.

'No, your worship,' the inspector said. 'Their present whereabouts are unknown.'

'H'm. Does the defendant plead guilty or not guilty?'

'Guilty, your worship,' Shankran said, 'on the charge of causing the accident; not guilty on the charge of intoxication.'

'Will the defendant please approach?'

Shankran nudged me, and I went forward and stood in front of the dais.

'You plead guilty to the charges against you?'

'Except to that of intoxication, your worship,' I said.

'What caused your car to collide with these men?'

'A pariah dog, your worship. It ran out in the road, and in my efforts to avoid it, caused the accident.'

'Why did you drive on, instead of stopping to assist the men you had injured?'

'I lost my nerve, your worship.'

'Why didn't you report to the police?'

'Same reason, your worship.'

'H'm. Well, in the absence of further witnesses, the case will have to be adjourned in order that the question of compensation be discussed among the parties concerned.'

Shankran jumped up again, wiping his glasses like mad.

'Your worship,' he said. 'Cannot the question of compensation be discussed without delay? My client has suffered considerable inconvenience as a result of this case and we would sooner proceed to its conclusion without further postponement.'

'Very well,' the magistrate said. He looked over at the coolies. The one with the broken leg had it done up in plaster of Paris and the other one had some of the bandages taken off his face and looked a bit better.

'Let us say then,' the magistrate stroked his chin, 'the sum of three hundred and fifty rupees.'

He repeated it in Tamil and looked again at the coolies and at the old mother who was sitting with the family on the front bench. She nodded and started to cry again and the rest of the family began to argue and talk in Tamil.

The magistrate rapped for order and said: 'You are also fined one hundred and fifty rupees for driving an automobile to the common danger and fifty rupees for failing to report an accident to the police. These sums should be paid to the clerk of the court. Case dismissed,' so it cost me eight hundred and fifty chips altogether, including three hundred for the inspector, and on top of that came Shankran's fee. By God, it was worth it though. I went on the binge for a bloody month afterwards, I was so relieved at getting off. In fact that's what got me the sack eventually, not the accident at all. Sir Alec was damn decent about it on the whole, he said he couldn't keep me in the circumstances, but gave me a damned good reference just the same. That's how I come to be home again.

Don't know of any good jobs going, do you?

O Dreams, O Destinations

C. DAY LEWIS

I

FOR infants time is like a humming shell
Heard between sleep and sleep, wherein the shores
Foam-fringed, wind-fluted of the strange earth dwell
And the sea's cavernous hunger faintly roars.
It is the humming pole of summer lanes
Whose sound quivers like heat-haze endlessly
Over the corn, over the poppied plains –
An emanation from the earth or sky.
Faintly they hear, through the womb's lingering haze,
A rumour of that sea to which they are born:
They hear the ringing pole of summer days,
But need not know what hungers for the corn.
They are the lisping rushes in a stream –
Grace-notes of a profound, legato dream.

2

Children look down upon the morning-grey
Tissue of mist that veils a valley's lap:
Their fingers itch to tear it and unwrap
The flags, the roundabouts, the gala day.
They watch the spring rise inexhaustibly –
A breathing thread out of the eddied sand,
Sufficient to their day: but half their mind
Is on the sailed and glittering estuary.
Fondly we wish their mist might never break,
Knowing it hides so much that best were hidden:
We'd chain them by the spring, lest it should broaden
For them into a quicksand and a wreck.

But they slip through our fingers like the source,
Like mist, like time that has flagged out their course.

3

That was the fatal move, the ruination
Of innocence so innocently begun,
When in the lawless orchard of creation
The child left this fruit for that rosier one.
Reaching towards the far thing, we begin it;
Looking beyond, or backward, more and more
We grow unfaithful to the unique minute
Till, from neglect, its features stale and blur.
Fish, bird or beast was never thus unfaithful –
Man only casts the image of his joys
Beyond his senses' reach; and by this fateful
Act, he confirms the ambiguous power of choice.
Innocence made that first choice. It is she
Who weeps, a child chained to the outraged tree.

4

Our youthtime passes down a colonnade
Shafted with alternating light and shade.
All's dark or dazzle there. Half in a dream
Rapturously we move, yet half afraid
Never to wake. That diamond-point, extreme
Brilliance engraved on us a classic theme:
The shaft of darkness had its lustre too,
Rising where earth's concentric mysteries gleam.
Oh youth-charmed hours, that made an avenue
Of fountains playing on us to love's full view,
A cypress walk to some romantic grave –
Waking, how false in outline and in hue
We find the dreams that flickered on our cave:
Only your fire, which cast them, still seems true.

5

All that time there was thunder in the air;
Our nerves branched and flickered with summer lightning.
The taut crab-apple, the pampas quivering, the glare
On the roses seemed irrelevant, or a heightening
At most of the sealed-up hour wherein we awaited
What? – some explosive oracle to abash
The platitudes on the lawn? heaven's delegated
Angel – the golden rod, our burning bush?
No storm broke. Yet in retrospect the rose
Mounting vermilion, fading, glowing again
Like a fire's heart, that breathless inspiration
Of pampas grass, crab-tree's attentive pose
Never were so divinely charged as then –
The veiled Word's flesh, a near annunciation.

6

Symbols of gross experience! – our grief
Flowed, like a sacred river, underground:
Desire bred fierce abstractions on the mind,
Then like an eagle soared beyond belief.
Often we tried our breast against the thorn,
Our paces on the turf: whither we flew,
Why we should agonize, we hardly knew –
Nor what ached in us, asking to be born.
Ennui of youth! – thin air above the clouds,
Vain divination of the sunless stream
Mirror that impotence, till we redeem
Our birthright, and the shadowplay concludes.
Ah, not in dreams, but when our souls engage
With the common mesh and moil, we come of age.

7

Older, we build a road where once our active
Heat threw up mountains and the deep dales veined:
We're glad to gain the limited objective,
Knowing the war we fight in has no end.
The road must needs follow each contour moulded
By that fire in its losing fight with earth:
We march over our past, we may behold it
Dreaming a slave's dream on our bivouac hearth.
Lost the archaic dawn wherein we started,
The appetite for wholeness: now we prize
Half-loaves, half-truths – enough for the half-hearted,
The gleam snatched from corruption satisfies.
Dead youth, forgive us if, all but defeated,
We raise a trophy where your honour lies.

8

But look, the old illusion still returns,
Walking a field-path where the succory burns
Like summer's eye, the blue lustre-drops of noon,
And the heart follows it and freshly yearns:
Yearns to the sighing distances beyond
Each height of happiness, the vistas drowned
In gold-dust haze, and dreams itself immune
From change and night to which all else is bound.
Love, we have caught perfection for a day
As succory holds a gem of halcyon ray:
Summer burns out, its flower will tarnish soon –
Deathless illusion, that could so relay
The truth of flesh and spirit, sun and clay
Singing for once together all in tune!

9

To travel like a bird, lightly to view
Deserts where stone gods founder in the sand,
Ocean embraced in a white sleep with land;
To escape time, always to start anew.
To settle like a bird, make one devoted
Gesture of permanence upon the spray
Of shaken stars and autumns; in a bay
Beyond the crestfallen surges to have floated.
Each is our wish. Alas, the bird flies blind,
Hooded by a dark sense of destination:
Her weight on the glass calm leaves no impression,
Her home is soon a basketful of wind.
Travellers, we're fabric of the road we go;
We settle, but like feathers on time's flow.

Fern Hill

DYLAN THOMAS

Now as I was young and easy under the apple boughs
About the lilting house and happy as the grass was green,
    The night above the dingle starry,
      Time let me hail and climb
    Golden in the heydays of his eyes,
And honoured among wagons I was prince of the apple towns
And once below a time I lordly had the trees and leaves
      Trail with daisies and barley
    Down the rivers of the windfall light.

And I was green and carefree, famous among the barns
About the happy yard and singing as the farm was home,
    In the sun that is young once only,
      Time let me play and be
    Golden in the mercy of his means,
And green and golden I was huntsman and herdsman, the calves
Sang to my horn, the foxes on the hills barked clear and cold,
      And the sabbath rang slowly
    In the pebbles of the holy streams.

All the sun long it was running, it was lovely, the hay
Fields high as the house, the tunes from the chimneys, it was air
    And playing, lovely and watery
      And fire green as grass.
    And nightly under the simple stars
As I rode to sleep the owls were bearing the farm away,
All the moon long I heard, blessed among stables, the nightjars
      Flying with the ricks, and the horses
    Flashing into the dark.

And then to awake, and the farm, like a wanderer white
With the dew, come back, the cock on his shoulder: it was all
      Shining, it was Adam and maiden,
          The sky gathered again
        And the sun grew round that very day.
So it must have been after the birth of the simple light
In the first, spinning place, the spellbound horses walking warm
      Out of the whinnying green stable
        On to the fields of praise.

And honoured among foxes and pheasants by the gay house
Under the new made clouds and happy as the heart was long,
      In the sun born over and over,
        I ran my heedless ways,
       My wishes raced through the house high hay
And nothing I cared, at my sky blue trades, that time allows
In all his tuneful turning so few and such morning songs
      Before the children green and golden
        Follow him out of grace,

Nothing I cared, in the lamb white days, that time would take me
Up to the swallow thronged loft by the shadow of my hand,
      In the moon that is always rising,
        Nor that riding to sleep
     I should hear him fly with the high fields
And wake to the farm forever fled from the childless land.
Oh as I was young and easy in the mercy of his means,
      Time held me green and dying
     Though I sang in my chains like the sea.

The Yogi and the Commissar

ARTHUR KOESTLER

1 The Static Spectrum

I LIKE to imagine an instrument which would enable us to break up patterns of social behaviour as the physicist is able to break up a beam of rays. Looking through this sociological spectroscope we would see spread out under the diffraction-grate the rainbow-coloured spectrum of all possible human attitudes to life. The whole distressing muddle would become neat, clear and comprehensive.

On one end of the spectrum, obviously on the infra-red end, we would see the Commissar. The Commissar believes in Change from Without. He believes that all the pests of humanity, including constipation and the Oedipus complex, can and will be cured by Revolution, that is by a radical reorganization of the system of production and distribution of goods; that this end justifies the use of all means, including violence, ruse, treachery and poison; that logical reasoning is an unfailing compass and the Universe a kind of very large clockwork in which a very large number of electrons once set into motion will forever revolve in their predictable orbits; and that whosoever believes in anything else is an escapist. This end of the spectrum has the lowest frequency of vibrations and is, in a way, the coarsest component of the beam; but it conveys the maximum amount of heat.

On the other end of the spectrum, where the waves become so short and high-frequent that the eye no longer sees them, colourless, warmthless but all-penetrating, crouches the Yogi, melting away in ultra-violet. He has no objection to calling the universe a clockwork, but he thinks that it could be called, with about the same amount of truth, a musical-box or a fishpond. He believes that the End is unpredictable and that the Means alone count. He rejects violence under any circumstances. He believes that logical reasoning loses its compass value in the same degree as the mind approaches the magnetic pole of Truth or the Absolute, which alone matters. He believes that nothing can be improved by exterior organization and everything by the individual effort from within; and that whosoever believes in anything else is an escapist. He believes that the debt-servitude imposed upon the peasants of India by the moneylenders should not be abolished by financial legislation but by spiritual means. He believes that each individual is alone but attached to the all-one by an invisible umbilical cord; and that his only task during his earthly life is to avoid any action which might lead to a breaking of the cord. This avoidance has to be maintained by a difficult, elaborate technique, the only kind of technique which he accepts.

Between these two extremes are spread out in a continuous sequence the spectral lines of the more sedate human attitudes. The more we approach its centre, the more the spectrum becomes blurred and woolly. On the other hand, this increase of wool on the naked spectral bodies makes them look more decent and intercourse with them more civilized. You cannot argue with a naked Commissar – he starts at once beating his chest and next he strangles you, whether you be friend or foe, in his deadly embrace. You cannot argue with the ultra-violet skeleton either, because words mean nothing to him. You can argue with post-war planners, Fabianists, Quakers, Liberals and Philanthropists. But the arguments will lead nowhere, for the real issue remains between the Yogi and the Commissar, between the fundamental conceptions of Change from Without and Change from Within.

It is easy to say that all that is wanted is a synthesis – the synthesis between saint and revolutionary; but so far this has never been achieved. What has been achieved are various motley forms of compromise – the blurred intermediary bands of the spectrum – compromise but not synthesis. Apparently the two elements do not mix, and this may be one of the reasons why we have made such a mess of our History.

The reason why a synthesis has so far not been achieved can be given in various terms. What appears as a conflict of principles is very often only a conflict in emphasis, but it does not make the reconciliation easier. The Commissar's emotional energies are fixed on the relation between individual and society, the Yogi's on the relation between the individual and the universe. Again it is easy to say that all that is wanted is a little mutual effort. One might as well ask a homosexual to make a little effort towards the opposite sex, and vice versa.

But even if the balance of emphasis may be adjusted and a working compromise achieved, the contradiction in *method* remains. Every attempt to achieve an inner change of man by changing the exterior order has so far failed, from Spartacus' Sun State through Inquisition and Reformation to Soviet Russia. This failure seems to be rooted in two disturbing phenomena which Kant could have called the Antinomies of Applied Reasoning. The first is the Antinomy of the Serpentine; the second the Antinomy of the Slopes.

The peak of Utopia is steep; the serpentine-road which leads up to it has many tortuous curves. While you are moving up the road you never face the peak, your direction is the tangent, leading nowhere. If a great mass of people is pushing forward along the Serpentine they will, according to the fatal laws of inertia, push off their leader from the road and then follow him, the whole movement flying off at the tangent into the nowhere. That is what happened to most revolutionary movements, where the mass-impulse is strong and the inertia of the mass is converted into a violent centrifugal force. In the more cautious reformist movements, on the other hand, the momentum soon fades out and the ascending spiral first becomes a wiry circling round and round the peak without gaining height until it finally degenerates into a descending spiral; i.e. the Trade Unionist movement.

The prophets of Change from Within who try to use the vehicle of organized ascent are caught by the antinomy of the serpentine and share the vehicle's fate: either they fly off the road with it – Inquisition; or slide gradually down with it – State Churches in the Liberal era.

The second root of the failure is the Antinomy of the Slopes, or of Ends and Means. Either the Means are subordinated to the End, or vice versa. Theoretically you may build up elaborate dialectical, liberal, conventional or religious half-way houses; but if burdened with responsibility, and confronted with a practical decision to take, you have to choose one way or the other. Once you have chosen you are on the slope. If you have chosen to subordinate the Means to the

nd, the slope makes you slide down deeper and deeper on a moving
arpet of common-sense propositions, for instance: the right of self-
efence – the best defence is attack – increase of ruthlessness shortens
he struggle, etc. Another well-known slope pattern starts with the
Healer's Knife' and ends with the Moscow Purges. The fatal
nechanism of this slope was already known to Pascal: 'Man is
either angel nor brute and his misery is that he would act the angel
ut acts the brute.'

The alternative method has, to our knowledge, only once been
ried on a large scale, by Gandhi. His slope started with Satyagraha
nd gradually made him slide down to his present position of non-
iolence towards the Japanese aggression: the Japanese might kill a
:w million Indians but some day they would get tired of it and thus
he moral integrity of India would be saved.

Obviously the prospects for the masses of common people are not
righter under this inverted Machiavellianism than under the leader-
hip of the Commissars. One slope leads to the Inquisition and the
'urges; the other to passive submission to bayoneting and raping;
› villages without sewage, septic childbeds and trachoma. The Yogi
nd the Commissar may call it quits.

II The Spectrum in Motion

ut they don't. Unable to form a synthesis and unsatisfied by the
atched-up compromises in the medium bands of the spectrum,
ey attract and repel each other in rhythmical intervals. This strange
ninuet is one of the more exciting aspects of History which Marxism,
therwise the most serviceable guide, falls short of explaining.

Under certain historic climates mass-migrations start from one
nd of the spectrum to the other, general displacements from infra-
ed to ultra-violet or vice versa, like mighty trade-winds travelling
ver the seas. The nineteenth century brought such a general dis-
lacement towards the Commissar or infra-red end. The present
limate favours the opposite direction. Since the early thirties we are
ll travelling, more or less consciously, more or less willingly, to-
vards the ultra-violet end.

The less consciously we drift with the wind the more willing
we do it; the more consciously the less willingly. Personally
belong to the latter type; I wish one could still write an honest infr
red novel without an ultra-violet ending. But one can't, just as ▪
honest scientist can now publish a book on physics without a met▪
physical epilogue, no honest Socialist can write a survey of the Lef▪
defeats without accounting for the irrational factor in mas
psychology. He who clings blindly to the past will be left behin
but he who abandons himself too readily will be carried away like
dry leaf; all one can do is to travel even more consciously and ev▪
less willingly.

But again, is such intentional readaptation possible? Are tho▪
who survive the great spectral displacements the fittest or merely t▪
glibbest? Thinking of some fellow writers who achieved the journe
from the pink decade to the Yogi decade with such monkey-lil
agility one is tempted to say: Let the dead bury their dead. Th▪
answer: But we mean it – and there is no doubt that, at least, the
believe that they mean it. Yet what writer has ever written a li▪
without at least meaning to mean it? Hence one feels first disgu▪
with them; then one finds out that one was disgusted for the wror
reasons; and after that one is still disgusted because they were
quick to find the right reasons for their ex-patriation from the infr
red to the ultra-violet. In these matters clumsiness is respectable ar
glibness abject. They never seriously attempted to sail against t▪
wind; they abandoned themselves to its first breeze, which bro▪
them gently from their stems, and whirled them round and dropp▪
them gently at the other end; that is perhaps why, when you he▪
their whisper, it sounds so much like the rattling of dead leaves.

For the political Commissars the spectral displacement has mo▪
tragic results than for the arty Commissars. I don't mean that the
necessarily feel deeper about it; perhaps it is rather the other wa
round. In ages of distress when values crumble and survival has a
ever so slight but still perceptible touch of glibness and betraya
artists are often tempted by suicide but rarely commit it, whereas t▪
revolutionary is rarely tempted by suicide, but when it happens ▪
has usually no other choice. In a sense spiritual life can be defined ▪
the training for the acceptance of death; the Commissar is the huma

type least advanced in this training and yet by force of circumstances most advanced towards its aim. This is the core of the Commissar's tragedy.

Thus the artist shows the least resistance against being carried away; the revolutionary the greatest. Perhaps because the artist *qua* artist has to leave the tap open for those underground currents which, in times of displacements, inundate the whole vessel and sweep it away, whereas the revolutionary *qua* revolutionary has to keep the tap tightly closed. Indeed the Commissar can be defined as the human type which has completely severed relations to the subconscious. This is the more remarkable as the constant danger under which he lives – I think Lenin used the phrase 'we are dead men on furlough' – is a constant temptation to communicate with those forbidden zones. In fact he is condemned to live in a permanent state of repressed puberty. While in a normal curriculum the great crisis of adolescence, the confrontation with the tragic and insoluble problems of existence only occurs once – a limited process like teething – the revolutionary spends all his life in this tropical climate and those tragic problems remain his daily bread and butter. The ordinary citizen, once the transcendental teething is over, evolves a smooth *modus vivendi* towards the absolute; hence the best the Commissar can hope is to find a smooth *modus moriendi*.

Yet though living in a climate of perpetual adolescence, his behaviour is as unadolescent, unecstatic and unromantic as can be imagined. One has the feeling that his subconscious has been dealt with not on the analyst's sofa but on the surgeon's table with the amputating knife. In fact one of his often recurring problems is not to give himself away by sleep-talking or other subconscious automatisms; and if he is a good Commissar he succeeds. He is a marvel of unneurotic repression: one of the most admirable achievements of the human species.

Now if life becomes impossible without pity, it is perhaps equally impossible without a grain of self-pity. The Commissar is not immune against suffering, but what he experiences is more the echo of pain than pain itself, like the aching of an amputated limb. He compels admiration, but also pity, that tender pity which the weak sometimes feel for the strong. Faced with giant figures like Blanqui, Luxembourg, Vera Figner, we can do nothing but shut up and realize what futile, frivolous dwarfs we are; yet pity remains.

That this instinct is justified becomes apparent when the Commissar faces the crisis of his life. This is a tragic and complicated process, often misunderstood. The forms it may take vary individually, but basically it is always the same: it is the revenge of the amputated organ. In a story of Gerard de Nerval's, which I remember only vaguely, a judge sentences a thief to have his hand cut off; the amputated hand then pursues the judge and finally strangles him. In the Commissar's case judge and victim are one person and the cut-off organ is not a hand; it is, if we examine it closer, the Yogi's umbilical cord, his means of communication with the Absolute, with the 'Oceanic Feeling' to use Freud's sober term. The Commissar lived in the conviction that it was a luxury-organ, but when the crisis comes he realizes that it is not. The Man-Society connexion suddenly proves to be not enough to procure psychic metabolism; the Man-Universe connexion has to be re-established.

At this point one of two things might happen. Either the cut connexion is re-established, and as an act of atonement the Man-Society connexion broken off; this is the classical case of the Revolutionary turning into a Mystic, the total jump from Commissar to Yogi. Or the connexion is *not* re-established – then the dead cord coils up and strangles its owner. This is the equally classical case of the ex-revolutionaries whose souls died of suffocation. They might appear as cadaverous as Sinowjew at the Moscow trials; or satanic and cynical like Laval and Doriot; or as impotent and desiccated as the Left party-bureaucracy. Since Rosa Luxembourg there has risen no man or woman endowed with both the Oceanic feeling and the momentum of action.

Unfortunately we have as yet no scientific terminology to describe these processes, which are of vital importance for the understanding of the 'subjective factor' in History. Hence the more soberly one tries to describe them the more vague imagery one has, *faute de mieux*, to use. The enormous literature of the three main contemporary schools in psychology contains not a single case-history of this non-hysterical conversion, the revolutionary's transformation into a cynic or mystic, whereas history, past and present, abounds in examples. Jung comes nearest to the question: his interpretation of the subconscious bears most resemblance to the 'umbilical cord', but he prefers to study its effects on the most unsuitable human type, the wealthy middle-aged Babbitts. And this for good reason: were he to choose his patients among the type which inhabits the German or Russian concentration camps, not only would his therapy prove to be inadequate but he would have to introduce so many new determining factors into his system that both his terminology and his *Weltanschauung* would go to blazes. The Commissar's spectral displacements are *terra nova* for the psychologist.

Turning to the more muddled, intermediary bands of the spectrum we find that their reactions to the mystic current are of a very revealing nature. In the pink regions the reaction first manifests itself by an intense consciousness of the Left's serial defeats, of disgust with the old parties, disgust with their worn-out leaders, with plans and promises, ideas and ideals and most of all with one's own foolish and frustrated hopes. This pink hangover is the emotional starting point. Next comes the realization that 'there must have been something basically wrong in our approach to the Masses'. Next to this the discovery that on the very point where they failed – activation of the masses – Fascism was horribly successful. Now the feelings which success inspires in the unsuccessful is envy. If we look at things closely we find indeed that the pink attitude to Fascism is envy rather than hatred.

What we envy we try to imitate. The fascination of Fascism was obviously its emotional, irrational, mystic type of appeal – the ultra-violet component of Fascism. Here the development ends for the moment. It has not gone further yet; but it has gone as far as this. Which proves that in certain constellations the displacement towards the ultra-violet has very dangerous aspects. Those who underestimate this danger – the dangers of the pink hangover – have not realized yet that just as a crowd or mass is more than the sum total of the individuals which compose it, in the same way the constellation 'Left' is more than the sum total of the Left parties, an entity of a higher order with its own laws of movement.

There is one definite profiteer of the spectral displacement: the Scientist. In a certain sense it was he started the movement; then its momentum carried him further than he probably liked. One should remember that the irrational or ultra-violet element which so strongly taints present-day physics, biology, psychology, was not a philosophical fashion smuggled into the laboratories, but grew out of the laboratories themselves and created the new philosophical climate. The most striking example is the development of physics which was an enormously successful rational Commissar-science up to the closing years of the last century and has become since more and more of a Yogi-science. Matter, substance, time, space, causality, precision of measurement and the belief in the predictability of behaviour of the Measured, have run like sand through the physicist's fingers until nothing remained but a group of formal statements of this type: 'If a small poker-dice is so constructed that we have no reason to assume a preference on its part for falling on the ace-side, then we are entitled to expect that, in the course of a great number of casts, it will show no preference for falling on the ace-side.'

This is undeniably a very precise statement but one must admit that it is a rather modest one in relation to our hunger for having the mysteries of the Universe explained to us. The modern physicist of course denies that his task should be to 'explain' anything, and he takes a masochistic delight in producing formulae which establish with precision the degree of unprecision in his statements, i.e. the inadequacy of physics not only to explain, but even to describe what is going on in the physical world. Some time ago Laplace thought that if a superior intelligence counted all atoms and their velocities at a given moment he could predict all future events to the end of the world, including the brand of Mr Churchill's cigars. Physicists and Philosophers of the last Commissar period tried to jolly around the fatalistic trap of physical determinism, but there was no escape from it. In nineteenth-century physics the world was running down like clockwork without any freedom, except the arbitrariness of the initial state and of the initial choice of a certain set of 'Natural Laws' which governed the mechanism. In twentieth-century physics this initial arbitrariness or freedom is evenly distributed in minute quantities over all possible cross-sections in time and space; the initial creation has become a *creatio continua*. 'Freedom' and 'arbitrariness' are of course merely terms to indicate the presence of factors which cannot be described or accounted for in the physicist's terminology. Nineteenth-century physics describes a sharply defined world with a blurred initial stage; contemporary physics describes an evenly blurred world, like a film with coarse granulation. (The granulation being indicated by the Quantum of Action 'h' and defined in Hiesenberg's Uncertainty Principle.) To describe this world as 'Pantheistic', 'Free', 'Undetermined', 'Statistical', 'Spiritual' or 'Voluntaristic' is more or less a matter of taste. What really matters is that the physicist's instruments of measurement indicate the presence of physically unmeasurable factors. And this is the reason why the physicist travels perhaps more consciously than anybody else towards the ultra-violet.

III The Pendulum

The Commissar, the Artist, the vague Man of Goodwill, the Scientist, not only seem to react in different ways to the great spectral displacement, but their motives for participating in it seem also different in nature. Is there a common reason for this pilgrimage? To a certain extent the revolution in physics has certainly affected the artist, the revolution in psychology has influenced political outlook, and similar cross-influences are easy to discover. They form a pattern of diagonal lines of forces, but this pattern is that of a network, not a causal chain running from Quantum Mechanics to the self-accusations of Bucharin, but in a direct way they are all linked together by diagonals. We cannot ask for a common reason, we can only ask for a common denominator in the variety of reasons.

In the critical years of the Weimar Republic, when a Communist or Fascist Revolution seemed equally possible and the only impossibility the continuation of the worn-out régime, a certain Ernst Juenger coined the phrase of the 'anti-capitalistic nostalgia of the masses'. This vague but violent longing was indeed shared by groups of people of otherwise very different tendencies. Perhaps the common denominator we are looking for can best be described as an

'anti-materialistic nostalgia'. It is idiosyncratic against the rational
ism, the shallow optimim, the ruthless logic, the arrogant self
assurance, the Promethean attitude of the nineteenth century; it i
attracted by mysticism, romanticism, the irrational ethical values
by medieval twilight. In short it is moving towards the very thing
from which the last-but-one great spectral displacement towards the
infra-red has moved away. Apparently these movements have
pendular rhythm.

The swinging of this pendulum from rationalistic to romanti
periods and back is not contradictory to the conception of a basi
dialectic movement of History. They are like the tidal waves on
river which yet flows into the sea. One of the fatal lacunae in th
Marxist interpretation of history is that it was only concerned wit
the course of the river, not with the waves. The mass-psychologica
aspect of Nazism is not desirable in Marxist terms, in terms of th
river's course; we need the tidal waves to account for it. On th
other hand our pendulum alone is no guide to history. We mus
know about the river before we talk of the waves.

Perhaps it is too hazardous to assume that these pendular change
in the mass-psychological spectrum are a process analogous to th
rhythmical change of waking and sleep in the individual. Th
irrational or romantic periods of mass-psychology are periods o
sleep and dream. The dreams are not necessarily peaceful; more ofte
they are nightmares; but without these periodic plunges into th
subconscious the vital saps would not be provided for the nex
wideawake Promethean or Commissar period. Perhaps every Gothi
period is followed by a Renaissance period and they are but th
succession of yoga-nights and commissar-days in the curriculum o
the race. And perhaps this, our present civilization, is not dying, onl
sleepy.

The Collier

VERNON WATKINS

When I was born on Amman hill
A dark bird crossed the sun.
Sharp on the floor the shadow fell;
I was the youngest son.

And when I went to the County School
I worked in a shaft of light.
In the wood of the desk I cut my name:
Dai for Dynamite.

The tall black hills my brothers stood;
Their lessons all were done.
From the floor of the school when I ran out
They frowned to watch me run.

The slow grey bells they rang a chime
Surly with grief or age.
Clever or clumsy, lad or lout,
All would look for a wage.

I learnt the valley flowers' names
And the rough bark knew my knees.
I brought home trout from the river
And spotted eggs from the trees.

A coloured coat I was given to wear
Where the lights of the rough land shone.
Still jealous of my favour
The tall black hills looked on.

They dipped my coat in the blood of a kid
And they cast me down a pit,
And although I crossed with strangers,
There was no way up from it.

Soon as I went from the County School
I worked in a shaft. Said Jim,
'You will get your chain of gold, my lad,
But not for a likely time.'

And one said, 'Jack was not raised up
When the wind blew out the light
Though he interpreted their dreams
And guessed their fears by night.'

And Tom, he shivered his leper's lamp
For the stain that round him grew;
And I heard mouths pray in the after-damp
When the picks would not break through.

They changed words there in darkness
And still through my head they run,
And white on my limbs is the linen sheet
And gold on my neck the sun.

The Young and the Old

W. J. TURNER

THE young are serious but the old are not frivolous,
They see what they saw in the days of their youth,
Yet all things appear to them in different proportion.
Is it wise they have grown or have they measured devotion?
No, they are the same as they were before,
But contained like a wave in the welter of the ocean
To appear and to vanish in the swell of their truth,
But youth is a billow that breaks on the shore.

The young are passionate but the old are not shallow –
I speak not of those from whom life has ebbed.
Violent and strange is a youthful sorrow,
Age is a seabird whose feet are webbed:
Smoothed with the touch of every wild billow
At peace in a curve of the water's uproar,
Till a balm from the air its truth seems to borrow,
But youth is a billow that breaks on the shore.

The young are impatient, but the old are not desperate,
Though they see in the distance the rock which divides.
And their voyage, they know, was predestined by fate,
But they, too, determined what fate decides.
With his ship the sailor forever abides –
No escape from the doom and the burden he bore!
Life's lie from its truth age seeks not to sever,
But youth is a billow that breaks on the shore.

To My Mother

GEORGE BARKER

Most near, most dear, most loved and most far,
Under the window where I often found her
Sitting as huge as Asia, seismic with laughter,
Gin and chicken helpless in her Irish hand,
Irresistible as Rabelais, but most tender for
The lame dogs and hurt birds that surround her, –
She is a procession no one can follow after
But be like a little dog following a brass band.

She will not glance up at the bomber, or condescend
To drop her gin and scuttle to a cellar,
But lean on the mahogany table like a mountain
Whom only faith can move, and so I send
O all my faith and all my love to tell her
That she will move from mourning into morning.

To T. S. Eliot

GEORGE BARKER

EXPECTING a bomb or angel through the roof,
Cold as a saint in Canterbury Cathedral,
This gentleman with Adam on his mind
Sits writing verses on cats that speak: lives
By the prolonged accident of divine proof,
A living martyr to the biological.
Hell spreads its horrors on his window blind
And fills his room with interrogatives.

St Thomas doubting and not doubting,
Confident of God, but dubious of human,
I render my tongue as merely minor flame
To glorify this inglorious martyrdom:
And when the bomb or angel breaks the vaulting
Trust he remembers, among the others, my name.

The Saint

V. S. PRITCHETT

When I was seventeen years old I lost my religious faith. It had been unsteady for some time and then, very suddenly, it went as the result of an incident in a punt on the river outside the town where we lived. My father was a small furniture manufacturer in the place, always in difficulties about money but convinced that in some way God would help him. And this happened. An investor arrived who belonged to a sect called the Church of the Last Purification, of Toronto, Canada. Could we imagine, this man asked, a good and omnipotent God allowing his children to be short of money? We had to admit we could not imagine this. The man paid in the money and we were converted. Our family were the first Purifiers – as they were called – in the town. Soon a congregation of fifty or more were meeting every Sunday in a room at the Corn Exchange.

At once we found ourselves isolated and hated people. Everyone made jokes about us. We had to stand together because we were sometimes dragged into the courts. What the unconverted could not forgive in us was first that we believed in successful prayer and, secondly, that our revelation came from Toronto. The success of our prayers had a simple foundation. We regarded it as 'Error' – our name for Evil – to believe the evidence of our senses and if we had influenza or consumption, or had lost our money or were unemployed, we denied the reality of these things, saying that since God could not have made them they therefore did not exist. It was exhilarating to look at our congregation and to know that what the vulgar would call miracles were performed among us, almost as a matter of routine, every day. Not very big miracles, perhaps; but up in London and out in Toronto, we knew that deafness and blindness, cancer and insanity, the great scourges, were constantly vanishing before the prayers of the more advanced Purifiers.

'What!' said my schoolmaster, an Irishman with eyes like broken glass and a sniff of irritability in the bristles of his nose. 'What! do you have the impudence to tell me that if you fell off the top floor of this building and smashed your head in you would say you hadn't fallen and were not injured?'

I was a small boy and very afraid of everybody but not when it was a question of my religion. I was used to the kind of conundrum the Irishman had set.

'I *would* say so,' I replied with coldness and some vanity, 'and my head would not be smashed.'

'You would not say so,' answered the Irishman, 'You would not say so.' His eyes sparkled with pure pleasure. 'You'd be dead.'

The boys laughed but they looked at me with admiration.

Then, I do not know how or why, I began to see a difficulty. Without warning and as if I had gone into my bedroom at night and had found a gross ape seated in my bed and thereafter following me about with his grunts and his fleas and a look relentless and ancient scored on his brown face, I was faced with the problem which prowls at the centre of all religious faith. I was faced by the difficulty of the origin of evil. It was an illusion, we were taught. But even illusions have an origin. The Purifiers denied this.

I consulted my father. Trade was bad at the time and this made his faith peremptory. He frowned as I spoke.

'When did you brush your coat last?' he said. 'You're getting slovenly about your appearance. If you spent more time studying the books' – that is to say, the Purification literature – 'and less with your hands in your pockets and playing about with boats on the river, you wouldn't be letting Error in.'

All dogmas have their jargon; my father as a business man loved the trade terms of the Purification. 'Don't let Error in' was a favourite one. The whole point about the Purification, he said, was that it was scientific and therefore exact; in consequence it was sheer weakness to admit discussion. Indeed, betrayal. He unpinched his pince-nez, stirred his tea and indicated I must submit or change the subject. Preferably the latter. I saw, to my alarm, that my arguments had defeated my father. Faith and doubt pulled like strings round my throat.

'You don't mean to say you don't believe that what our Lord said was true?' my mother asked nervously following me out of the room. 'Your dad does, dear.'

I could not answer. I went out of the house and down the main street to the river where the punts were stuck like insects in the summery flash of the reach. Life was a dream, I thought; no, a nightmare, for the ape was beside me.

I was still in this state, half sulking and half exalted, when Mr Hubert Timberlake came to the town. He was one of the important people from the headquarters of our Church and he had come to give an address on the Purification at the Corn Exchange. Posters announcing this were everywhere. Mr Timberlake was to spend Sunday afternoon with us. It was unbelievable that a man so eminent would actually sit in our dining room, use our knives and forks, and eat our food. Every imperfection in our home and our characters would jump out at him. The Truth had been revealed to man with scientific accuracy – an accuracy we could all test by experiment – and the future course of human development on earth was laid down, with finality. And here in Mr Timberlake was a man who had not merely performed many miracles – even, as it was said, with proper reserve, having twice raised the dead – but who had actually been to Toronto, our headquarters, where this great and revolutionary revelation had first been given.

'This is my son,' my father said introducing me. 'He thinks, he thinks, Mr Timberlake, but I tell him he only thinks he does ha, ha.' My father was a humorous man. 'He's always on the river,' my father continued. 'I tell him he's got water on the brain. I've been telling Mr Timberlake about you, my boy.'

A hand as soft as the best quality chamois leather took mine. I saw a wide upright man in a double-breasted navy blue suit. He had a pink square head with very small ears and one of those torpid, enamelled smiles which were so common in our sect.

'Why, isn't that just fine?' said Mr Timberlake dryly. Owing to his contacts with Toronto he spoke with an American accent. 'What say we tell your father it's funny he thinks he's funny.'

The eyes of Mr Timberlake were direct and colourless. He had the look of a retired merchant captain who had become decontaminated from the sea and had reformed and made money. His defence of me had made me his at once. My doubts vanished. Whatever Mr Timberlake believed must be true and as I listened to him at lunch I thought there could be no finer life than his.

'I expect Mr Timberlake's tired after his address,' said my mother.

'Tired?' exclaimed my father brilliant with indignation. 'How can Mr Timberlake be tired? Don't let Error in!'

For the merely inconvenient in our faith was just as illusory as a great catastrophe would have been, if you wished to be strict, and Mr Timberlake's presence made us so.

I noticed then that, after their broad smiles, Mr Timberlake's lips had the habit of setting into a long depressed sarcastic curve.

'I guess,' he drawled, 'I guess the Almighty must have been tired sometimes for it says He relaxed on the seventh day. Say, do you know what I'd like to do this afternoon?' he said turning to me. 'While your father and mother are sleeping off this loin of pork let's you and me go on the river and get water on the brain. I'll show you how to punt.'

Mr Timberlake, I saw to my disappointment, was out to show he understood the young. I saw he was planning 'a quiet talk' with me about my problems.

'There are too many people on the river on Sundays,' said my father uneasily.

'Oh, I like a crowd,' said Mr Timberlake giving my father a tough look. 'This is the day of rest, you know.' He had had my father gobbling up every bit of gossip from the sacred city of Toronto all the morning.

My parents were incredulous that a man like Mr Timberlake should go out among the blazers and gramophones of the river on a Sunday afternoon. In any other member of our church they thought this would be sin.

'Waal, what say?' said Mr Timberlake. I could only murmur.

'That's fixed,' said Mr Timberlake. And on came the smile as simple, vivid and unanswerable as the smile on an advertisement. 'Isn't that just fine!'

Mr Timberlake went upstairs to wash his hands. My father was

deeply offended and shocked but he could say nothing. He unpinched his glasses.

'A very wonderful man,' he said. 'So human,' he apologized.

'My boy,' my father said, 'this is going to be an experience for
you. Hubert Timberlake was making a thousand a year in the insur-
ance business ten years ago. Then he heard of the Purification. He
threw everything up, just like that. He gave up his job and took
up the work. It was a struggle, he told me so himself this
morning. "Many's the time," he said to me this morning, "when
I wondered where my next meal was coming from." But the
way was shown. He came down from Worcester to London and
in two years he was making fifteen hundred a year out of his
practice.'

To heal the sick by prayer according to the tenets of the Church
of the Last Purification was Mr Timberlake's profession.

My father lowered his eyes. With his glasses off the lids were
small and uneasy. He lowered his voice too.

'I have told him about your little trouble,' my father said quietly
with emotion. I was burned with shame. My father looked up and
stuck out his chin confidently.

'He just simply smiled,' my father said. 'That's all.'

Then we waited for Mr Timberlake to come down.

I put on white flannels at my father's request, and soon I was
walking down to the river with Mr Timberlake. I felt that I was
going with him under false pretences; for he would begin explaining
to me the origin of evil and I would have to pretend politely that he
was converting me when already, at the first sight of him, I had
believed. A stone bridge whose two arches seem like an owlish pair
of eyes gazing up the reach, crosses the river at the landing stage and
I thought as I got the tickets for our punt that it was a pity the
flannelled men and the sun-burned girls there did not know that this
man in the navy blue suit, the bowler hat and the brown boots was
the Mr Timberlake who had been speaking in the town that very
morning. I looked round for him and when I saw him I was a little
startled. He was standing at the edge of the water looking at it with
an expression of empty incomprehension. Among the white crowds
his air of brisk efficiency had gone. He looked middle-aged, lonely and

insignificant. But the smile switched on when he saw me. He was God's sales manager once more.

'Ready?' he called. 'Fine!'

I had the feeling that inside him there must be a gramophone record that went round and round inside him, stopping at that word.

He stepped into the punt and at once took charge.

'Now I want you to paddle us over to the far bank,' he said, 'and then I'll show you how to punt.'

Everything that Mr Timberlake said still seemed unreal to me. The fact that he was sitting in a punt of all commonplace material things was incredible. That he should propose to pole us up the river was terrifying. Suppose he fell into the river? At once I checked the thought. A leader of our church under the direct guidance of God could not possibly fall into the river.

The stream is wide and deep in this reach but on the southern bank there is a manageable depth and a hard bottom. Over the clay banks the willows hang making their basket work print of sun and shadow on the water, while under the gliding boat lie cloudy, chloride caverns. The hoop-like branches of the trees bend down until their tips touch the water like fingers making musical sounds. Ahead in midstream, on a day sunny as this one was, there is a path of strong light which is hard to look at unless you half close your eyes, and down this path on the crowded Sundays, go the launches with their parasols and their pennants and also the rowing boats with their beetle-leg oars which seem to dig the sunlight out of the water as they rise. Upstream one goes, on and on, between gardens and then between fields kept for grazing. On the afternoon when Mr Timberlake and I went out to settle the question of the origin of evil, the meadows were packed densely with buttercups.

'Now,' said Mr Timberlake decisively, when I had paddled to the other side. 'Now I'll take her.'

He got over the seat into the well at the stern.

'I'll just get you clear of the trees,' I said.

'Give me the pole,' said Mr Timberlake, standing up on the little platform and making a squeak with his boots as he did so. 'Thank you, sir. I haven't done this for eighteen years but I can tell you, my lord, in those days I was considered some poler.'

He looked around and let the pole slide down through his hands. Then he gave the first, difficult push. The punt rocked pleasantly and we moved forward. I sat facing him, paddle in hand, to check any inward drift of the punt.

'How's that, you guys?' said Mr Timberlake, looking round at our eddies and drawing in the pole. The water swished down it.

'Fine,' I said. Deferentially I had caught the word.

He went on to his second and third strokes, taking too much water on his sleeve, perhaps, and uncertain in his steering, which I corrected, but he was doing well.

'It comes back to me,' he said. 'How am I doing?'

'Just keep her out from the trees,' I said.

'The trees?' he asked.

'The willows,' I replied.

'I'll do it now,' he said. 'How's that? Not quite enough? Well, how's this?'

'Another one,' I said. 'The current runs strong this side.'

'What? More trees?' he exclaimed. He was getting hot.

'We can shoot out past them,' I answered. 'I'll ease us over with the paddle.'

Mr Timberlake did not like this suggestion.

'No, don't do that. I can manage it,' he said.

I did not want to offend one of the leaders of our Church, so I put the paddle down; but I felt I ought to have taken him further along, away from the irritation of the trees.

'Of course,' I said, 'we could go under them. It might be nice.'

'I think,' said Mr Timberlake, 'that would be a very good idea, my lord.'

He lunged hard on the pole and took us towards the next archway of willow branches.

'We may have to duck a bit, that's all,' I said.

'Oh I can push the branches up,' replied Mr Timberlake.

'It is better to duck,' I said.

We were gliding now quickly towards the arch, in fact I was already under it.

'I think I should duck,' I said. 'Just bend down for this one.'

'What makes the trees lean over the water like this?' asked Mr

Timberlake. 'Weeping willows – I'll give you a thought there. How Error likes to make us dwell on sorrow. Why not call them *laughing* willows?' discoursed Mr Timberlake as the branch passed over my head.

'Duck,' I said.

'Where? I don't see them,' said Mr Timberlake, turning round.

'No, your head,' I said. 'The branch,' I called.

'Oh, the branch. This one?' said Mr Timberlake, finding a branch just against his chest, and he put out a hand to lift it. It is not easy to lift a willow branch and Mr Timberlake was surprised. He stepped back as it gently and firmly leaned against him. He leaned back and pushed from his feet. And he pushed too far. The boat went on. I saw Mr Timberlake's boots leave the stern as he took an unthoughtful step backwards. He made a last-minute grab at a stronger and higher branch; and then, there he hung a yard above the water, round as a blue damson that is ripe and ready, waiting only for a touch to make it fall. Too late with the paddle and shot ahead by the force of his thrust, I could not save him.

For a full minute I did not believe what I saw; indeed our religion taught us not to believe what we saw. Unbelieving I could not move. I gaped. The impossible had happened. Only a miracle, I found myself saying, could save him.

What was most striking was the silence of Mr Timberlake as he hung from the bough. I was lost between gazing at him and trying to get the punt out of the small branches of the tree. By the time I had got the punt out there were several yards of water between us and the soles of his boots were very near the water as the branch bent under his weight. Boats were passing at the time but no one seemed to notice us. I was glad about this. This was a private agony. The face of Mr Timberlake was thickened but not empurpled and it was squeezed between his shoulders and his hanging arms. I saw him blink and look up at the sky. His eyelids were pale like a chicken's. He was tidy and dignified as he hung there, the hat was not displaced and the top button of his coat was done up. He had a blue silk handkerchief in his breast pocket. So unperturbed and genteel he seemed that as the tip of his shoes came nearer and nearer to the water, I became alarmed. He could perform what are called miracles.

He would be thinking at this moment that only in an erroneous and illusory sense was he hanging from the branch of the tree over six feet of water. He was probably praying one of the closely reasoned prayers of our faith which were more like conversations with Euclid than with God. The calm of his face suggested this. Was he (I asked myself) within sight of the main road, the town Recreation Ground, and the landing stage crowded with people, was he about to re-enact a well-known miracle? I hoped that he was not. I prayed that he was not. I prayed with all my will that Mr. Timberlake would not walk upon the water. It was my prayer and not his that was answered.

I saw the shoes dip, the water rise above his ankles and up his socks. He tried to move his grip now to a yet higher branch – he did not succeed – and in making this effort his coat and waistcoat rose and parted from his trousers. A seam of shirt with its pant loops and brace tabs broke like a crack across the middle of Mr Timberlake. It was like a fatal flaw in a statue, an earthquake crack which made the monumental mortal. The last Greeks must have felt as I felt then when they saw a split across the middle of some statue of Apollo. It was at this moment that I realized that the final revelation about man and society on earth had come to nobody and that Mr Timberlake knew nothing at all about the origin of evil.

All this takes long to describe but it happened in a few seconds as I paddled towards him. I was too late to get his feet on the boat and the only thing to do was to let him sink until his hands were nearer the level of the punt and then to get him to change hand holds. Then I would paddle him ashore. I did this. Amputated by the water, first a torso, then a bust, then a mere head and shoulders, Mr Timberlake, I noticed, looked sad and lonely as he sank. He was a declining dogma. As the water lapped his collar – for he hesitated to let go of the branch to hold the punt – I saw a small triangle of deprecation and pathos between his nose and the corners of his mouth. The head resting on the platter of water had the sneer of calamity on it, such as one sees in the pictures of a beheaded saint.

'Hold on to the punt, Mr Timberlake,' I said urgently. 'Hold on to the punt.'

He did so.

'Push from behind,' he directed in a dry business-like voice. They were his first words. I obeyed him.

Carefully I paddled him towards the bank. He turned and, with a splash, climbed ashore. There he stood, raising his arms and looking at the water running down his swollen suit and making a puddle at his feet.

'Say,' said Mr Timberlake coldly. 'We let some Error in that time.' How much he must have hated our family.

'I am sorry, Mr Timberlake,' I said. 'I am most awfully sorry. I should have paddled. It was my fault. I'll get you home at once. Let me wring out your coat and waistcoat. You'll catch your death . . .'

I stopped. I had nearly blasphemed. I had nearly suggested that Mr Timberlake had fallen into the water and that to a man of his age this might be dangerous.

Mr Timberlake corrected me. His voice was impersonal addressing the laws of human existence rather than myself.

'If God made water it would be ridiculous to suggest He made it capable of harming his other creatures. Wouldn't it?'

'Yes,' I murmured hypocritically.

'O.K.' said Mr Timberlake. 'Let's go.'

'I'll soon get you across,' I said.

'No,' he said, 'I mean let's go on. We're not going to let a little thing like this spoil a beautiful afternoon. Where were we going? You spoke of a pretty landing place farther on. Let's go there.'

'But I must take you home. You can't sit there soaked to the skin. It will spoil your clothes.'

'Now, now,' said Mr Timberlake, 'do as I say. Go on.'

There was nothing to be done with him. I held the punt into the bank and he stepped in. He sat like a bursting and sodden bolster in front of me while I paddled. We had lost the pole of course.

For a long time I could hardly look at Mr Timberlake. He was taking the line that nothing had happened and this put me at a disadvantage. I knew something considerable had happened. That glaze, which so many of the members of our sect had on their faces and persons, their minds and manners, had been washed off. There was no gleam for me from Mr Timberlake.

'What's that house over there?' he asked. He was making conversation. I had steered into the middle of the river to get him into the strong sun. I saw steam rise from him.

I took courage and studied him. He was a man, I realized, in poor physical condition, unexercised and sedentary. I remember he had said at lunch:

'A young woman I know said, "Isn't it wonderful. I can walk thirty miles a day without being in the least tired." I said, "I do not see that bodily indulgence is anything a member of the Church of the Last Purification should boast about."'

Yes, there was something flaccid, passive and slack about Mr Timberlake. Bunched in swollen clothes, he refused to take them off. It came to me as he looked with boredom at the water, the passing boats and the country, that he had not been in the country before. That it was something he had agreed to do but wanted to get over quickly. He was totally uninterested. By his questions: What is that church? Are there any fish in this river? Is that a wireless or a gramophone? I understood that Mr Timberlake was politely and formally acknowledging a world he did not live in. It was too interesting, too eventful. His spirit, inert and preoccupied, was elsewhere in an eventless and immaterial habitation. He was a dull man, duller than any man I have ever known; but his dullness was a sort of earthly deposit left by a being whose mind was engrossed in abstract matters. There was a slightly pettish look on his face as (to himself, of course) he declared he was not wet and that he would not catch pneumonia.

Mr Timberlake spoke little. Sometimes he squeezed water out of his sleeve. He shivered a little. He watched his steam. I had planned when we set out to go up as far as the lock, but now the thought of another two miles of this responsibility was too much. I pretended I wanted to go only as far as the bend which we were approaching, where one of the richest buttercup meadows was. I mentioned this to him. He turned and looked with boredom at the field. Slowly we came to the bank.

We tied up the punt and we landed.

'Fine,' said Mr Timberlake. He stood at the edge of the meadow just as he had stood at the landing stage – lost, stupefied, uncomprehending.

'Nice to stretch our legs,' I said. I led the way into the deep flowers. So dense were the buttercups there was hardly any green. Presently I sat down. Mr Timberlake looked at me and sat down also. Then I turned to him with a last try at persuasion. Respectability, I was sure, was his trouble.

'No one will see us,' I said. 'This is out of sight of the river. Take off your coat and trousers and wring them out.'

Mr Timberlake replied firmly.

'I am satisfied to remain as I am.'

'What is this flower?' he asked to change the subject.

'Buttercup,' I said.

'Of course,' he replied.

I could do nothing with him. I lay down full length in the sun and, observing this and thinking to please me, Mr Timberlake did the same. He must have supposed that this was what I had come out in the boat to do. It was only human. He had come out with me, I saw, to show that he was human.

But as we lay there I saw the steam still rising. I had had enough.

'A bit hot,' I said, getting up.

He got up at once.

'Do you want to sit in the shade,' he asked politely.

'No,' I said. 'Would you like to?'

'No,' he said, 'I was thinking of you.'

'Let's go back,' I said. We both stood up and I let him pass in front of me. When I looked at him again I stopped dead. Mr Timberlake was no longer a man in a navy blue suit. He was blue no longer. He was transfigured. He was yellow. He was covered with buttercup pollen, a fine yellow paste of it made by the damp, from head to foot.

'Your suit,' I said.

He looked at it. He raised his thin eyebrows a little, but he did not smile or make any comment.

The man is a saint, I thought. As saintly as any of those gold leaf figures in the churches of Sicily. Golden he sat in the punt; golden he sat for the next hour as I paddled him down the river. Golden and bored. Golden as we landed at the town and as we walked up the street back to my parents' house. There he refused to change his clothes or to sit by a fire. He kept an eye on the time for his train back to London. By no word did he acknowledge the disasters or the beauties of the world. If they were printed upon him it was as upon a husk.

Sixteen years have passed since I dropped Mr Timberlake in the river and since the sight of his pant loops destroyed my faith. I have not seen him since, and today I heard that he was dead. He was fifty-seven. His mother, a very old lady with whom he had lived all his life, went into his bedroom when he was getting ready for church and found him lying on the floor in his shirtsleeves. A stiff collar with the tie half inserted was in one hand. Five minutes before, she told the doctor, she had been speaking to him.

The doctor who looked at the heavy body lying on the single bed, saw a middle-aged man, wide rather than stout and with an extra-ordinarily broad, box-like, thick-jawed face. He had got fat, my father told me, in later years. The heavy liver-coloured cheeks were like the chaps of a hound. Heart disease, it was plain, was the cause of the death of Mr Timberlake. In death the face was lax, even coarse and degenerate. It was a miracle, the doctor said, that he had lived as long. Any time during the last twenty years a sudden shock might have killed him.

I thought of our afternoon on the river. I thought of him hanging from the tree. I thought of him, indifferent and golden, in the meadow. I understood why he had made for himself a protective, sedentary blandness, an automatic smile, a collection of phrases. He kept them on like the coat after his ducking. And I understood why – though I had feared it all the time we were on the river – I understood why he did not talk to me about the origin of evil. He was honest. The ape was with us. The ape that merely followed me was already inside Mr Timberlake eating at his heart.

Walking at Whitsun

DAVID GASCOYNE

La fontaine n'a pas tari
Pas plus que l'or de la paille ne s'est terni
Regardons l'abeille
Et ne songeons pas à l'avenir ...

Apollinaire

... THEN let the cloth across my back grow warm
Beneath such comforting strong rays! new leaf
Flow everywhere, translucently profuse,
And flagrant weed be tall, the banks of lanes
Sprawl dazed with swarming lion-petalled suns,
As with largesse of pollen-coloured wealth
The meadows; and across these vibrant lands
Of Summer-afternoon through which I stroll
Let rapidly gold glazes slide and chase
Away such shades as chill the hillside trees
And make remindful mind turn cold ...

                              The eyes
Of thought stare elsewhere, as though skewer-fixed
To an imagined sky's immense collapse;
Nor can, borne undistracted through this scene
Of festive plant and basking pastorale,
The mind find any calm or light within
The bone walls of the skull; for at its ear
Resound recurrent thunderings of dark
Smoke towered waves rearing sheer tons to strike
Down through Today's last dyke. Day-long
That far thick roar of fear thuds, on-and-on,
Beneath the floor of sense, and makes
All carefree quodlibet of leaves and larks

And fragile tympani of insects sound
Like Chinese music, mindlessly remote
Drawing across both sight and thought-like gauze
Its unreality's taut haze.

                              But light!
O cleanse with widespread flood of rays the brain's
Oppressively still sickroom, wherein brood
Hot festering obsessions, and absolve
My introspection's mirror of such stains
As blot its true reflection of the world!
Let streams of sweetest air dissolve the blight
And poison of the News, which every hour
Contaminates the aether.

                                 I will pass
On far beyond the village, out of sight
Of human habitation for a while.
Grass has an everlasting pristine smell.
On high, sublime in his bronze ark, the sun
Goes cruising across seas of silken sky.
In fields atop the hillside, chestnut trees
Displace the splendour of their branches piled
With blazing candle burdens. – Such a May
As this might never come again . . .

                            I tread
The white dust of a weed-bright lane; alone
Upon Time-Present's tranquil outmost rim,
Seeing the sunlight through a lens of dread,
While anguish makes the English landscape seem
Inhuman as the jungle, and unreal
Its peace. And meditating as I pace
The afternoon away, upon the smile
(Like that worn by the dead) which Nature wears
In ignorance of our unnatural tears.
From time to time I think! How such a sun

Must glitter on their helmets! How bright-red
Against this sky's clear screen must ruins burn . . .

How sharply their invading steel must shine!

Marshfield, May 1940

Bowen, Morgan and Williams

GLYN JONES

AFTER what I had done the night before I couldn't very well refuse.
Benja Bowen and I had come home from Imperato's about nine
o'clock and I had gone straight into the front room to slip my canvas
boots into the window flower-pot with my school cap on top of
them because my father didn't like me going boxing. (I used to keep
Benja's boots there too, because his people were very strict and
religious, much narrower than mine – his father tried to start a sect
that believed there were thirteen Persons in the Trinity, and he made
Benja go to chapel on Saturdays.) There in the parlour my mother
was sitting with our new electric light on full-float, talking to two
visitors from our chapel – Miss Phillips (M'Liza, William the Rates's
sister) and Mrs Rees the Come-inside, who had heard about her
tumble. My mother was in her oil talking to them; she looked
beautiful with her crinkly auburny hair and the summerspots on her
eyelids, but she made me blush because she had her dress on backwards. Mrs Rees was a sour, knowing-looking woman, red and
stoutish, with a sultry expression on her face as though she was having
bad heartburn. She had untidy grey hair like the stuff that comes
out of a rip in the sofa, and clothes that seemed, but for the heavy
brooches with which she bolted them on, as though they were going to
slide off her body. She had on now her husband's panama hat with a
barricade of hen's feathers stuck upright into the ribbon and a gnawed
fur coat hanging half-way down her back the way our masters wore
their gowns. She kept an ironmonger shop and everybody called
her the Come-inside, because if you stood looking in at her window
for a few seconds she would waddle out on to the pavement in her
mangy coat and whisper, 'Come inside, come inside'. She had a long
stocking, but she was stingy with her money, and she and her husband
lived in a little shed at the top of the garden behind their mansion.

Miss Phillips, William's sister, was very genteel and polite, but
poor-looking as well and very old-fashioned and dowdy. Summer

and winter she wore a long, voluminous, greenish-black skirt, a riding-coat of the same colour trimmed with wide braid like flat spanish, and a squashed velvet hat that looked as though she had found it under the cushion. I used to make fun of her with her elastic boots and tall umbrella, and then be ashamed because really she was fine and I liked her very much. Her thin face was refined and white as ivory, very genteel, with a prim expression on it, because before William's leg got bad she used to be a governess.

I wanted to back out directly I had got inside the room, both because I had the boxing-boots under my arm and because I remembered in a flash that the mouthy Come-inside had seen Benja and me from her shed smoking up the mountain where we used to go to shave one another, but it was too late.

'How do you do, Mr Williams?' said Miss Phillips, holding out her thin white hand to me. (She was so polite she used to reply to my mother with 'Yes'm' and 'No'm', and started to call me Mister as soon as I got into the grammar school.) I told her I was all right, and I asked her how she was, of course.

'Thank you for your kind inquiry,' she answered. 'If you mean my physical health, I am very well indeed. And now will you allow me to take this opportunity of congratulating you upon your recent success?'

I was taken aback for the moment – this speech seemed so elegant after Imperato's – but I realized she meant my passing senior at last. I blushed again and thanked her, but I was relieved to see the Come-inside looking as though her water-brash was a bit easier on her, as she too wished me well. After a bit more handshaking amongst us and dropping the boxing-boots all over the floor, I got out into the cool passage.

I went into the kitchen, avoiding the puddles, and there Mam Evans, my mother's washerwoman, was crouching, eating toasted cheese out of a tin plate by the glow of the fire because she was afraid to turn the electric light on. I did it for her, and then I sat down on the couch and began pumping her about the time she went to the seaside and about her mother when she was a shindry girl. She was a big, fleshy old woman now with a bun at the back of her head and a hot smell to her blouse. She had a soft, shapeless face looking as though

315

there were no bones in it, the flabby flesh beginning to hang into her goitrous neck, which was really a good bit wider than her head. There were no teeth or lips to her mouth; it was only a pleat in her skin right under her nose. She couldn't see much with her pale watery eyes, so that my mother often had to wash the clothes over after her, and when she had scrubbed our kitchen floor she used to leave it swimming with puddles and with small heaps of brown snuff like little molehills scattered all over it. When she had finished her cheese, she took off her sack apron with the holes in the knees and wrapped it in newspaper, asking me what time it was. I told her it was nine o'clock, and she swore in her faulty old-fashioned way because she would be too late to buy twist for her poor mother, alone in the dark house with an empty clay pipe in her head. She hurried out the back way in her cap and shawl, and then I began to tease the canary a bit, hoping M'Liza and the Come-inside would go, so that I could have my supper, but he was too sleepy to respond. Then alongside my father's trombone in the corner I saw my mother's new vacuum cleaner, and I began examining that. I fixed a sort of plug with a wire on it into the wall, and then I turned on the current by means of a button I found under the handle. The engine started to hum, but almost at once there was a loud snap and a blue flash and the electric light went out in the kitchen. I dropped the handle in my fright, and then when I had recovered a bit I tried to put the light on at the switch, but nothing happened. I crept out of the kitchen in the darkness and tried the light in the middle room, but nothing happened there either. Just then my mother opened the door of the parlour, which I could see was also in complete darkness, and shouted out, 'Evan, Evan, now stop that nonsense. Put the lights on at once, will you?'

*

The next morning my mother's foot was a lot better, and she said, 'Ev, take these roses up to your Uncle Sam's and ask how his asthma is, will you?' (She was holding the canary under the tap to revive him as she said this, because she had turned on the gas-ring and forgotten to light it and the poor little dab had fallen off his perch in a faint.) The roses were all right, some of my father's best, each bloom bursting out like a coloured cabbage and bound together into a huge bouquet nearly three feet in girth. But remembering the night before and not being able to think of an excuse, I said I would go. So I heaved up the flowers off the table and started out the lane way to see my Uncle Sam, who lived the other end of the town. Before I got to the main street I passed the Come-inside's husband on the prowl for back-rents, and the half-grin I fancied I saw on his face made me blush a bit. But I soon remembered seeing him looking silly in the Big Seat in chapel with a white price-ticket four inches by five still sewn on the tail of his new frock-coat, and that cheered me up again. Before crossing over High Street I hung the flowers negligently half-way behind my legs to conceal them a bit and hurried over towards the tram-road, not looking to right or left. This tram-road ran parallel with the main street almost all the way to my uncle's house, and it wasn't bad walking there with no one about and the sun yellow as electric light on the walls, although the place itself was shabby and dusty. The only thing that made me really uncomfortable was that my mother had been darning my socks again and my right foot felt as though I had a poultice on it. My mother was lovely, with freckles and auburn hair, but it was wonderful my brother and I were alive with all the things she had done to us. When our Rhysie was a baby, so she said, and she was tidying the dresser, she slipped him in the knife-drawer to answer the milkman, and when she came back into the kitchen she began to search all over the place, behind the blower and in the boot-cupboard, because she couldn't remember where she had put him.

At the back of the Temperance Hall I met Madame Jones-Edwards (Llinos Cwm Du, the majestic ex-singer), who had married three husbands, all of them little men about half her weight, each one before the last was cold. She was a tall, stately woman leaning on an ebony walking-stick, wearing a starched collar and a tie like a man, a costume of crimson plush and a cartwheel hat with red seagulls skewered on to it. She rolled over slowly from side to side as she walked, like a boy riding a bike too big for him. She was so sparkling and highly coloured she looked a bit out of place on the grimy tram-road, which was only a narrow lane for the colliers' train with the backs of shops and houses on each side of it. Her hands were covered with rings; there was a gold chain looped many times over her chest and a long pair of droppers shaped like golden indian clubs swung on chains from the lobes of her ears. When she saw the roses she came slowly to rest upright, and asked me with an elegant sort of bow if she might smell them. She had a soft-skinned, creamy face covered with fine lines as thin as hairs, and black bossy eyes, very glittering and watchful. The smell of the roses seemed to give her great raptures; she kept her face buried a long time in the massive bunch closing her eyelids and letting her head loll on one side. She asked me where I had got them from, and I thought she wanted to find out who I was too, but I didn't tell her much because she was so gushing and I didn't know what she would do if she discovered my father played the trombone. At last I got away, leaving even her scent behind, but I felt better after meeting her because these roses were silver-bowl winners after all, something to be proud of. My father grew about the best blooms in town, in the whole valley perhaps, and Llinos Cwm Du had liked them and she had been all over the world singing in her young days and had received bouquets too, no doubt, like the actresses Arthur and I saw in the Theatre Royal. She wasn't bad at all except that she was too dramatic in everything she did, but you could see she was a good judge of roses, so that was nothing. But when I came round the next bend I saw Arthur Vaughan Morgan crossing the tram-road on the way up from High Street with his bull-terrier on the lead beside him. I dodged and marked time, but it was no good; Arthur had seen me and he was waiting with a faint smile on his face, looking at me as though I was something that had crawled out of the long grass. It was the same sort of look as he had for the kid who tagged on to us when we were small the first day we were in the grammar school. 'Which way are you going?' he said to him. 'We're going the other way.' He greeted me now with his lids half down over his deep blue eyes. 'Hullo, Williams,' he said. 'Going to a wedding?'

When I told him I was on my way up to my Uncle Sam's, he said he would come with me after he had slipped home to give a message to his father. So for a start I had to carry my roses up to Arthur's house.

*

The first time I ever saw Arthur was when we were little boys and there was a Coronation fête and gala on in town. I was with my father going among the crowds after the procession and we met Arthur doing the same with his father, a well-known character the people called Tommy White-hat. The first thing I noticed about Arthur was that he had a much better Union Jack than I had, with a real gilded wooden point on the end of his flag-stick and not a bit of pointed cardboard like mine. He was dressed in a sailor suit with long trousers and a thick whistle-cord hanging out of his pocket.

His father was a tall, big man, wearing pale spats, a white felt hat pushed on the side of his head, and a thin grey suit with a collar to the waistcoat and a scarlet carnation in the buttonhole. He was smoking a thin cigar like a pencil, which he was using to point with, and which he kept passing from hand to hand as he made jokes and explained things to Arthur and me, bending down with his bright blue eyes close to mine and his breath smelling of scented cachous. He had a gold band on one of his fingers with a little hailstone in it, and he laughed and talked all the time in a rich-sounding way, showing a lot of gold in his big teeth. I thought him lovely then, more beautiful than a mermaid, with his mannish smell, and his handsome cheeks pink as blotting-paper, and his thick curly hair like grey tobacco.

When Arthur and I got to the grammar school Mr Vaughan Morgan always talked to me in a grown-up way and asked about my mother and father in his rich throaty voice, very cheerful and friendly. I always thought then he came right off the top shelf; but whenever I mentioned him at home my mother would turn on me and say, 'Hark at him! He likes Tommy Vaughan Morgan, who feeds the children on bread and spit and works poor Annie's hands into holes so that he can live among the *crachach*. *Ach y fi*.' I couldn't believe it at first when my mother said the Morgans didn't have tuppence to put in the gas at the same time and we could easily buy them up, because although I knew the wolf was a long way from our door we seemed to live pretty close to the ground compared with them – my father came home from work dirty and never wore a gold ring on his tie and smoked cigars like Mr Vaughan Morgan, and we didn't have a big house like theirs either with red tilings on the roof and a white flagstaff in the garden. (Although when I thought about it, I saw it was true their place was battered about by the children, and whenever you went there you might find a bucket on the piano and perhaps nearly break your neck with the holes in the carpet. And upstairs you would see the marks of running water in streaks down all the bedroom wallpaper from the winter the Vaughan Morgans had a big hole in the roof where the gutters joined and they tied a zinc bath with rope to the rafters to catch the rain coming in through it. Because when the bath was full and Cuckoo and his father went up the manhole to fetch it down they upset it between them in getting it off the ropes and the bathful of water poured in gallons through all the ceilings and down the bedroom walls). Then once my father came in from practice laughing, saying he had just met Tommy White-hat and then acting what had happened for my mother, exaggerating everything, as he always did. Mr Vaughan Morgan had seemed as gay as usual when they had met, but when my father asked him how Annie was he changed altogether and looked very downhearted. His blue eyes filled up with tears and he could hardly speak as he said he had just come from the hospital, where they told him she had coughed up one of her lungs that very morning, poor girl. Likely enough she had coughed up the other by now, he said, throwing away his cigar and taking his bandanna out of his breast pocket to mop his eyes with. He spoke for a long time, crying salt and describing how all his life he had lived under the showers and how Annie had been his only comfort, so no wonder he was shedding the tears nearest his heart. My father sympathized with him and invited him down to our house for a meal of food. He thanked my father again and again for this with his hand on his shoulder, and wiping his eyes and shaking hands, he said, 'Thank you, Rhys, for your kindness in my trouble. Poor Annie, poor girl! How she's suffered – years and years of it! Nobody knows.' Here he gave a deep sigh and a final blow to his nose, and putting his spotted handkerchief away took out his gold half-hunter. 'I don't think I'll come down today, Rhys, my boy,' he said, 'if you don't mind. Thank you all the same. You see, I must hurry off to catch the special – I want to see the final between the Wanderers and the Thursdays.' My father watched him swaggering down the road with his white hat on the side of his head, lighting another cigar.

'The dirt,' said my mother. 'No *dal* on the White-hat.'

But Arthur was always distant with people: he wasn't much like his father, friends with everybody, except that he was handsome too, and always wore smart clothes, with a bit of handkerchief showing at his breast-pocket. (I noticed his nice suits because my mother used to try to make my school clothes herself until I refused to wear them after she put the two sleeves of my jacket in backwards, so that I looked like a cripple.) He was a tall slim boy with black wavy hair, pale skin, and red lips, and a habit of lowering his long-lashed lids over his eyes when he was talking to you. His dog was a classy-looking bull-terrier, shapely and milk-white, called Tiger, and when he saw me and my roses he winked his pink eyes and wagged his tail in an indifferent way. He was a dog who had fits and didn't seem quite right in the head by the way he behaved off the lead. Everybody hated him except the Vaughan Morgans, and once or twice they had found him laid out flat in the gutter a long way from home.

*

Arthur's house was in a row of big villas, where the people lived on bloaters and were in debt. We squeezed in through the swollen door that had a bulged knob, a broken fanlight, and a panel the dog had scratched into a hole with his claws, and went through to the large sunny dining-room overlooking the lawn at the back. Here Arthur left me, saying he wouldn't be long, and went upstairs with Tiger to look for Mr Vaughan Morgan.

In this big bare room, where the white ceiling-paper hung down at the corners like the flaps of a huge envelope, Nicholas y Glo, one of the lodgers, was sitting on a broken-backed chair reading the paper and eating his breakfast off dishes that were all of different colours, sizes, and designs. He had a bad stomach, and before him, holding up the newspaper on a bit of tablecloth, were a lot of medicines – some peppermint ovals, a cup of bicarbonate of soda, and a bottle of wind-and-water pills. I said good morning to him, lifting a heap of washing on to the sewing machine so that I could get into the armchair, which had a hollow arm and all its springs on the floor. As

I sat there carefully with the championship roses across my knees, I noticed on the table the blue sugar-bag and the loaf started at both ends as usual, and the tin alarm clock ticking upside-down on the sideboard, and the crack in the big mirror that Mostyn, Arthur's younger brother, had made in walking across the mantelpiece with the coal-hammer in his hand. And on the wall below the American clock, whose pendulum and workings had all fallen into the glass case at the bottom, were a lot of drawings of actresses in pencil and the huge purplish splash caused by the black-currant wine-bottle exploding against the wall-paper four or five Christmases ago.

The sun's rays were pouring in so strongly upon Nicholas's waxy little head that it glistened under his thin hair and the yellow skin looked as though it had started melting. 'Good morning,' he said to me, and then he became so bashful he blushed and started whistling the bass part of the 'Men of Harlech' to himself. One reason he never said much was that he had a high falsetto voice coming out through his nose, so that whenever he spoke he sounded as though he was trying to imitate somebody. He was very nervous and he always acted queer when there were visitors about, cracking his fingers and playing with his watch-chains and tapping the table with the dishes. He was as flustered now as a fly caught in a glass of water because he knew I was watching him, and in his embarrassment he picked up his silver serviette ring and screwed it into his right eye, staring round at the cobwebs and the ceiling flies through the hole with a deep blush on his face. But I didn't take much notice of him; my mother said he was never the same after he fell through the trapdoor outside the Ship and Castle. All the boys thought him a bit queer because if there was a window rattling in chapel or the sun was disturbing the preacher, he would pull off his boots, blushing like a girl, and creep about the gallery in his black stockings full of big holes to fasten the catch or pull the curtains, the joints of his feet giving off loud snaps on the floorboards at every step. He was a very tall thin man with legs like whips, wearing a black coat and striped trousers, a cream flannel waistcoat with a bunch of gold chains across it, and a very high white collar which looked as though he had stepped into it and slid it up his body into its position under his head. He had a small square face, very thin and wrinkled, and all the time he sat whistling and beating on the table with his alphabet plate, and glaring at the newspaper like a one-eyed spider. I was afraid that if his jawbone lost contact with the top edge of the massive collar on which it was supported, his whole head would disappear inside and perhaps shave off his gristly ears as it did so. The moustache on his long upper lip was perfect, neatly trimmed and waxed out, but minute, a tiny coloured model, hardly visible at all in the shadow of his nose, and yet perfect in every detail like a tiny grub or a fly seen under a microscope. His hair was long and dry-looking, but not very plentiful; it was pressed lifeless and wiglike on to the wax of his bony scalp. But it wasn't its shape or its texture that used to attract my attention, but its colour, because it was a deep and sombre green.

There was always a lot of noise in Arthur's house, people were always coming in and out of rooms and banging doors and shouting, and all the time I watched Mr Nicholas as he squirmed and blushed on his broken-backed chair that creaked like the unoiled ratchet of a winch at every move, I could hear the bump-bumping noise from the other side of the wall that Mostyn was making riding round the drawing-room on his bike. Then someone started pounding on the piano, and one of Arthur's sisters thundered up the stairs two at a time shouting out to stop it, and a fierce argument started on the landing with 'By Babylon's Wave' coming louder and louder out of the piano all the time. I hoped neither of the elder girls would burst into the dining-room and catch me with my flowers, because they were very smart and witty. They had always heard everything before and they used to use French words like *blasé* and *à la mode* that I wasn't sure of the meaning of.

At last there was a deafening crash as the hallstand fell over in the passage and Mostyn came skirmishing into the room fighting with Tiger.

'Hullo, Williams,' he said, staring hard at my flowers, and I only said, 'Hullo, Cuckoo,' because I didn't want to see him. He had yellow curls and blue eyes like a girl, but he was dirty and objectionable, always smashing things and getting into a mess, and Arthur ignored him, he didn't like him at all. If one of the masters at school said, 'Arthur, is your brother present this morning?' he would answer, 'I don't know; I'll find out for you if you wish me to.' And if we happened to pass Mostyn on the other side of the street, perhaps with his thumb to his nose on the top of a lamp-post or showing off on his yellow racer, and I said, 'Arthur, there's Cuckoo over there,' he would reply, 'I've seen him before,' without troubling to look across. And then, when we had passed him, he would start quoting dirty Latin.

Mostyn started pulling Tiger across the room by the ears, and trying to get him to jump on to the table, where he knelt with his knee in the butter. He was giggling all the time and whispering something to the dog about my roses, and I could feel myself colouring because of it. He was always a nuisance, doing silly things that made Arthur sneer at him, like putting a handful of the black-beetles that were always running about the house into Nicholas's cup of tea, or tying Crumpy's front door-knocker to the lamp-post. And he was the boy with a face like an angel who had five rulers stuck down his neck as soon as the master left the classroom, and his shirt pulled up over his belly and a tin box of instruments pushed into the front of his trousers.

'That will keep, Cuckoo,' I said, showing him I had heard.

At that Mr Nicholas's blush became so plentiful it looked as though it would pass into his hair and collar and dye those scarlet too. And in his embarrassment he screwed Mr Morgan's serviette ring into his other eye and glared hard at the newspaper before him like a goggle-eyed insect, bending his fingers so far back I was afraid they would snap off and squirt blood at the knuckles. But he was too nervous to say anything and Mostyn only laughed.

For a bit there was complete silence in the house, and in the quiet I heard the tin alarm-clock stop, change gear, and then begin ticking again with a deeper and more important note. But the noises started almost at once. There were two heavy bumps right above us like a couple of people falling out of bed, and in a moment or two Mr Vaughan Morgan came into the room with a gale behind him, rubbing his gold-ringed hands and lowering the full skin-bags of his lids over his deep blue eyes against the sunglare. 'Hullo, hullo, hullo,' he said, smiling, the glitter of his rings and his golden corner teeth bright like brass in the sunshine. 'Your father's roses, Evan?'

he said. 'How is the old pilgrim? Don't move, my boy.' Without asking, he took a little folding cigar cutter from his waistcoat pocket, snipped off the best bud he could see and put the crimson flower in his buttonhole. His skin looked fresh, as though he had just come from the bath; he was wearing a pale pair of spats, a thin light grey suit with sharp creases down his trousers, and a spotted bow-tie round his wing-collar. His handsome face was as pink as lint; it was clean-looking and faintly powdered after shaving and there was some sweet-smelling oil rubbed into his thick grey hair.

He went round the table, patting Nicholas on the back and putting a thin cigar out beside his plate. 'How do you feel today, Nat?' he said to him.

'Common,' said Mr Nicholas in a falsetto voice like the sound squeezed out of a conjurer's dummy. The sun shone bright as a burning-glass on the green back of his head and on his collar, swelling out and narrowing as he gulped his bicarbonate of soda, as though someone were pumping air through it. Then, feeling embarrassed, he got up and stood reading the news before the huge marble fireplace and the cracked mirror, his big ears burning scarlet like a pair of cart-lamps hung one each side of his head. Mr Vaughan Morgan was tall, but Mr Nicholas was taller. When I glanced at him standing there on the hearthrug, long and narrow as a vinegar-drinker, the flushes all the time coming up out of his collar and disappearing into his green hair, I thought he had his boots on the wrong feet, but when I looked again I saw his long legs were crossed behind the paper.

Everybody knew that being in the same room as Tommy Vaughan Morgan was like living at the foot of the waterfall, because he could talk by the hour. His bass voice was rich and resonant, he seemed to have three or four throats when he was speaking, with a deep note bubbling out of each of them, making his voice into a harmony like a handful of keys sounded together on an organ. 'What are you trying to do, Mostyn?' he asked, ruffling his curls. But Mostyn pushed his hand away; although he was from the bottom of the nest he was always cheeky to his father. 'Like this, look,' Mr Morgan went on. He got up from the table again and began calling the bull-terrier to entice him towards the casement window, which he managed to open after a lot of tugging that made the handle come off in his hand. It was through this window that I once saw him throwing out the dinner when Mrs Morgan was alive. Arthur and I were below near the flagstaff on the lawn when we saw Mr Morgan through the open window coming into the dining-room. He had been at the Bull, potting, by the look of him, because his white felt was low down on his ears like a comedian's bowler, his pince-nez were hanging out of his pocket, and his face was sulky and flushed purple. 'Annie,' we heard him shout in his high-class way, 'what's for dinner today?' Arthur's mother was a quiet little woman, always pattering about the house in silence; she never went out except to meet the trains in when Tommy had been away. 'Ham, my love,' she said meekly, holding before him a dish with a big piece of ham on it. 'Damn the ham,' said Tommy, and he threw the meat out of the window.

'My father,' said Arthur, 'under the influence of words or liquor, exhibits a strange vehemence of behaviour.'

He began fondling the dog, and when he had got him near the wall he shouted, 'Cats, Tiger! Cats!' The dog gave a growl and with a clever spring disappeared through the window on to the lawn, but when he found he had been fooled he dived back into the room again. Tommy laughed and, taking the breadsaw off the table, started to comb him with it.

'This is the most wonderful dog in the valley, Evan,' he went on, going over to the sideboard that had a row of cigar burns across the edge. 'Now, where are those snaps of him, Mostyn?' He took the cigar from the table and Mostyn lit it for him with a match. With his spring pince-nez on he began searching about first in the bulgy tea-caddy and then in the shallow drawers, piling the contents on to the table – a dog's bone, a gym-shoe, some gas-mantle cases, two or three pigeon-rings, a mass of clockwork, a toffee hammer and a cigar-box holding a wad of letters and a handful of watch-wheels. He couldn't find the photographs, but among the letters was a tele-gram which he handed to me. 'Read that, Evan,' he said. 'From our Arthur when he matriculated.' (There was one word in the telegram – *Undergraduate*.) 'This is what I was going to say. You know Mam Evans, Evan?'

'My mother's washerwoman,' I said, and Mr Nicholas put his newspaper behind him to listen.

'On the tram-road yesterday,' he went on, 'I saw her with Sian her mother in a pair of chairs outside the house. I got my watch ready, because she always wants to know the time. And it's a trick to tell her the time, you know. Have you tried it, Evan?'

'Stick to your story, Tommy,' said Mostyn.

Mr Morgan laughed. 'Mostyn *bach*,' he said, pulling at his cigar. 'The lamb teaching the sheep to graze.' Then he began again, imitating the impediment of the old woman. 'If ever she asks you, tell her to the nearest quarter of an hour – she's got no looks on minutes. "Thomas Vaughan," she says to me – "Thomas Vaughan, have you got the right time, please?" So I take out my watch to tell her.'

Here Mr Morgan opened his half-hunter, but the belly fell out on the table. He pushed it back in again and stared at it down the side of his pink Roman nose, but before he could say anything Mr Nicholas made his middle finger go off snap behind his back with a crack like a pistol shot. Tommy was startled by the noise, and Nicholas went red and looked as though he would like to fold the big flaps of his ears over his face to hide his blushes, but he didn't dare open his beak. Then as he was getting behind the paper again, Arthur came into the room and motioned me out. I got off the armchair, which gave out a long chorus of pings like a number of pitchforks struck in a cluster as the springs worked up one by one through the plush again, and Mr Morgan recovered himself at the noise.

'"Well, Mam Evans," I say,' he went on, mocking the way she said *s* and *r*, '"it's now precisely eleven minutes past five." That won't do for her at all. Not at all. "Eleven minutes past five indeed," she says, rubbing that old scab on her chin. "What sort of time is that? Tell us the right time now, boy." I don't know what in the world to tell her, so I say, "Well, I *have* told you the right time, Mam Evans, it's now nearly twelve minutes past five." "There's funny you are getting, Thomas Vaughan," she complains, disgusted with me. "Tell us the right time now tidy and don't be so dull, boy." We go on like this until it's quarter past, and then she's satisfied.'

Tommy was in a *hwyl* by now with a story to act and an audience to listen; his blue eyes were glittering like stars and his mouth was full of spit. When he was like this he seemed overflowing with energy and I had seen him posting a letter in the middle of a tale as though he was going to stuff his arm up to the elbow into the pillar-box, and turning the kitchen tap on so that the word COLD went round and round and the water splashed all over the kitchen.

Slowly I edged round to the door, Tommy talking like the pit of the sea, telling us how the old women had walked out of the house because Tiger had come in and was lying fast asleep by the fire in the kitchen. I stumbled over the hymn-book holding up the leg of the table, but at last I stood by Arthur near the door, ready to slip out. Before us in the liquidy sunshine of the room I could see the others as though they were in a play, Mostyn smoothing the dog wth the match-box, Tommy pink with acting his story, a trellis of lines clear on the soft bags under his blue eyes, and Nicholas y Glo in an up-right coil on the mat, his hair green as seaweed and his collar like a white legging rising above the paper. And then our chance came, because we saw Mostyn setting fire with a match to the bottom edge of the paper Nicholas was again holding spread out before him. The sheets kindled at once, they flared up like celluloid, divided into two by the flames, and when Nicholas saw he held a blazing mass in each hand his face went crimson, he let out a terrified shriek in his high-pitched voice and began waving the burning sheets around his head so that I was afraid his hair would catch fire. He danced up and down on the mat, shouting out, 'I'm on fire, I'm on fire! Holy water! Holy water!' loudly through his nose. Mostyn laughed, the dog set up a howl and dived out through the window, and Tommy stopped with his cigar up, his golden fangs and the flat band on his finger flashing like signals in the sun. Arthur and I bolted out into the passage, but as we were coming on to the path through the front door it stuck fast, and Arthur pulled it after him with such a bang that six feet of iron down-pipe dropped off the wall and nearly knocked me cold.

When we got to the end of the road Tiger was waiting for us, wagging his tail and blinking.

*

As soon as we got back on to the tram-road we met Benja Bowen on his way home. It was a Tuesday in the holidays, but he said he had been to chapel. I didn't feel much like taking him to my Uncle Sam's house because he was such a clown and you couldn't trust him. (Once when he came with me to my Mamgu Williams's he tried to creep into her sleeve by showing her a balancing trick with some of her cut-glass tumblers, and he smashed them all.) But he said, 'Going towards up?' and when we told him we were he said he would be with us as soon as he had changed his clothes. I couldn't think of anything to say, so we went back with him to the shop.

Benja was a bit misshapen; he was short, thick-set, and bull-necked, with arms hanging down to his knees like an ape. His short, powerful legs were rather bandy because he had broken both of them and he had a great wrinkled cone of ginger hair piled up on top of his huge head like stiff coconut matting. His bottom jaw, covered with blond unshaved cub-fur, stuck out beyond his top and his cheeks were red, but if you called him Rosie or Cochyn he would punch you on the muscles. He had his best clothes on, an Eton collar, a black coat and vest and striped trousers stinking of tobacco, and a pair of button boots that someone had ordered from his father and never called for. His father was a bootmaker, and you could always see the top of him showing above the green-painted window of their shop, his bald head very shiny and dirty as though he had polished it a bit with the heel-ball. He was an evangelist too, and you had to keep your hat straight when you were talking to him. One night my mother called round at his house to look for our groceries, and when he said they hadn't been left there, my mother thought he was teasing and said, 'Go on, Mr Bowen; aren't they here indeed?' 'Mrs Williams,' said Benja's father, 'my yea is yea, and my nay is nay,' and he slammed the door and bolted it after him. My mother said wfft to him; she had no looks on Bowen the bootmaker after that.

But he was very strict with his children too, and sometimes Benja would turn up to play for the school wearing his ordinary clothes and only one football boot, because that was all he had been able to smuggle out of the house. And perhaps even then he had jumped out of the upstairs window. He was stupid in school, he didn't have much under his hair except for games (once when the Welsh master asked him if his home was bi-lingual, he said, 'No, sir; by the Ship

and Castle'), and on the morning the school reports came out Benj
would be seen skulking in the shop doorway asking people if the
had seen the postman.

We thought Benja would be quicker if we didn't go inside hi
house, so we sat on a box in the little backyard with Tiger betweer
us. Benja's father was a queer man, and before he tried to start hi
own religion he used to come to our chapel and disturb the meeting
by shouting out 'Amen', and beating his breast and groaning wher
the minister mentioned Judas Iscariot. You never knew what h
would do next, and once when it was nearly midnight we heard fron
our house a great crash and Mrs Bowen ran down to my mother in
fright asking if she could come in. She said her husband had got uj
out of bed and suddenly started sweeping the soot out of the flues
and with a mighty heave of the brush he had pushed the bac'
kitchen chimney over into the glass-house next door.

But whatever he did himself, he always sat very tight on the tail
of the children, and one Sunday at tea-time he asked Benja if he hac
been that afternoon to the *gymanfa ganu* rehearsal at Bethel, a chape
a couple miles up the valley. Benja said yes he had, and he enjoyec
the singing too. 'Where were you sitting?' asked his father. 'Behinc
the clock on the gallery,' said Benja. His father landed him a stinge
with his heavy stitching hand on the side of the head, and chased hin
with a walking-stick from the table up into the bedroom. Benja wa
startled out of his wits up there, hearing his father roaring abou
downstairs and the furniture smashing, and after a couple of hours
as he sat bewildered on the bed with a kettle boiling in his hot ear, h
heard his sister at the keyhole whispering his name. 'What's all tha
noise down there?' he asked. 'What's happening?' 'It's our dad,
she answered. 'He's gone mad and he's attacking the back of the
piano with the hatchet.' 'What's the matter with him?' askec
Benja. 'What did he hit me across the ear like that for?' 'There'
no gallery in Bethel,' she said. 'I was there.'

But that was a long time ago, when Benja used to spend the time
he wasn't in chapel swimming in the canal where the hot wate
poured out of the boiler-house, and teasing the pawn-broker by
spitting on his crossed fingers outside the shop-window.

After a bit Benja came out dressed in his holiday clothes instead

f his dark suit and Eton collar. He was wearing over his pile of
inger hair a man's tweed cap with the broken peak pointing sky-
wards, and his grey suit so shrunken with boiling that the tight bandy
rousers were above his boots and the cuffs almost up to the elbows
f his monkey arms. And under his jacket he had a white cycling
weater tied with waxed thread round his waist to stop it hanging
own to his knees like a shirt.

The three of us started out again for my uncle's with Tiger
rotting behind us like a back sergeant, and as we passed the front of
Senja's shop we could see the dirty top of his father's head showing
bove the green paint; it was bald and shining as though he had held
: hard against the spinning brushes he kept for polishing the leather
a the shop. We turned into the tram-road once more, just where I
ad met the crimson singer, passing Dai Ben Tip nursing the baby
vith the shawl wrapped all round him, and M'Liza's brother, Will-
am the Rates, resting his bad leg on a window-sill. He had a big
lack beard and hair all over him, and he growled all day long like a
ig dog who wants you to spit on a stone and throw it for him. As
ve passed by Benja said something cheeky and the old man hit him
cross the behind with his walking-stick. But Benja only laughed
nd soon he began smoking a cigarette nip, pulling hard at it,
rimacing, hollowing his ginger-haired cheeks, and wrinkling up
is eyes as though it was a hard job to suck any smoke out of it.

After a while he began telling us again about the time he went
broad to play for the country against the French schoolboys (his
ather didn't know till after; he thought he was bad with the bile in
is Auntie Blod's in the next valley), and how they gave him so much
randy over there they couldn't keep him in his seat at the banquet
nd before he was sick he wanted to fight the Mayor of Paris. He
lways made me laugh with this story, but Arthur didn't take any
otice of him.

Then, to annoy me and Benja, Arthur started talking about
Horace and Catullus, and we didn't know anything about those
poets because he had got up into a form above us now. We were
orry they had separated us, because you could get fun out of the
ool way Arthur always spoke to the masters, like when he cheeked
Crumpy in the Latin lesson and told him of course he had a crib and

331

he found he couldn't do without it. Besides, Benja didn't have any
one to copy off now. Benja never had much time to do his homework
because he was always in chapel or boxing over Imperato's, so h
used to scribble Arthur's lessons out behind the fives court durin
dinner-time, fetching a pen and an inkwell stuffed with paper out o
school for the job. He was always in such a hurry that he used t
make a broth of it with blots and smudges, and when he had finishe
he used to throw the inkwell away into the bushes and hurry dow
town without us for a smoke and a game of billiards. (I wouldn't g
with him now, because the only time I went I found a couple o
yellow snooker balls in my schoolbag when I got home).

Very soon Benja had had a bellyful of Horace and Catullus, and h
started talking about the footwork of Maxy Imperato, because tha
was the only thing he knew more about than Arthur. I didn't muc
care what they talked about as long as it wasn't my bunch of roses
but presently Arthur said, 'What did you say was the matter wit
your uncle, Williams?'

'Asthma,' I said. 'Chronic.'

'Asthma,' he said, 'and you're taking him flowers. Don't yo
know things like that plastered with pollen will bring on an attac
for him?'

I was angry with him and I said that was old-fashioned talk, fly
me, like spitting on warts and having a potato for rheumatism, but
knew for sure somehow he was right. I felt cross with my mother; i
was just like her to do this to me. (I couldn't help remembering th
time my cousins were coming for Christmas when I was small, an
she gave me and Rhysie a sleeping-draught to stop us getting excited
But she gave us so much we slept fast for three days and never saw
our cousins at all.)

'I've never seen anyone having an attack of asthma,' said Benja
in a thoughtful way, grinning and picking at his bad teeth. So I wa
feeling worried when at last we got outside my uncle's house and a
I wanted to do was to get away as soon as I could.

*

My Uncle Sam's stone house was very small and so full of furnitur
that there were only narrow passages in between the hulking

ressers and the chests of drawers for you to move about in. Every shelf and flat space had a big Bible on it, or a collier's lamp, or a crowd of photographs and china mementos, and you could hardly see the wall-paper anywhere because of the family enlargements and the Rechabites' calendars and the massive furniture, big enough for a palace or a castle. My Auntie Maggie was very clean and always smelling of carbolic; she was for ever smoothing the table oil-cloth with her apron, and using her goose's wing on the curtains, and scouring the handles of her sweeping-brushes with red sand to keep them white. And though it was misty in her kitchen now, as dim as the inside of a bottle, still every piece of wood and every strip of metal shone like polished glass in the smoky gloom, especially the heavy brass airing-rail, and the steel stand and fender, and the gleaming fringe of brass around the mantelpiece. My uncle and auntie always lived in this little box of a kitchen, which had a bosh in the corner smelling of soap, and white stoning swirls on the floor, and a square of drying wires on the ceiling, and a chimney that was always blowing down clouds of stife into the room in winter. They had a nice parlour too, but my auntie only used that to let the jellies set in, and whenever you went in there your feet stuck to the oil-cloth and all the ornaments trembled.

I liked my Uncle Sam ever since I was small and he taught me corkwork. He used to draw a flag for me then, and the *gwdihw*, and Harlequin, or swallow his watch on the end of a string and let me hear it ticking in his belly. He was my favourite uncle, although I knew he was a born liar. When he was a young man he had run away because my Mamgu Thomas used to beat him for buying bottle beer with the money from his drapery round. But he was old now and bald, and a bit deaf; he looked very respectable drowsing in the rocking-chair by the fire with a snowy shawl round his shoulders and a jug of herb beer in his hand. He was wearing a washed suit after my father and a pair of old carpet slaps, and round his neck there was a black knitted tie but no collar. And although he hadn't done a tap for years now, you could tell it was true he had once been working underground because there was a jagged blue mark running like quartz across his forehead and continuing in a thick blue vein down his cheek. He had yellow eyeballs, a red nose as bright as a

berry, and brown bamboo marks mottling the skin of his long
hanging cheeks. His moustache was small now (when he was on h
wanderings it had been a huge one shaped like the horns of the Buffs
and because he hadn't shaved his bristling chin sparkled like a stubb
of hoar frost. He had been ailing so long he smiled with pleasur
when he saw us, showing his bad teeth under his moustache. All m
uncle's teeth were of different colours and sizes. Some were brow
some yellow, and some slatish, and one buff-coloured tooth wou'
be twice the height of the little black stump standing next to it.

My Auntie Maggie made us go inside the kitchen, dog and all,
talk to Uncle Sam. She was always dressed in baggy black, and sh
was fat and soft all over with a lap like a feather bed. Her face wa
clean and handsome, she had a lot of grey horse-hair, a big curve
nose, and a lovely smile, but there was something the matter wit
one of her eyes: the right ball was fixed and pitch-black; it stoo
bulging out of her head and shining with the polish of the big black
leaded pebble that kept the back door open and it never slid abou
into the corners at all. Sometimes after chapel on Sunday nights m
uncle and auntie used to come down to our house to sing hymr
round the parlour harmonium while my father accompanied us on th
trombone. My auntie had a lovely soprano voice, but her favourit
Sunday night solo was called "'Tis heaven or hell with you and me'
and she used to frighten the life out of me with that song, becaus
the great polished knob of her stuck eye was fixed fast upon me th
whole time she was singing it, making me remember all the times
had smoked and told lies and even gone up the woods mitching.
knew where I was going, and in the dead silence after her song, wit
only the gas-shade ringing, I could feel my hair creeping about or
my head.

But all that was years ago and I knew now my auntie was innocent
she would believe anything. And she waited on my uncle hand, foo
and finger, saying, 'You'll come, come you,' to him all the time t
cheer him up a bit. She was a lovely woman and she put the roses ou
the back where Mam Evans was getting the washing ready, withou
hurting my feelings, although Benja wanted to take them in th
kitchen for my uncle to have a good smell.

Although I was so anxious to get away, we had a tidy little time talking to my Uncle Sam. We could hear the two women banging about among the buckets outside the window behind us, my auntie using the cane brush like mad on the back, and every now and then popping the big black knob of her horse-eye up against the pane and staring through the geranium leaves to see how we were getting on. The three of us sat in a row on the couch opposite my uncle and he told us interesting lies with gusto about America and Woolangong and other places, but none of us believed him; we had the yarn about the man who worked in the airways and the tale of how my uncle found that week's *Football Echo* in the middle of the Australian bush when he was a lost man out there. (Benja grinned at that, his teeth like barnacles on his gums. 'And now tell us the one about the three bears,' he said.)

At times my uncle would get so excited he would have to stop his tale for a bit of puff, or to take a swig out of his herb jug, sucking his soaking moustaches into his mouth after he had done it. 'The old bellows,' he would mutter, pointing to his chest and smiling. With the fire lit, the door closed, and the sun shining hot outside, the boxy little room was becoming warmer and warmer and I would move to go while my uncle was drinking, but Benja would say, 'Take a blow, Evan; I think he's got an attack coming on,' although he was hot in his white sweater. But nothing happened and I would have to sit down again, while my uncle hooked his hand like the skinny yellow claw of a boiling fowl around his ear trying to catch what Benja was saying.

When we made my uncle understand who Arthur was, he rolled his amber eyeballs with pleasure and laughed, shaking his hanging mottled cheeks. He knew Tommy Morgan well, and his father the Gentleman Miner before him, and he began telling stories about him when he was a young cutter, before he got his tail into the mud. Arthur smiled, very polite, hanging on to Tiger's collar, but he didn't say much. He was too indolent to shout, although really he was a fine conversationalist; he used to talk very far back and use phrases you couldn't understand, like 'the perihelion of Mercury' and 'the pucelage and virginity of women'.

But Benja didn't mind shouting and he began showing off like a red-headed ape, telling my uncle fairy-tales about his family, and

turning round to show the scar on the back of his ginger head that he
said his mother had done when she crowned him with the frying-pan
because he couldn't remember the three headings of a sermon on
charity. (Arthur and I knew that really he had bolted some second-
hand spring expanders up in the attic on the sly, and when he went
to use them the hook had pulled out of the wood and nearly brained
him.) He had started his clowning as soon as he had come in, shaking
hands with my uncle and auntie with the wrong hand like a big-
headed gnome, and grinning at them as though he were an idiot, the
gaps in his teeth showing like book-backs missing from a shelf. He
was daft now and his nonsense made me hotter than ever, although
I had to laugh when he rolled up his tight trousers and showed the
birthmark on his bandy leg shaped like the Caspian Sea that he said
had made him top of the class when he copied it on to his geography
paper.

'Come on, Benja,' I said, standing up, wanting to peg him back
a bit because my uncle was laughing and sweating at the same time;
his snowy shawl was down behind him in the bars of the rocker and
he was holding his chest with his bright yellow fist, his eyes shut
tight, his cheeks puffed out, and his puce tongue showing under his
moustache with a fit of coughing. But before I could get him to
move my auntie padded smiling and bulge-eyed into the kitchen,
sidling with her tin tray among the massive mahogany, and gave us
a slice of apple tart each, and a fork to get it up with. Then she went
over to my uncle and tidied him up a bit, wiping his ripe red nose
and dusting his face with her apron as though he were a piece of
furniture, persuading him to have another dose of 'Cough-no-more'
as she draped the shawl around his shoulders. Then when we had
started eating Mam Evans came in with some of the things *she* liked,
bread and cheese and a jampot of pickle cabbage which she put down
on the table for us. They never had anything with vinegar in it in
Benja's because Bowen the bootmaker had found out the word
meant 'sour wine', so when no one was looking Benja threw his
piece of tart under the couch and started enjoying the pickle cabbage.

'Bowen,' said Arthur, 'why do you catch your fork so low down?'

I didn't notice that Benja held his fork low down, but I always used
to look at his finger with the top off.

Mam Evans, who stood by the table as we were eating, dipping now and then into the pickle cabbage with a spoon and a piece of bread, had a face like rubber or fresh putty. She had no teeth, and because her mouth was right up under her nose she seemed to be chewing with her nostrils. And her flabby head with the watery blue eyes in it and the toe-nail growing out of her chin seemed narrow compared with her neck, because on each side she had a smooth and solid wen. She was wearing a pair of clogs, her black flannel working clothes with a canvas apron round her and a man's cap fastened with a hat-pin through her bun.

She listened to my uncle telling Arthur and Benja the old story of how he fell down and kissed the railway line in *hiraeth* when he was abroad because he saw by the stamp on it it was rolled not fifty yards from my Mamgu's house, and then she interrupted him, chewing all over her face. 'Sam Thomas,' she said loudly, 'you won't laugh at me, will you?'

My uncle stopped his story and we all looked at her.

'Laugh at you, Mam Evans?' he said, when he understood her broken English. 'What do you mean? Laugh at you?'

'Well, if I ask you a question you won't laugh at me, will you?' She had big baggy hands like coal-gloves and she played with her scabby chin.

'Of course not,' said my Uncle Sam, all his different coloured teeth showing like a street skyline. 'What do you want to know?'

'Well, you've been to America abroad, haven't you?'

'Yes, I have, Mam Evans,' my uncle answered, his yellow talon hung on his ear.

'And you know the sun and the moon?'

My uncle nodded. 'Yes, I do, of course.'

'You won't laugh at me, will you?'

'No, no; I won't laugh. Go on.'

'Well, do they have the same sun and moon in America as we do have by here?'

We all laughed at that, my uncle and all, and Benja threw his feet in their button boots into the air. My uncle said yes, they had the same sun and moon, and at that Mam Evans clumped back to her work, chewing and grumbling at us and taking snuff, her skirts down at the sides and up at the back.

My auntie stood by smiling too as we were eating, landed that we were enjoying ourselves, and then she began questioning me about Rhysie and my mother. Anybody else would see I didn't want to talk about our mam just then, but my auntie was so innocent she didn't notice. Our door-knocker was a solid brass hand with a palmed brass ball in it, and when I couldn't hold her off any longer I had to blurt out my mother's foot was bad because when she was going to chapel she pulled the front door after her and the knocker came away as she did it. She came a cropper down our five steps and landed up with her leg under the gate, and she had to limp to chapel with the brass knocker weighing three or four pounds in her overcoat pocket. I was ashamed to say what had happened, because everyone would say it was just like my mother, so I ended by turning to Benja and saying, 'Don't start on that culff, Benja. Let's go home.'

He shook his big head, his cheeks full of bread and his bad teeth quarrying the cheese. 'Take a blow, mun,' he growled like a prompter. 'The bloke that made time made plenty of it.'

Arthur had let go his hold on Tiger to eat his tart, and the dog had his paws up on the couch, hoping for a bit of it. Suddenly he growled and quivered all over, and without any more warning jumped on to the couch alongside us and then bolted straight out through the window from between the geraniums. He took a header clean through the glass as though it were not there at all and disappeared out of sight. The pane shattered into fragments, leaving only a fringe of jagged pieces like a paper hoop around the edges, and there was the deafening clatter of an accident with trays among the buckets in the back-yard. We all jumped up and stared out of the window, feeling the cool air at once on our faces, my uncle behind us gripping our arms and wheezing with excitement. Arthur began whistling through the broken pane after the dog, which had galloped up the path and was now standing rigid near the garden wall on which the next door's tabby was sitting and gradually getting smaller in safety. 'Tiger, Tiger,' he called coolly. 'Come here, boy. Come here, boy.' And at last Tiger turned round and came bounding and diving back down the garden path towards the kitchen again. He saw Arthur

standing by the broken glass of the window, and without any hesi-
tation he plunged back into the room through the other pane,
bursting it like a water-bubble and bringing all the geraniums down
on to the couch behind him as he tumbled over on to the mat. Arthur
gripped him by the collar and began slapping him about the head, his
black hair hanging in curves like the claws of a pair of callipers over
his face.

My auntie, who used to pick my uncle up at the doorstep when it
was raining and battle her way through the passage with him on
her back to keep the oilcloth clean, didn't know what to do. She just
sat down on the stool and said, 'O wel ta wir,' with her face in a twist
and her glued eye staring at the mess on the floor. Because it was a
sad sight to her, as bad as a pig's breakfast spoiling the stoning on
her lovely hearth. There were pieces of glass scattered all over her
spotless kitchen, and the geranium pots in falling had split open and
the earth lay spread in dollops all over the hearthrug mixed with
fragments of cheese and red cabbage and flakes of pastry. And the
dog, who had opened his bowels with fright on the mat when he
crashed like a cannon-ball back into the room, made my uncle fall
over backwards into the rocker, overturning the little table behind
him and sending all the crockery to the floor, including the Mabon
milk-jug, and splashing the herb beer all over the wall and the cupboard and the black-leaded fireplace, where it ran down the oven in
long tears.

Just then Mam Evans put her head on the end of her wide wenny
neck around the door, a snuff-stain on her nose, and her bottom lip
fitted up over her top like the flap of a bandage.

'Maggie Thomas,' she said, not noticing anything with her pale
half-liquid eyes, 'I want a bit of soda. Have you got a bit of soda?'

But my auntie took no notice of her, she sat glaring downwards
with her black ornamental eye and muttering to herself, 'O wel ta wir.
O wel ta wir.'

Suddenly, in the middle of all the mess, I noticed Benja's face. He
wasn't paying any attention to my auntie, or to Mam Evans squinting
round the corner, or to Arthur slapping the dog; he was gaping at my
Uncle Sam's bald head starting to simmer, and his blue wound
growing brilliant on his forehead, and his boiling chest beginning

to bubble like a kettle as his shoulders heaved up under his ears. He sat fascinated with his short finger in his nose, his lower jaw hung out like a balcony, and a daft smile of satisfaction on his face as the attack began to develop.

Two Decisions

VERNON WATKINS

I MUST go back to Winter,
The dark, confiding tree,
The sunflower's eaten centre
That waved so tenderly;
Go back, break fellowship
With bud and leaf,
Break the loud branch and strip
The stillborn grief.
I must restore the thorn,
The naked sentinel,
Call lash of hail, wind-scorn
To laughter's lintel;
End argument in a way
Sudden and swift,
Leave stillness, go away
Beyond this leaf-drift,
Leave the ten-windowed house
And merely remark,
The ivy grew too close:
The house was dark.
Then I look out:
Rut, road and hill I see.
Tracks turn about.
Winter must come to me.
I shall not go,
I shall wait here
Until the snow
Bury the old year,
Until the swallows are gone
And the lintels wet
Tell that the rain that has blown

341

Is blowing yet.
Let me be nowhere
A melodramatic guest
Since here as anywhere
The light is best.
Though distant things entreat
The afraid, the fanciful,
The near is faithful:
Do not deny it.

The Poet

C. DAY LEWIS

FOR me there is no dismay
Though ills enough impend.
I have learned to count each day
Minute by breathing minute –
Birds that lightly begin it,
Shadows muting its end –
As lovers count for luck
Their own heart-beats and believe
In the forest of time they pluck
Eternity's single leaf.

Tonight the moon's at the full.
Full moon's the time for murder.
But I look to the clouds that hide her –
The bay below me is dull,
An unreflecting glass –
And chafe for the clouds to pass,
And wish she suddenly might
Blaze down at me so I shiver
Into a twelve-branched river
Of visionary light.

For now imagination,
My royal, impulsive swan,
With raking flight – I can see her –
Comes down as it were upon
A lake in whirled snow-floss
And flurry of spray like a skier
Checking. Again I feel
The wounded waters heal.

Never before did she cross
My heart with such exaltation.

Oh, on this striding edge,
This hare-bell height of calm
Where intuitions swarm
Like nesting gulls and knowledge
Is free as the winds that blow,
A little while sustain me,
Love, till my answer is heard!
Oblivion roars below,
Death's cordon narrows: but vainly,
If I've slipped the carrier word.

Dying, any man may
Feel wisdom harmonious, fateful
At the tip of his dry tongue.
All I have felt or sung
Seems now but the moon's fitful
Sleep on a clouded bay,
Swan's maiden flight, or the climb
To a tremulous, hare-bell crest.
Love, tear the song from my breast!
Short, short is the time.

The Dark

The Death of the Moth

VIRGINIA WOOLF

MOTHS that fly by day are not properly to be called moths; they do not excite that pleasant sense of dark autumn nights and ivy-blossom which the commonest yellow-underwing asleep in the shadow of the curtain never fails to rouse in us. They are hybrid creatures, neither gay like butterflies nor sombre like their own species. Nevertheless the present specimen, with his narrow hay-coloured wings, fringed with a tassel of the same colour, seemed to be content with life. It was a pleasant morning, mid-September, mild, benign-ant, yet with a keener breath than that of the summer months. The plough was already scoring the field opposite the window, and where the share had been, the earth was pressed flat and gleamed with moisture. Such vigour came rolling in from the fields and the down beyond that it was difficult to keep the eyes strictly turned upon the book. The rooks too were keeping one of their annual festivities; soaring round the tree tops until it looked as if a vast net with thousands of black knots in it had been cast up into the air; which, after a few moments sank slowly down upon the trees until every twig seemed to have a knot at the end of it. Then, suddenly, the net would be thrown into the air again in a wider circle this time, with the utmost clamour and vociferation, as though to be thrown into the air and settle slowly down upon the tree tops were a tremen-dously exciting experience.

The same energy which inspired the rooks, the ploughmen, the horses, and even, it seemed, the lean bare-backed downs, sent the moth fluttering from side to side of his square of the window-pane. One could not help watching him. One was, indeed, conscious of a queer feeling of pity for him. The possibilities of pleasure seemed that morning so enormous and so various that to have only a moth's part in life, and a day moth's at that, appeared a hard fate, and his zest in enjoying his meagre opportunities to the full, pathetic. He flew vigorously to one corner of his compartment, and, after waiting there a second, flew across to the other. What remained for him but to fly to a third corner and then to a fourth? That was all he could do, in spite of the size of the downs, the width of the sky, the far-off smoke of the houses, and the romantic voice, now and then, of a steamer out at sea. What he could do he did. Watching him, it seemed as if a fibre, very thin but pure, of the enormous energy of the world had been thrust into his frail and diminutive body. As often as he crossed the pane, I could fancy that a thread of vital light became visible. He was little or nothing but life.

Yet, because he was so small, and so simple a form of the energy that was rolling in at the open window and driving its way through so many narrow and intricate corridors in my own brain and in those of other human beings, there was something marvellous as well as pathetic about him. It was as if someone had taken a tiny bead of pure life and decking it as lightly as possible with down and feathers, had set it dancing and zig-zagging to show us the true nature of life. Thus displayed one could not get over the strangeness of it. One is apt to forget all about life, seeing it humped and bossed and garnished and cumbered so that it has to move with the greatest circumspection and dignity. Again, the thought of all that life might have been had he been born in any other shape caused one to view his simple activities with a kind of pity.

After a time, tired by his dancing apparently, he settled on the window ledge in the sun, and, the queer spectacle being at an end, I forgot about him. Then, looking up, my eye was caught by him. He was trying to resume his dancing, but seemed either so stiff or so awkward that he could only flutter to the bottom of the window-pane; and when he tried to fly across it he failed. Being intent on other matters I watched these futile attempts for some time without thinking, unconsciously waiting for him to resume his flight, as one waits for a machine, that has stopped momentarily, to start again without considering the reason of its failure. After perhaps a seventh attempt he slipped from the wooden ledge and fell, fluttering his wings, on to his back on the window sill. The helplessness of his attitude roused me. It flashed upon me that he was in difficulties; he could no longer raise himself; his legs struggled vainly. But, as I stretched out a pencil, meaning to help him to right himself, it came over me that the failure and awkwardness were the approach of death. I laid the pencil down again.

The legs agitated themselves once more. I looked as if for the enemy against which he struggled. I looked out of doors. What had happened there? Presumably it was midday, and work in the fields had stopped. Stillness and quiet had replaced the previous animation. The birds had taken themselves off to feed in the brooks. The horses stood still. Yet the power was there all the same, massed outside indifferent, impersonal, not attending to anything in particular. Somehow it was opposed to the little hay-coloured moth. It was useless to try to do anything. One could only watch the extraordinary efforts made by those tiny legs against an oncoming doom which could, had it chosen, have submerged an entire city, not merely a city, but masses of human beings; nothing, I knew, had any chance against death. Nevertheless after a pause of exhaustion the legs fluttered again. It was superb this last protest, and so frantic that he succeeded at last in righting himself. One's sympathies, of course, were all on the side of life. Also, when there was nobody to care or to know, this gigantic effort on the part of an insignificant little moth, against a power of such magnitude, to retain what no one else valued or desired to keep, moved one strangely. Again, somehow, one saw life, a pure bead: I lifted the pencil again, useless though I knew it to be. But even as I did so, the unmistakable tokens of death showed themselves. The body relaxed, and instantly grew stiff. The struggle was over. The insignificant little creature now knew death. As I looked at the dead moth, this minute wayside triumph of so great a force over so mean an antagonist filled me with wonder. Just as life had been strange a few minutes before, so death was now as strange. The moth having righted himself now lay most decently and uncomplainingly composed. O yes, he seemed to say, death is stronger than I am.

Elegy for Mrs. Virginia Woolf

SIDNEY KEYES

UNFORTUNATE lady, where white crowfoot binds
Unheeded garlands, starred with crumpled flowers,
Lie low, sleep well, safe from the rabid winds
Of war and argument, our hierarchies and powers.

Let the clear current spare you, once
A water spirit, spare your quiet eyes;
Let worm and newt respect your diffidence –
And sink, tired lovely skull, beyond surprise.

Over that head, those small distinguished bones
Hurry, young river, guard their privacy;
Too common, by her grave the willow leans
And trails its foliage fittingly.

In time's retreat, a stickleback's
Most complicated house, she lies:
Colours and currents tend her; no more vex
Her river-mind our towns and broken skies.

Little Gidding

T. S. ELIOT

I

MIDWINTER spring is its own season
Sempiternal though sodden towards sundown,
Suspended in time, between pole and tropic.
When the short day is brightest, with frost and fire,
The brief sun flames the ice, on pond and ditches,
In windless cold that is the heart's heat,
Reflecting in a watery mirror
A glare that is blindness in the early afternoon.
And glow more intense than blaze of branch, or brazier,
Stirs the dumb spirit: no wind, but pentecostal fire
In the dark time of the year. Between melting and freezing
The soul's sap quivers. There is no earth smell
Or smell of living thing. This is the spring time
But not in time's covenant. Now the hedgerow
Is blanched for an hour with transitory blossom
Of snow, a bloom more sudden
Than that of summer, neither budding nor fading,
Not in the scheme of generation.
Where is the summer, the unimaginable
Zero summer?

    If you came this way,
Taking the route you would be likely to take
From the place you would be likely to come from,
If you came this way in may time, you would find the hedges
White again, in May, with voluptuary sweetness.
It would be the same at the end of the journey,
If you came at night like a broken king,
If you came by day not knowing what you came for,

It would be the same, when you leave the rough road
And turn behind the pig-sty to the dull façade
And the tombstone. And what you thought you came for
Is only a shell, a husk of meaning
From which the purpose breaks only when it is fulfilled
If at all. Either you had no purpose
Or the purpose is beyond the end you figured
And is altered in fulfilment. There are other places
Which also are the world's end, some at the sea jaws,
Or over a dark lake, in a desert or a city –
But this is the nearest, in place and time,
Now and in England.

          If you came this way,
Taking any route, starting from anywhere,
At any time or at any season,
It would always be the same: you would have to put off
Sense and notion. You are not here to verify,
Instruct yourself, or inform curiosity
Or carry report. You are here to kneel
Where prayer has been valid. And prayer is more
Than an order of words, the conscious occupation
Of the praying mind, or the sound of the voice praying.
And what the dead had no speech for, when living,
They can tell you, being dead: the communication
Of the dead is tongued with fire beyond the language of the living.
Here, the intersection of the timeless moment
Is England and nowhere. Never and always.

II

      Ash on an old man's sleeve
      Is all the ash the burnt roses leave.
      Dust in the air suspended
      Marks the place where a story ended.
      Dust inbreathed was a house –
      The wall, the wainscot and the mouse.

The death of hope and despair,
 This is the death of air.

There are flood and drouth
Over the eyes and in the mouth,
Dead water and dead sand
Contending for the upper hand.
The parched eviscerate soil
Gapes at the vanity of toil,
Laughs without mirth.
 This is the death of earth.

Water and fire succeed
The town, the pasture and the weed.
Water and fire deride
The sacrifice that we denied.
Water and fire shall rot
The marred foundations we forgot,
Of sanctuary and choir.
 This is the death of water and fire.

In the uncertain hour before the morning
 Near the ending of interminable night
 At the recurrent end of the unending
After the dark dove with the flickering tongue
 Had passed below the horizon of his homing
 While the dead leaves still rattled on like tin
Over the asphalt where no other sound was
 Between three districts whence the smoke arose
 I met one walking, loitering and hurried
As if blown towards me like the metal leaves
 Before the urban dawn wind unresisting.
 And as I fixed upon the down-turned face
That pointed scrutiny with which we challenge
 The first-met stranger in the waning dusk
 I caught the sudden look of some dead master
Whom I had known, forgotten, half recalled

Both one and many; in the brown baked features
The eyes of a familiar compound ghost
Both intimate and unidentifiable.
So I assumed a double part, and cried
And heard another's voice cry: 'What! are *you* here?'
Although we were not. I was still the same,
Knowing myself yet being someone other –
And he a face still forming; yet the words sufficed
To compel the recognition they preceded.
And so, compliant to the common wind,
Too strange to each other for misunderstanding,
In concord at this intersection time
Of meeting nowhere, no before and after,
We trod the pavement in a dead patrol.
I said: 'The wonder that I feel is easy,
Yet ease is cause of wonder. Therefore speak:
I may not comprehend, may not remember.'
And he: 'I am not eager to rehearse
My thought and theory which you have forgotten.
These things have served their purpose: let them be.
So with your own, and pray they be forgiven
By others, as I pray you to forgive
Both bad and good. Last season's fruit is eaten
And the fullfed beast shall kick the empty pail.
For last year's words belong to last year's language
And next year's words await another voice.
But, as the passage now presents no hindrance
To the spirit unappeased and peregrine
Between two worlds become much like each other,
So I find words I never thought to speak
In streets I never thought I should revisit
When I left my body on a distant shore.
Since our concern was speech, and speech impelled us
To purify the dialect of the tribe
And urge the mind to aftersight and foresight,
Let me disclose the gifts reserved for age
To set a crown upon your lifetime's effort.

First, the cold friction of expiring sense
Without enchantment, offering no promise
But bitter tastelessness of shadow fruit
As body and soul begin to fall asunder.
Second, the conscious impotence of rage
At human folly, and the laceration
Of laughter at what ceases to amuse.
And last, the rending pain of re-enactment
Of all that you have done, and been; the shame
Of motives late revealed, and the awareness
Of things ill done and done to others' harm
Which once you took for exercise of virtue.
Then fools' approval stings, and honour stains.
From wrong to wrong the exasperated spirit
Proceeds, unless restored by that refining fire
Where you must move in measure, like a dancer.'
The day was breaking. In the disfigured street
He left me, with a kind of valediction,
And faded on the blowing of the horn.

III

There are three conditions which often look alike
Yet differ completely, flourish in the same hedgerow:
Attachment to self and to things and to persons, detachment
From self and from things and from persons; and, growing between
    them, indifference
Which resembles the others as death resembles life,
Being between two lives – unflowering, between
The live and the dead nettle. This is the use of memory:
For liberation – not less of love but expanding
Of love beyond desire, and so liberation
From the future as well as the past. Thus, love of a country
Begins as attachment to our own field of action
And comes to find that action of little importance
Though never indifferent. History may be servitude,
History may be freedom. See, now they vanish,

The faces and places, with the self which, as it could, loved them,
To become renewed, transfigured, in another pattern.

Sin is Behovely, but
All shall be well, and
All manner of thing shall be well.
If I think, again, of this place,
And of people, not wholly commendable,
Of no immediate kin or kindness,
But some of peculiar genius,
All touched by a common genius,
United in the strife which divided them;
If I think of a king at nightfall,
Of three men, and more, on the scaffold
And a few who died forgotten
In other places, here and abroad,
And of one who died blind and quiet,
Why should we celebrate
These dead men more than the dying?
It is not to ring the bell backward
Nor is it an incantation
To summon the spectre of a Rose.
We cannot revive old factions
We cannot restore old policies
Or follow an antique drum.
These men, and those who opposed them
And those whom they opposed
Accept the constitution of silence
And are folded in a single party.
Whatever we inherit from the fortunate
We have taken from the defeated
What they had to leave us – a symbol:
A symbol perfected in death.
And all shall be well and
All manner of thing shall be well
By the purification of the motive
In the ground of our beseeching.

IV

The dove descending breaks the air
With flame of incandescent terror
Of which the tongues declare
The one discharge from sin and error.
The only hope, or else despair
   Lies in the choice of pyre or pyre –
   To be redeemed from fire by fire.

Who then devised the torment? Love.
Love is the unfamiliar Name
Behind the hands that wove
The intolerable shirt of flame
Which human power cannot remove.
   We only live, only suspire
   Consumed by either fire or fire.

V

What we call the beginning is often the end
And to make an end is to make a beginning.
The end is where we start from. And every phrase
And sentence that is right (where every word is at home,
Taking its place to support the others,
The word neither diffident nor ostentatious,
An easy commerce of the old and the new,
The common word exact without vulgarity,
The formal word precise but not pedantic,
The complete consort dancing together)
Every phrase and every sentence is an end and a beginning,
Every poem an epitaph. And any action
Is a step to the block, to the fire, down the sea's throat
Or to an illegible stone: and that is where we start.
We die with the dying:
See, they depart, and we go with them.

We are born with the dead:
See, they return, and bring us with them.
The moment of the rose and the moment of the yew-tree
Are of equal duration. A people without history
Is not redeemed from time, for history is a pattern
Of timeless moments. So, while the light fails
On a winter's afternoon, in a secluded chapel
History is now and England.

With the drawing of this Love and the voice of this Calling

We shall not cease from exploration
And the end of all our exploring
Will be to arrive where we started
And know the place for the first time.
Through the unknown, remembered gate
When the last of earth left to discover
Is that which was the beginning;
At the source of the longest river
The voice of the hidden waterfall
And the children in the apple-tree
Not known, because not looked for
But heard, half-heard, in the stillness
Between two waves of the sea.
Quick now, here, now, always –
A condition of complete simplicity
(Costing not less than everything)
And all shall be well and
All manner of thing shall be well
When the tongues of flame are in-folded
Into the crowned knot of fire
And the fire and the rose are one.

Ignorance of Death

WILLIAM EMPSON

THEN there is this civilizing love of death, by which
Even music and painting tell you what else to love.
Buddhists and Christians contrive to agree about death

Making death their ideal basis for different ideals.
The communists however disapprove of death
Except when practical. The people who dig up

Corpses and rape them are I understand not reported.
The Freudians regard the death-wish as fundamental,
Though 'the clamour of life' proceeds from its rival 'Eros'.

Whether you are to admire a given case for making less clamour
Is not their story. Liberal hopefulness
Regards death as a mere border to an improving picture.

Because we have neither hereditary nor direct knowledge of death
It is the trigger of the literary man's biggest gun
And we are happy to equate it to any conceived calm.

Heaven me, when a man is ready to die about something
Other than himself, and is in fact ready because of that,
Not because of himself, that is something clear about himself.
Otherwise I feel very blank upon this topic,
And think that though important, and proper for anyone to bring
up,
It is one that most people should be prepared to be blank upon.

Poem

G. S. FRASER

Now cry your heart out if you can,
Cry for many a simple man.
I would weep, too, for my part,
But too soon I drained my heart,
Seeing only beauty could
Rouse or touch my tender blood,
Seeing that my coward will
Kept me far from beauty still
And my awkward limbs and tongue
Were not framed to charm the young;
Seeing all that beauty had
Time and circumstance forbade,

Me to touch or me to taste,
Seeing all my youth ran waste.
Many a fool as dull as I
Now must rouse himself to die,
Now must seek a colder bed
Than the loneliest he had,
Now must learn to die alone
In the nakedness of bone,
Or through nights of terror wake
When harder things than hearts can break;
When the inventive eye and head
Yield to duller lumps of lead,
When snaffling hand, and lying tongue,
And labyrinth gut, and bellows lung,
About the inhuman landscape spread
A natural history of the dead.

Time Will Not Grant

SIDNEY KEYES

TIME will not grant the unlined page
Completion or the hand respite:
The Magi stray, the heavens rage,
The careful pilgrim stumbles in the night.

Take pen, take eye and etch
Your vision on this unpropitious time;
Faces are fluid, actions never reach
Perfection but in reflex or in rhyme.

Take now, not soon; your lost
Minutes roost home like curses.
Nicolo, Martin, every unhoused ghost
Proclaims time's strange reverses.

Fear was Donne's peace; to him,
Charted between the minstrel cherubim,
Terror was decent. Rilke tenderly
Accepted autumn like a rooted tree.
But I am frightened after every good day
That all my life must change and fall away.

October, 1941

Europe's Prisoners

SIDNEY KEYES

NEVER a day, never a day passes
But I remember them, their stoneblind faces
Beaten by arclights, their eyes turned inward
Seeking an answer and their passage homeward:

For being citizens of time, they never
Would learn the body's nationality.
Tortured for years now, they refuse to sever
Spirit from flesh or accept our callow century.

Not without hope, but lacking present solace,
The preacher knows the feel of nails and grace;
The singer snores; the orator's facile hands
Are fixed in a gesture no one understands.

Others escaped, yet paid for their betrayal:
Even the politicians with their stale
Visions and cheap flirtation with the past
Will not die any easier at the last.

The ones who took to garrets and consumption
In foreign cities, found a deeper dungeon
Than any Dachau. Free but still confined
The human lack of pity split their mind.

Whatever days, whatever seasons pass,
The prisoners must stare in pain's white face:
Until at last the courage they have learned
Shall burst the walls and overturn the world.

May, 1941

The Sweet War Man is Dead

PAUL DEHN

THEIR stricken bones lie all about the world,
Who were my friends in England; and the law
Permits me to have loved them, who lack flesh.

Eyes winked, once, in the skull. Ribs that are curled
Under the sand, under the sea, under the hairy paw
Of Death who sent the flies, who sent the fish,

Had once a heart. Pluck me that heart, now,
From bird's beak, eel-gut and the maggot's mouth;
Put back those eyes, where the eternal tide

Sings in the sockets; on the crackpot brow
Pencil the leaf-light shadow-lines of youth;
For these bare bones were children, when they died.

So must I mourn among the glutted gulls,
Cry to a shark, weep with the fat, white worm
Who turns and nods to me across the stones.

They feasted and are full. Only these skulls
Ring emptily and need no requiem,
Being at peace. Lie easy now, poor bones.

Tell it to a Stranger

ELIZABETH BERRIDGE

THE war had been on nearly three years when Mrs Hatfield, on one of her periodic visits home, found a young reserve policeman whistling on her front doorstep and leaning against the splintered door. He had news for her: the house had been ransacked. After a moment's coldness in her stomach, Mrs Hatfield raised her eyebrows.

'Perhaps you would allow me to come in and see for myself,' she said.

The young policeman knocked the door open and stood aside for her. He wondered how long she would take to dissolve into an understandable hysteria. But she went through the whole house, noting silver ornaments missing, seeing the drawers pulled out, photograph albums and old accounts lying with West Indian shells over the floor. Upstairs her linen savagely mauled, cashmere shawls gone, the one good fur cape. Cut glass bottles, beautiful wine-glasses that responded finely to a flick of the thumbnail – this seemed the full extent of the haul. In her bedroom she stood in silence a long while. She saw that although her carpet was ripped across one corner it could be repaired. This was not a total loss – but by the evening it would be, when she told the story to her fellow-guests at Belvedere.

The policeman was saying: 'Helped himself to the whisky all right. Sergeant finished off the rest.' He grinned amicably, 'Must've worked in a raid,' he said, and again grinned, this time in admiration. 'Some nerve.'

Really, thought Mrs Hatfield through her preoccupation, if he wasn't a policeman I do believe he would become a criminal. She said curtly: 'I suppose you would like a list of the things missing?'

'Well, you don't have to do it at once, ma'am.' He was a little put out by her lack of emotion. 'But I'll have to ask you to step round to the station with me to have your finger-prints taken . . .' That touched her, pricked the present into her calm, and he felt obscurely pleased. It always got them that way. A look of horror, of flinching,

364

ame into her eyes. Again, the thought of the evening comforted her
- how would they take it, she wondered.

'That's quite all right,' she said, and without another look at the
urniture, now stripped of its shrouds, she went out into the streets
vith him.

That evening on the train she felt even more exhilarated than
vhen she had seen the dogfight in the sky. How they had listened
s she described the tiny metal flashes high over the town, how they
ad sighed when the smoke poured out, like lifeblood into the clear
ky.

Mrs Hatfield had moved out to Belvedere just before the bombing
tarted, when it was a not very successful guest house, despite the
alms in the coffee room and the planned garden. But when the
uests at the promenade hotels saw the sun pick out the bitter
pikes of barbed wire set in concertina rolls along the beach, and
eard the cry of rising gulls as shells whistled deadly out at sea, every
oom at Belvedere was taken, and an annexe planned.

Sitting back in the blue-lighted train, Mrs Hatfield thought back
over those two years. There was no doubt about it, she was a happier
woman, more alive than she had ever been. It's a dreadful thing to
ay, she told herself, but this war's been a blessing to some. Hastily
he brushed away all thought of the shadier blessings, and fixed
irmly on the unemployed. You're happy when you're working, she
hought. As the train stopped, the jerk shattered her conclusion:
fack had hated working. Although in the colonies you never did
nuch anyway. I never could please him, she thought with sudden
pain. She pleased the others, her friends now. Mr McAdam, Miss
Blackett, Doreen, and Mrs Kent. She almost loved Mrs Kent, for
ndirectly all her happiness hinged on her. For if she had not kept on
with Belvedere – Mrs Hatfield almost shuddered.

'I've been ransacked, my dears, everything – ' slowly the train
slid on its way, like a cowed animal, unobtrusive as possible. Then
from the outer darkness the rise and fall of a distant siren swept
across the country, starting from the coast, and as in a relay race,
handing on the warning to towns nearer the capital.

For a moment Mrs Hatfield felt panic, the country lay so dark
either side of the track and there was no stopping. The clank and

swing of wheels over points drowsed her into a numb sense o
security. This could go on forever, this invisible rushing throug
dark fields, wooden stations, hidden towns – it was all so effortles
and smooth. She lifted her feet and looked at them; they were no
walking, yet she was being carried incredible distances.

Almost imperceptibly another sound wove itself into the dark
ness, a gentle hum-humming, fast gaining on them. The trai
attempted to go even faster, but at this the humming increased unt
the whole countryside lay petrified under the heavy *throb-throb*
throb. Deliberately, delicately, the air rushed down, and somewher
to the right earth fountained up like oil from a gusher. Again, neare
the track this time, and clods of rich meadow grass and clay fe
heavily onto the roof of the train, plastering windows and doors. A
third and fourth followed swiftly, the full effect dulled by the sogg
earth. Then came machine-gun fire, sharp and tearing as sudde
rain on corrugated iron.

'This is war,' thought Mrs Hatfield, and her heart lifted an
throbbed in time with the great steel heart in the sky. But her fee
were cold and numb and hung heavily on to the floor. She heard th
guard go by, calling in a low voice, as if fearful of being overheard
'All blinds down. Screen all lights. Jerry overhead.' He repeated thi
with flat authority as he ducked along the corridor. How stupid
thought Mrs Hatfield; she almost laughed, a dry bad-tasting tremo
of her tongue. Who else could it be? Doggedly the train went on
Passengers, white lipped, told each other it was impossible to hit a
moving object in the dark. Besides, the Hun flashboards weren'
fitted with proper sights, everyone knew that.

In her compartment Mrs Hatfield sat erect. For a moment she fel
almost petulant; this was too much to tell. She could not allow thi
episode to crowd out the other. I have been ransacked, she tol
herself firmly. My beautiful wineglasses, Jack's last present to me
But she was listening to the sudden quietness, the suspense through
out the whole train, spreading from carriage to carriage. The hum
humming was growing less. It was lost in the nightwind.

Immediately the corridors were filled with strung voices, som
jaunty with relief, others low and shaken. The train had stopped
'Good heavens,' said Mrs Hatfield aloud. 'This must be my station.

She called from the doorway to make quite sure, and then got out of the train. It drew away silently, some of its windows broken by bullets which were now souvenirs. She watched it go, her ears still blocked with the noise of the thrumming sky.

Shaking a little, she went over the humped bridge and along the road. Overhead the wires sang between her and the faint moon, cold as the rime on the hedges.

'I'll be better when I get home,' she thought, and it warmed her to speak of Mrs Kent, of Belvedere, as home. They were waiting for her, she knew it, waiting for her to walk in between the palms and bring them news of the world at war. News without the slickness and positivity of the radio, the newspapers, which contained, as they felt, an oblique reproach.

She had something to tell this time. Here was some real news directly touching her, and through her, every person at Belvedere. The war had at last affected them personally; they were no longer grouped outside it, they shared in the general lawlessness. Lack of respect for property. What are we coming to? Police finishing off the whisky, wouldn't be surprised if – and so it would grow, filling more than an evening, filling the days, recreating their lives, and more important, affirming their belief in the past.

As Mrs Hatfield hurried down the lanes she felt exultant, almost like an envoy back from untold perils. She looked ahead and thought: I must have come the wrong way. For there was a glow in the sky. A haystack, she thought again. Then she stopped thinking and hurried on, for somehow she knew it was not a haystack burning, and she never came the wrong way.

She ran into the drive of Belvedere, and said stupidly, 'But there's nothing there.' It was the wooden annexe burning, the flames driving back the ambulance men and village firemen.

'You can't go any nearer, ma'am,' said one of them, struggling with a hose.

'Where are they?' asked Mrs Hatfield. She was white and the bones showed through the flesh of her cheeks. The man shook his head and motioned to the heaps of bricks and blazing rafters. 'Better ask the ambulance people,' he said, and wrenched the hose round.

'They can't drop bombs on Belvedere,' cried Mrs Hatfield, with tears suddenly released and streaming down her face. She started to shout, to drown the flames with noise, 'Doreen! Mrs Kent! I've got some news – some news – ' One of the ambulance men came over from a group of silent people.

'Now then, now then,' he said, 'we're doing our best. Got one or two out, but they can't do much until the fire dies down.'

Mrs Hatfield ran to the stretchers she saw on the ground. A maid, one of the newer arrivals, a porter. 'Chance in a million,' she heard one of the onlookers say.

'I've been ransacked,' said Mrs Hatfield to herself, gently, conversationally, 'ransacked.' She looked round at the people staring at the fire. They would not care. She ran up to a pile of rubble – maybe it was the lounge – and started to tear away the bricks and glass. As the hole grew deeper a childhood tale flashed through her mind. *The Emperor has asses ears*, the poor little barber who had to shout his secret into the earth, and the song of the corn repeating it. *The Emperor has asses ears*.

The firemen watched her incredulously.

'There's pluck for you,' said one. 'Poor old girl, friend of hers, I suppose.'

He went over to her. It was singeing hot even here. He seized her beneath the armpits.

'You can't!' he shouted as the flames found fresh ground.

Mrs Hatfield looked up at him.

'My lovely wineglasses,' she said.

What is Terrible

ROY FULLER

LIFE at last I know is terrible:
The innocent scene, the innocent walls and light
And hills for me are like the cavities
Of surgery and dreams. The visible might
Vanish, for all it reassures, in white.

This apprehension has come slowly to me,
Like symptoms and bulletins of sickness. I
Must first be moved across two oceans, then
Bored, systematically and sickeningly,
In a place where war is news. And constantly

I must be threatened with what is certainly worse:
Peril and death, but no less boring. And
What else? Besides my fear, my misspent time,
My love, hurt and postponed, there is the hand
Moving the empty glove; the bland

Aspect of nothing disguised as something; that
Part of living incommunicable,
For which we try to find vague adequate
Images, and which, after all,
Is quite surprisingly communicable.

Because in the clear hard light of war the ghosts
Are seen to be suspended by wires, and in
The old house the attic is empty: and the furious
Inner existence of objects and even
Ourselves is largely a myth: and for the sin

To blame our fathers, to attribute vengeance
To the pursuing chorus, and to live
In a good and tenuous world of private values,
Is simply to lie when only truth can give
Continuation in time to bread and love.

For what is terrible is the obvious
Organization of life: the oiled black gun,
And what it cost, the destruction of Europe by
Its councils; the unending justification
Of that which cannot be justified, what is done.

The year, the month, the day, the minute at war
Is terrible and my participation
And that of all the world is terrible.
My living must bear the laceration
Of the herd, and always will. What's done

To me is donē to many. I can see
No ghosts, but only the fearful actual
Lives of my comrades. If the empty whitish
Horror is ever to be flushed and real,
It must be for them and changed by them all.

Musée des Beaux Arts

W. H. AUDEN

ABOUT suffering they were never wrong,
The Old Masters: how well they understood
Its human position; how it takes place
While someone else is eating or opening a window or just walking
    dully along;
How, when the aged are reverently passionately waiting
For the miraculous birth, there always must be
Children who did not specially want it to happen, skating
On a pond at the edge of the wood:
They never forgot
That even the dreadful martyrdom must run its course
Anyhow in a corner, some untidy spot
Where the dogs go on with their doggy life, and the torturer's horse
Scratches its innocent behind on a tree.

In Breughel's *Icarus*, for instance: how everything turns away
Quite leisurely from the disaster; the ploughman may
Have heard the splash, the forsaken cry,
But for him it was not an important failure; the sun shone,
As it had to on the white legs disappearing into the green
Water; and the expensive delicate ship that must have seen
Something amazing, a boy falling out of the sky,
Had somewhere to get to, and sailed calmly on.

Memento

STEPHEN SPENDER

REMEMBER the blackness of that flesh
Tarring the bones with a thin varnish
Belsen Theresenstadt Buchenwald where
Faces were a clenched despair
Knocking at the bird-song-fretted air.

Their eyes sunk jellied in their holes
Were held up to the sun like begging bowls
Their hands like rakes with finger-nails of rust
Scratched for a little kindness from the dust.
To many, in its beak, no dove brought answer.

The War God

STEPHEN SPENDER

WHY cannot the one good
Benevolent feasible
Final dove descend?

And the wheat be divided?
And the soldiers sent home?
And the barriers torn down?
And the enemies forgiven?
And there be no retribution?

Because the conqueror
Is an instrument of power,
With merciless heart hammered
Out of former fear,
When today's vanquished
Destroyed his noble father,
Filling his cradle with anguish.

His irremediable victory
Chokes back sobbing anxiety
Lest children of the slain
(When the ripe ears grow high
To the sickles of his own
And the sun goes down)
Rise in iron morning
To stain with blood the sky
And avenge their fathers again.

His heart broke before
His raging splendour.

The virgins of prayer
Fumble vainly for that day
Buried under ruins,
Of his pride's greatest murder
When his heart which was a child
Asking and tender,
He hunted and killed.

The lost filled with lead
On the helpless field
May dream the pious reason
Of mercy, but also
Their eyes know what they did
In their own proud season,
Their dead teeth bite the earth
With semen of new hatred.

For the world is the world
And not the slain
Nor the slayer, forgive,
Nor do wild shores
Of passionate histories
Close on endless love;
Though hidden under seas
Of chafing despair,
Love's need does not cease.

Notes on Contributors

WYSTAN HUGH AUDEN (1907–73): The outbreak of the war revealed the irony of the two leading poets of the modernist movement entering into deeper commitments with each other's native land. Eliot, the New Englander, became the old Anglican of the *Four Quartets* while Auden, his most brilliant disciple, began his controversial process of becoming an American poet. Louis MacNeice defended Auden and the other migrants – '. . . an artist ought either to live where he has live roots or where he has no roots at all. . . . In England today the artist feels essentially lonely, twisted in dying roots, always in opposition to a group; that in America he is just as lonely, but so, says Auden, is everybody else. . . . It is no question of *il gran rifiuto*; he feels he can work better here than in Europe, and that is all there is to it.'

Eliot was tangibly anchored to his new country by a masterpiece, *The Waste Land*. Auden arrived in New York with a reputation for witty propagandist engagement in moral and political affairs, and glittering technical ability, but with no major achievement. The war was not to alter his delight in ingenious techniques or to check his bursts of facility, but it did mark a different kind of seriousness as the influences of Rilke, Kierkegaard and modern Christian apologists replaced those of Freud and Marx. In *The Age Of Anxiety* (1948) Auden describes war-time New York with all its guilt and peculiar isolation. No other twentieth century poet has so closely identified himself with the mood of his time. It is only in the context of such unflinching identification that his strange harvest of doggerel tract and faultless lyric can be understood.

A stretcher-bearer during the Spanish Civil War, Auden was to serve with the Strategic Bombing Survey of the U.S. Army in Germany in 1945.

Poetry: *Selected Poems*, 1940; *Another Time*, 1940; *New Year Letter*, 1941; *For The Time Being*, 1944.

Critical Prose: *Journey To A War* (With Christopher Isherwood), 1939.

DONALD BAIN (b. 1922): Bain was an actor who served in the Royal Artillery and Gordon Highlanders. He helped to edit *Oxford & Cambridge Writing*, 1942.

GEORGE GRANVILLE BARKER (b. 1913): Barker was the 26-year-old Professor of English Literature at the Imperial Tohoku University, Japan, when the war broke out, and in the United States 1940-3. His work is mysterious and oratorical, dark and violent words for a dark and violent age. Barker often achieves the genuine 'word explosion' sought by the poets of the New Apocalypse whose apology, as described by G. S. Fraser in *Apocalypse in Poetry*, was 'The obscurity of our poetry, its air of something desperately snatched from dream or woven round a chime of words, are the results of disintegration, not in ourselves, but in society. . . .' Unlike the Apocalyptics, Barker could not accept that a world gone mad deserved 'a dialectical development of surrealism' any more than he believed in further doses of thirties poetry-politics. His mid-way course was religious and romantic, an organ continuo in the broken aisles of the West.

Poetry: *Lament and Triumph*, 1940; *Eros in Dogma*, 1944.

ELIZABETH BERRIDGE (b. 1921): Novelist and critic.
Miscellaneous Writings: *House of Defence*, 1945; *Selected Stories*, 1949.

ELIZABETH BOWEN (1899-1973): With what proved to be her best novels immediately behind her, *The House in Paris* (1935) and *The Death of the Heart* (1938), Elizabeth Bowen entered the forties as the most distinguished novelist following the 'sensibility' tradition in English fiction. '. . . it's not catastrophes, murders, deaths, diseases, that age and kill us,' writes Virginia Woolf in *Jacob's Room*, 'it's the way people look and laugh, and run up the steps of omnibuses.' Elizabeth Bowen agreed. Her sense of place – as it exists to a certain person at a crucial moment – was remarkable, and her stories of friends and lovers in blitzed London reflected in a unique manner the war's inner war of private standards versus shabby freedoms.

Short Stories: *Look At All Those Roses*, 1941; *The Demon Lover*, 1945; *Selected Stories*, 1946.
Miscellaneous Writings: *Bowen's Court*, 1942; *English Novelists*, 1942; *Seven Winters*, 1942.

BRYHER (WINIFRED) (b. 19—): Bryher is the daughter of Sir John Ellerman, the shipping magnate. Before and after the war she has made her home in Vaud, Switzerland. She spent the war years in London with the poet H.D. (Hilda Doolittle). Her experiences of the war from which the extract here was taken were not published until 1972. She made her name from a series of novels which she wrote in the 1950s.

Novels: *The Fourteenth of October*, 1952; *The Player's Boy*, 1953; *Beowulf*, 1956; *Gate to the Sea*, 1958.

ROY CAMPBELL (1901–57): This South African poet's pro-fascist sympathies during the Spanish Civil War and his noisy attacks on 'MacSpaunday' (Auden, MacNeice, Day Lewis and Spender) made many readers antipathetic to him during the forties. R. N. Currey called *Talking Bronco* 'the most vigorous single book of poems of the war ... and the most untypical'. Five years before his death Campbell published his translation of the *Poems of St John of the Cross* (1952). It is a revelation, not only of the saint, but of Campbell himself. He served in the King's African Rifles during the war.

Poetry: *Flowering Rifle*, 1939; *Talking Bronco*, 1946; *Collected Poems*, 1949.

CHARLES CAUSLEY (b. 1917): Served in the Navy throughout the war. *Farewell, Aggie Weston*, 1951.

WILLIAM CHAPPELL (b. 1908): Chappell's essay is a good example of personal writing at a time when a high degree of sensitivity is set in motion by destructive events. There is awareness and candid self-analysis, but none of that inviolable inner calm shared by poets like Keyes and Lewis. Countless young men guarding outlandish places, waking up in fetid nissen huts, unbelievingly finding themselves thrust across seas into deserts and jungles, caught in the prisoner's net or discovering the extent of a mutilation, experienced Chappell's questioning reaction.

'So that is all you are now,' I thought. 'A symbol! – a stranger . . . not only you, but you and you, and you . . . You belong to no one, and the world is no longer yours . . .'

'At least,' I thought, 'now you know who you are – you can, perhaps, understand yourself.'

Then my heart sank as I realized that it means very little, very little indeed, to understand nothing.

HERBERT CORBY (b. 1911): Corby's first poems, like those of Dylan Thomas, were accepted by Victor Neuburg – the 'Vickybird' – for the *Sunday Referee*. Rich accounts of this St John's Wood patron appear in a number of thirties memoirs and most recently in Constantine FitzGibbon's *Life of Dylan Thomas* (1965). Corby rejected the largely symbolist traditions of the Neuburg Group when the war began. His R.A.F. poetry, created from his experiences as an armourer in a bomber squadron, is quiet, unemphatic, precise.

Set in his turret he'd seen the whole sky alter,
The Dornier swoop oddly to the sea, and falter.

Poetry: *Hampdens Going Over*, 1945; *Time In A Blue Prison*, 1947.

TIMOTHY CORSELLIS (1921–41): This young poet, killed early on in the war, put the basic complaint with ironic exactness.

I was ready for death . . .
but
We sat together as we sat at peace
Bound by no ideal of service
But by a common interest in pornography and a desire to outdrink one
another.

and, as many a death-accepter found when bullshit and boredom
exacted their implacable dues,

The sacrifice is greater than I ever expected.

RALPH NIXON CURREY (b. 1907): Currey served as a gunner
officer in India. A South African who came to England between the
wars, he found the impact of the old civilization overwhelming. He
was to observe a similar cultural and hemispheric effect on many
servicemen in the East and his anthology of their impressions, *Poems
From India* (1945) is one of the best collections of war-time verse.
His British Council booklet, *Poets of the 1939-1945 War* (Long-
mans, 1960), is essential reading for students of the period.

Poetry: *Tiresias and Other Poems*, 1940; *This Other Planet*, 1945;
Indian Landscape, 1947.

CECIL DAY LEWIS (1904-72): C. Day Lewis rejected Audenism
very early in his career and could say, 'all my poems "rhyme and
scan"; . . . contrary to the preconceived opinions of some, they are
not always less experimental in nature when they are more traditional in idiom'. He was scathing about the frequent demands for
war poets made by politicians and journalists connected with, up
till then, poetry-abusing newspapers.

> They who in panic or mere greed
> Enslave religion, markets, laws,
> Borrow our language now and bid
> Us to speak up in freedom's cause.

His own fine war poem, *The Nabara*, was written during the Spanish Civil War. The forties found him somewhat cool and detached
as he edited books and pamphlets at the Ministry of Information. He
translated the *Georgics* and his work at this time is calm and contem-
plative.

Poetry: *Overtures To Death*, 1938; *Poems In Wartime*, 1940; *Word
Over All*, 1943; *Poems 1943-1947*, 1948; *Collected Poems*, 1954.
Translations: *The Georgics Of Virgil*, 1941; *Le Cimetière Marin* by
Paul Valéry, 1946.

PAUL DEHN (b. 1912): Dehn served as a major in the Intelligence Corps during the war and afterwards became the excellent but doomed *News Chronicle*'s film critic. Poetry, he has said, became his 'honest safety-valve' at a time when the full implications of training men to become saboteurs in Western Europe swept over him. His work is witty and compassionate. A drowned friend is bidden farewell with:

> Each on our way, my ghost, my grayling,
> You to the water, the land for me;
> I am the fat-knuckled, noisy diver
> But you are the quietest fish in the sea.

Poetry: *The Day's Alarm*, 1949; *Collected Poems*, 1965.

KEITH DOUGLAS (1920–44): Douglas is the Second World War poet who stands nearest in succession to Wilfred Owen. Current achievement and future promise are more evident in his work than in that of any other writer of his generation. His account of what happened when he ran away from a safe staff job to the fighting in the Western Desert is, perhaps, the most magnificent piece of battle description to come out of the war. His genius was to be able to harness a clear unsentimental vision to a direct pity. 'To be sentimental or emotional now is dangerous to oneself and to others,' he said in 1943. The result of such candour in his poetry and prose was a vigour, conviction, colour and attack which were unique in the literature of these years. He saw death with a brilliant inquisitiveness. Corpses on the sand drew his curiosity and understanding. The lover's and the killer's body is now the slain body. It is terrible – yet marvellous. And this is the tragedy. He was killed in Normandy on 9 June 1944.

Poetry and Prose: *Alamein to Zem-Zem*, 1946; *Collected Poems* (Ed. J. Waller and G. S. Fraser), 1951; *Selected Poems* (Ed. Ted Hughes), 1964.

THOMAS STEARNS ELIOT (1888–1965): W. B. Yeats died in 1939, and his death left an aspect of succession to Eliot, a poet who embodied the mood of his time in a way Yeats never did. Eliot's anti-romantic revolution had begun to take effect immediately after the First World War and by 1930 with *Ash Wednesday* there were quiet indications enough to show that the remainder of the poet's journey was not to offer the same excitements. Auden can be said to have taken over the revolution at this point with his *Poems* (1930). The climax of Eliot's retreat was *Four Quartets*, a profound Christian poetic statement ranking with Donne's *Holy Sonnets*, and which appeared during the darkest years of the century. At a time when state priorities threatened the true function of the poet he urged writers to remember their duty as 'men of letters'. 'The first responsibility of the man of letters is, of course, his responsibility towards his art, the same, which neither time nor circumstance can abate or modify . . .' This was a brave and challenging injunction for the time and circumstances of late 1943.

Poetry: *Old Possum's Book Of Practical Cats*, 1939; *East Coker*, 1940; *Burnt Norton* (first published in *Collected Poems* 1936), 1941; *The Dry Salvages*, 1941; *Little Gidding*, 1942; *Four Quartets*, 1943.
Plays: *The Family Reunion*, 1939.
Criticism, etc: *The Idea of a Christian Society*, 1939; *The Music of Poetry*, 1942; *The Classics and the Man of Letters*, 1942; *Reunion by Destruction*, 1942; *What is a Classic?* 1945.

WILLIAM EMPSON (b. 1906): Empson held the Chair of English Literature at Tokyo University 1931–4 and was Professor in English Literature at Peking National University 1937–9. During the war he was Chinese Editor at the B.B.C., returning to Peking in 1947. Empson's oriental concern for the patterns of meaning was expressed, before he went to the Far East, in *Seven Types of Ambiguity* (1930), written when he was twenty-six. It is a tantalus of a book and preceded poems which also resist a direct approach. Empsonian subtlety drew many imitators but no real rival, either here or in America. Huge events are made to look less formidable, or even vulgar, by a fastidious kind of under-statement. Nemesis and Thor, the thunderous and the crudely retributive, are mocked with urbanity and wit. Yet, as a recent critic has said, Empson's highly civilized world, for all its brave conceits, remains 'betrayed by a diffused sense of torment, helplessness, despair, of the impossibility of knowledge and judgement'.

Poetry: *The Gathering Storm*, 1940; *Collected Poems*, 1955.

GEORGE SUTHERLAND FRASER (b. 1915): Fraser was a founder member of the New Apocalypse movement at the beginning of the war. Supported by Henry Treece and J. F. Hendrey, this movement attempted what it called 'a dialectical development of Surrealism'. The moral collapse of society was to be accompanied by splintered poetry. Fraser retreated from this short-lived inarticulation and by the middle of the war had withdrawn to an austere personal position where certain verities outlast 'the interminable debate' and certain realities prove the continuity of meaning.

> . . . the country lying quiet and full of farms.
> This is the shape of a land that outlasts a strategy
> And is not to be taken by rhetoric or arms.

Poetry: *The Fatal Landscape*, 1942; *Home Town Elegy*, 1944; *The Traveller Has Regrets*, 1947.

ROY FULLER (b. 1912): Fuller served in the Navy, first as an ordinary seaman, later as an officer in the Fleet Air Arm. One of the war's most prolific poets, he could acknowledge its freedoms and excitements.

> I wipe my fingers on the hurrying faces,
> And implant the wish to be in different places.

Poetry: *Poems*, 1939; *The Middle of a War*, 1942; *A Lost Season*, 1944; *Epitaphs and Orations*, 1949.

DAVID GASCOYNE (b. 1916): The only English poet who was to any considerable extent influenced by the surrealist movement, Gascoyne's work during the early war years is marked by a curiously ecstatic fusion of beauty and terror. His only recently published *Paris Journal 1937–9* and *Journal 1936–1937* are wonderfully evocative of the atmosphere of the immediate pre-war days.

Poetry: *Poems 1937–1942*, 1948.

ROBERT GRAVES (b. 1895): For Robert Graves it was a prose war. He wrote a series of historical novels, none of which really approached the brilliance of the Claudius stories of 1934. Then, shortly after the armistice, and harmonizing well with the personal-mythological element which half-tragically, half-wittily, was insinuating itself into the intellectual climate of the latter forties, much of it stemming from *The Unquiet Grave*, came the fascinating *White Goddess* in which he traces the fluctuating honour which mortal man has paid to the supreme Mother deity, the giver of all, and the consequences of such fickleness. The poetry which Graves published during the war – mostly in magazines – was as casual in tone as it was expert in construction.

Novels: *Sergeant Lamb of the Ninth*, 1940; *Proceed, Sergeant Lamb*, 1941; *Wife to Mr Milton*, 1943; *The Golden Fleece*, 1944; *King Jesus*, 1946.

JAMES HANLEY (b. 1901): James Hanley was born in Dublin and brought up in Liverpool. At fourteen he followed his father to sea as a ship's boy. After ten years of drifting about in a harsh and terrible world he returned to Liverpool and became a recluse in order to learn to be a writer. His stories, built up with stark and sometimes clumsy sentences, were informed with a mixture of pity and realism which created a climate of loneliness and terror rarely found in English fiction. The theme of sea-isolation repeats itself throughout his work and is sometimes adapted to reveal other kinds of human solitude. In *No Directions* (1943) he used his 'adrift' plot to show a crowded Chelsea house raft-like in the welter of an air-raid. This novel followed *The Ocean* (1941), a superb work which many critics place with *Typhoon*. *Sailor's Song* (1943), from which the extract in this anthology is taken, is a daring bid to write about the sea and its victims – the latter not necessarily dead – in terms of pure sea-emotion. It marks the climax of Hanley's sea writing.

Novels: *Our Time is Gone*, 1940; *The Ocean*, 1941; *No Directions*, 1943; *Sailor's Song*, 1943; *What Farrar Saw*, 1946.
Short Stories: *At Bay*, 1944; *Crilley*, 1945.

RAYNER HEPPENSTALL (1911–82): Heppenstall served in the ranks, first in the Royal Artillery, then in the R.A.P.C. for the whole of the war. His poem *Instead of a Carol* is one of the few totally eloquent statements about the plight of the ordinary fighting man during the twentieth century. At the end of the war he sided somewhat warily with Guido de Ruggiero against the tempting romance of Existentialism – 'Existentialism is at its best a periodical reaffirmation of the individual against the impersonal absolute. At the worst, it is a handy rationalization for those who wish to adopt pessimistic conclusions for temperamental motives which they do not declare.'

Poetry: *Blind Men's Flowers are Green*, 1940; *Poems: 1933–45*, 1946.
Novels: *Saturnine*, 1943; *The Blaze of Noon*, 1942.

RICHARD HILLARY (1920–43): 'In times of war the dead recede quicker and myths form faster; already there is one growing around Hillary and it is easy to foresee that it will wax and expand, until his name has become one of the symbolic names of this war,' wrote Arthur Koestler in the spring of 1943. Hillary wrote against the flood of bestseller service memoirs because 'I got so sick of the sop about our "Island Fortress" and "The Knights of the Air".' *The Last Enemy* is a study of inverted heroism as well as being a painful enlargement of the nerve of the Battle of Britain. There is an added poignancy in remembering that this kind of battle is unlikely ever to take place again, so that already the Fighter Command young men, 'the long-haired boys', as Hillary called them, have in thirty-five brief years become as much a part of the obsolescent pageantry of arms as the Crécy archers and the wooden wall sailors. While the Spitfire itself now has the implacable quaintness which time reserves for old weapons. Hillary began his war self-consciously aware of belonging to a privileged generation – 'This then was the Oxford Generation which on September 3, 1939, went to war ...' – and ended it two years later as the authentic voice of the war's most exclusive brotherhood, the Few.

Autobiography: *The Last Enemy*, 1942.

GLYN JONES (b. 1905): Glyn Jones was born in Merthyr Tydfil and was one of a group of forties writers – others included Dylan Thomas and Vernon Watkins – whose work appeared in the magazine *Wales*. His stories display a richness of language and inventive vigour which typify the way some high-spirited writers reacted to the drabness and austerity of the war.

Poetry: *The Dream of Jake Hopkins*.
Short Stories: *The Blue Bed*, 1937; *The Water Music*, 1944.

SIDNEY KEYES (1922–43): 'If the word that Wilfred Owen made his own was "pity", Keyes' word is "pain",' wrote R. N. Currey, adding, 'Keyes' work is a continuation of Wilfred Owen's. Owen wrote from his own gradual conversion, under stress, to a surprised hatred of war – to such effect that Keyes, by the time he came to join the army, could start almost where Owen left off. He put on his uniform of pain before he was issued with battledress. . . .' Keyes died while on patrol in North Africa aged twenty-one, leaving behind an astonishing achievement, and sharing with Keith Douglas the greatest promise of all the poets of their generation. He was posthumously awarded the Hawthornden Prize.

Poetry: *The Iron Laurel*, 1942; *The Cruel Solstice*, 1943; *Collected Poems*, 1946.

ARTHUR KOESTLER (b. 1905): Koestler began his career as a foreign correspondent (1926–31) and later covered the Spanish Civil War for the *News Chronicle*. He was imprisoned by Franco and sentenced to death. He was living in France when the Germans invaded in 1940, and fled to England. The degree to which he was morally and physically caught up in the events which were changing Europe lent a unique authority to the novels and essays he wrote during the war years. Eventually he came to distrust all the various political and intellectual coteries and called for writers to 'cling more than ever to the ragged banner of independent thinking'.

Novels: *The Gladiators*, 1939; *Darkness at Noon*, 1940; *Scum of the Earth*, 1941.
Essays: *The Yogi and the Commissar*, 1945.

ALUN LEWIS (1915–44): Lewis was a young Welsh historian on whose imagination the landscapes of India and the Far East were to act like a burning glass. There is a fastidious, almost chaste element in his poetry. Outrage receives a quiet answer. He saw 'the gradual self-effacement of the dead' and, looking back at the death of Edward Thomas at Arras in 1917, he says coldly, 'a bullet stopped his song'.

Poetry: *Raider's Dawn*, 1942; *Ha! Ha! Among the Trumpets*, 1945; *In the Green Tree*, 1948.

Stories: *The Last Inspection*, 1943.

JULIAN MACLAREN-ROSS (d. 1965): The decadal voice of the forties, Maclaren-Ross has been described as a 'twentieth-century Aubrey' whose work was done 'with the slightly studied negligence of a snooker player idly knocking the balls about in the morning, before the pub fills up'. His autobiography and *The Life of Dylan Thomas* by Constantine FitzGibbon (1965) contain some of the best evocations of literary London at war (more frequently with itself than with the Axis Powers) in existence. Just before he died Maclaren-Ross described the fifties as 'a decade I could have done without'.

Short Stories: *The Stuff to Give the Troops*, 1944; *Better than a Kick in the Pants*, 1945; *The Nine Men of Soho*, 1946.

Novels: *Bitten by the Tarantula*, 1946; *Of Love and Hunger*, 1947.

Autobiography: *Memoirs of the Forties*, 1965.

LOUIS MACNEICE (1907–63): MacNeice was in Ireland during the autumn of 1939 and went from there to America, where he remained for nearly a year. In his apology for the emigré British writers he said that he found his pleasure in being back in England, and any regret he may have felt had he not returned, 'equally unethical'. From 1941–9 he was a B.B.C. feature writer and producer, helping to further important developments in the field of radio verse-drama. Some critics have regretted the extent to which MacNeice occupied himself with this work, feeling it to be an ephemeral use of his great gifts. He wrote brilliant descriptions of the London bombings in *Picture Post*. His poetry avoids the emphatic. His terrain is often melancholy, the Dover Beach of the thirties and forties.

Poetry: *Autumn Journal*, 1939; *Plant and Phantom*, 1941; *Springboard*, 1944; *The Dark Tower*, 1946.
Critical Writing: *W. B. Yeats*, 1941.

GEORGE ORWELL (Pseud. of Eric Blair) (1903–50): Orwell explored the popular by-paths of the British soul during the war. In *The Art of Donald McGill* (1941) he examined the permissive ribaldry of the seaside picture-postcard. In *Raffles and Miss Blandish* (1944) he studied the forerunners of James Bond, seeing in James Hadley Chase's sado-masochistic thugs and dames the antics of 'non-political fascists'. But his interpretation of *Boys' Weeklies* (1940) was to land him in an hilarious debate with Frank Richards, the creator of Billy Bunter. Orwell's Etonian-proletarian approach to the British complexity was complex in itself. He wrote the nightmarish *1984* when he was dying and when the Cold War fever was at its height. It created a great sensation but can now be seen, like H. G. Wells's *Mind at the End of its Tether* (1945), as a piece of hollow pessimism, and much inferior to *Animal Farm*.

Novels: *Coming Up For Air*, 1930; *Animal Farm*, 1945; *1984*, 1949.
Essays: *Inside the Whale*, 1940; *The Lion and the Unicorn*, 1941; *Critical Essays*, 1946.

MERVYN PEAKE (1911–68): Mervyn Peake was born and partly educated in China. *Titus Groan* and its sequel *Gormenghast* make up an imaginative achievement which would be rare in any decade but which in the romantic forties stood out with a violent Gothic power. Both novels, brilliant and original as they are, have until recently been curiously neglected. Peake's drawings, poems and stories are atavistic, the gargoyle on the church tower made flesh once more, while Bosch's imps ride the bomb. He scarcely exaggerates when he says:

> The paper is breathless
> Under the hand
> And the pencil is poised
> Like a warlock's wand.

Poetry: *Shapes and Sounds*, 1941; *Rhymes Without Reason*, 1944.
Novels: *Titus Groan*, 1946; *Gormenghast*, 1950.

F. T. PRINCE (b. 1912): F. T. Prince was born in Kimberley, South Africa and believes that his most important war-time experience was that he, an outsider by birth and education, achieved a European sense of belonging. Although 'Soldiers Bathing', which first appeared in *Poems from the Forces*, is considered by many to be the best single poem of the war, Prince himself is severe and modest about the work he did at this time.

Poetry: *Poems*, 1938; *Soldiers Bathing*, 1954; *The Door of Stone*, 1963.

V. S. PRITCHETT (b. 1900): Writing of Hašek's *The Good Soldier Schweik* in 1944, Pritchett said, 'The great comic characters of fiction are the imbeciles, the rogues and the lunatic martyrs. ... Beginning as fools they end as saints.' David Daitches has pointed out Pritchett's own 'half-ironical, half affectionate relish for the absurdities of human character'. Many of his best stories were written during the war and it was also during these years that the extraordinary range and catholicity of his literary judgements began to be felt. Pritchett grinds no axe.

Short Stories: *It May Never Happen*, 1945; *Collected Short Stories*, 1956.

JOHN PUDNEY (b. 1909): Pudney worked first as a B.B.C. producer and then as a journalist on the *News Chronicle* during the thirties. He served in the R.A.F. 1941–5. One of the most prolific poets of the war, he saw the whole disaster, as he was later to confess, in over-simplified terms. His work had an immediate appeal and one poem, 'For Johnny', has claim to be the most popular epitaph of the period.

> Do not despair
> For Johnny-head-in-air;
> He sleeps as sound
> As Johnny underground.
>
> Fetch out no shroud
> For Johnny-in-the-cloud;
> And keep your tears
> For him in after years.

Better by far
For Johnny-the-bright-star,
To keep your head
And see his children fed.

KATHLEEN RAINE (b. 1908): Kathleen Raine shared with many women writers at this time, Anne Ridler, Freda Laughton and Elizabeth Bowen in particular, a special grief and wonder at the fragility of the scene, streets vanishing into dust, conventions and institutions exploding like the bombs themselves, and all the pathetic impermanence –

Stairways into space, and windows into sky,
And the tear-wet streets, with cloud-torn moonlight shining;
Ways underground are open, and the trains are running
Oh to what end, in this dream-entangled city?

Poetry: *Stone and Flower*, 1943; *Living in Time*, 1946; *The Pythoness* 1949; *Collected Poems*, 1956.

HENRY REED (b. 1914): Reed's contact with the military was short, sharp and memorable, a few months' brush with the army inspiring; *The Naming of Parts* and a subsequent group of ironic poems which were an acute comment on the old soldier versus the civilian soldier clash. These poems, later to be known as *Lessons of the War*, are moving, witty and cool, breaking many of the rules of the pompous army game.

Poetry: *A Map of Verona*, 1945.

W. R. RODGERS (b. 1909): Rodgers was a Presbyterian minister in County Armagh until 1946, when he joined the B.B.C., where he helped to develop radio biography. His poetry, described by one critic as 'not on the whole characteristic of modern verse, its texture open, its tone that of courteous eloquence', was first seen in the early numbers of *Horizon* and in the magazine edited by Sean O'Faolain, *The Bell*.

Poetry: *Awake! and other Poems*, 1941.

ALAN ROOK (b. 1910): Alan Rook served as a staff major in the Royal Artillery. His response to the calamity was fatalistic –

> Do not think, gunner, thus to provoke
> any immediate answer from death . . .
> death shall come when the reaper is ripe for the corn.

Poetry: *Soldiers, This Solitude,* 1942; *These are my Comrades,* 1943; *We who are Fortunate,* 1945; *Not as a Refuge,* 1948.
He and Henry Treece were joint editors of the Oxford magazine *Kingdom Come.*

WILLIAM SANSOM (b. 1912): 'The short-storyist by birth, addiction and destiny. Such is William Sansom,' wrote Elizabeth Bowen. 'From his war-time London, National Fire Service and fly-bomb period we have those two masterpieces, "The Wall" and "Building Alive". . . . A Sansom story is a tour-de-force. It is not written *for* effect, he is dealing *in* it.' William Sansom gave his recreation as 'watching'.

Short Stories: *Fireman Flower,* 1944; *Three,* 1946; *Something Terrible, Something Lovely,* 1948.
Miscellaneous Writings: *Westminster at War,* 1947.

FRANCIS SCARFE (b. 1911): Scarfe served in the R.A.O.C. and in the R.A.E.C. from 1941–6, eventually as a Lt-Colonel. His poetry is marked by a brooding darkness which underlies the apparent calm with which its reminiscent statements are made.

Poetry: *Inscapes,* 1940; *Poems and Ballads,* 1941.
Criticism: *Auden and After,* 1942.

EDITH JOY SCOVELL (b. 1907):
Poetry: *Shadows of Chrysanthemums,* 1944; *The Midsummer Meadow,* 1946.

EDITH SITWELL (1887–1964): Edith Sitwell was a year older than T. S. Eliot when the war began, a middle-aged poet (fifty-two) who had come a long way from what David Daitches called 'the brilliant verbal clowning' of *Wheels*, the anthology she edited during World War I. She wrote prolifically during the forties, her work often reaching great depths of tragic expression. *Still Falls the Rain* protests against the seemingly endless re-crucifyings of the God of Love.

Poetry: *Poems New and Old*, 1940; *Green Song*, 1944; *The Song of the Cold*, 1945; *The Shadow of Cain*, 1947; *The Canticle of the Rose*, 1949.
Critical and Miscellaneous Writings: *Edith Sitwell's Anthology*, 1940; *Look, the Sun* (for children), 1941; *English Women*, 1942; *A Poet's Notebook*, 1943; *Planet and Glow-worm*, 1944; *Fanfare for Elizabeth*, 1946; *A Notebook on William Shakespeare*, 1948.

STEVIE SMITH (1902–71): To paraphrase E. M. Forster's celebrated description of Cavafy, Stevie Smith was an English lady . . . standing absolutely motionless at a slight angle to the universe. The view is often desperate.

Novels: *Novel on Yellow Paper*, 1936.
Poetry: *Tender Only to One*, 1938; *Mother, What is Man?* 1942; *Harold's Leap*, 1950.

JOHN SOMMERFIELD: After what could be called a typical thirties career as a writer, that is, working between bouts of casual employment as seaman, carpenter, stage-manager, etc. – as well as participating in events which produced a book entitled *Volunteer in Spain*, John Sommerfield spent the war years serving in the R.A.F.

STEPHEN SPENDER (b. 1909): Spender was co-editor of *Horizon* during the early months of its existence, and contributed poems and critical articles to it throughout the war. He also wrote regularly for *Penguin New Writing* in a section called 'Book Front'. These articles are now of great interest because they show thirties political and ethical literature giving way to the more personal and romantic literature of the forties. Spender's poetry during the latter decade retreated more and more into the strictly personal – the 'confessional' was how some critics preferred to call it – as he abandoned the tractarian intentions of the thirties. Spender's was the vulnerable unmasked face which had neither wit (like Auden) nor religious certainty (like Eliot) to defend it.

Poetry: *Poems for Spain*, 1939; *The Still Centre*, 1939; *Ruins and Visions*, 1941; *Poems of Dedication*, 1946; *The Edge of Being*, 1949; *Collected Poems*, 1954.
Novels: *The Backward Son*, 1940.
Autobiography: *World Within World*, 1951.

DYLAN THOMAS (1914–53): An American poet and critic, Kenneth Roxroth, described Dylan Thomas's descent on London during the late thirties and early forties as 'though something had escaped that had been locked up in Wild Wales since the Synod of Whitby, and was clanking its chains and yammering in the Rectory drawing-room'. Thomas regarded the war as a tremendous personal inconvenience at first – 'Dylan-shooting begins', he wrote to Pamela Hansford Johnson on 3 September 1939. Later, he used his 'sullen art' (and this included the florid splendour of his voice in many poetry broadcasts and film scripts) to mourn war's final interruption of the lives of others.

Poetry: *The Map of Love*, 1939; *The World I Breathe* (poems and stories), 1939; *New Poems*, 1942; *Deaths and Entrances*, 1946; *Selected Writings*, 1946; *Collected Poems*, 1953.
Short stories: *Portrait of the Artist as a Young Dog*, 1940.

TERENCE TILLER (b. 1916): Tiller held an appointment at the University of Cairo during the war and was associated with a group of other British writers living in a kind of Graeco-Egyptian exile at this time. They included Lawrence Durrell, Robert Liddell and Robin Fedden. Their work appeared in an occasional journal called *Personal Landscape*.

Poetry: *Poems*, 1941; *The Inward Animal*, 1943; *Unarm, Eros*, 1947.

HENRY TREECE (1912–66): Treece and J. F. Hendrey edited two anthologies connected with the 'New Apocalypse' movement, *The*

White Horseman and *The Crown and the Sickle*, and in 1946 he wrote *How I See Apocalypse*. The movement was in the nature of a rhetorical rebellion against the social poetry of the thirties. The true romantic liberation, itself an experimental thing, was forced through by Dylan Thomas and owed much of its spiritual colouring to George Barker. Treece also edited *Wartime Harvest*.

Poetry: *Invitation and Warning*, 1942; *The Black Seasons*, 1945; *Collected Poems*, 1946.

W. J. TURNER (1889–1946): Turner published some seventeen volumes of poetry between 1916 and 1937. In 1935 he wrote a brilliant fantastic novel called *Blow for Balloons*. He was also a musicologist. The occasional poems which he wrote at the end of his life show a hardening, if anything, of the individuality which had kept him out of various persuasive literary movements of his time.

FRED URQUHART (b. 1912): Urquhart's stories deal with the effect of war on remote communities, with prisoners at work on lonely farms and with one kind of primitivism working against another. His work is witty, poetic and laconic.

Short stories: *I Fell for a Sailor*, 1940; *Selected Stories*, 1946; *The Last G.I. Bride Wore Tartan*, 1948.

VERNON WATKINS (1906–67): Watkins was a scholarly religious Welsh poet of great technical accomplishment. He met Dylan Thomas in 1936, becoming a close friend and, in the words of Constantine FitzGibbon, 'provided the Welsh counterpoint to Dylan's roaring London friendships'. Watkin's poetry often makes strong and intellectual use of the ballad form. The approach is purposeful, challenging: 'I sing of the Good Samaritan, of Pity and the Fixed Stars. . . .'

Poetry: *The Ballad of the Mari Lwyd*, 1941; *The Lamp and the Veil*, 1945; *The Lady with the Unicorn*, 1948.

DENTON WELCH (1915–48): A bicycle accident in 1935 allowed Welch to retreat during the war to what Jocelyn Brooke called 'a

tiny exquisite world embalmed within a Victorian glass paperweight'.
He was a curious and intriguing figure, a pain-shattered child prop-
ping himself up on rococo crutches. He flaunted a certain preciosity
at the tough war-time world, yet his writing itself was plain and
direct, as well as being as colloquial and strongly evocative of the
times in its way as that of Julian Maclaren-Ross. He was a
narcissist who was bitterly truthful about what was reflected in
the black water.

Autobiography: *Maiden Voyage*, 1943.
Stories: *Brave and Cruel*; *In Youth is Pleasure*, 1950; *A Last Sheaf*,
1951.
Essays: *A Voice through a Cloud*, 1951.
The Denton Welch Journals, edited by Jocelyn Brooke, 1952.

VIRGINIA WOOLF (1882–1941): Early in 1941 Virginia Woolf
drowned herself in the little stream running by her garden at
Rodmell. For Eliot the tragedy contained the enormity of the
moment when somebody simply said, 'Coleridge is dead'. It meant,
he added, 'a change to the world which is also a damage to oneself.'
Her first novel, *The Voyage Out*, had been published in 1915 and
her greatest, *The Waves* in 1931. Both her work and her life were
concerned with the bridge by which one isolated personality can
reach another and destroy its loneliness, and (and this was profoundly important) at the same time in no way lessen the individual-
ism of either lover or friend. She brought the novel form to the
point where the dividing line between prose and poetry disappeared.
During the thirties she was guyed as the high priestess of literary
exclusivism, but didn't care. 'All this talk about Bloomsbury . . .'
she said to Rose Macaulay, 'I don't feel Bloomsbury; do you feel
Marylebone?' The retort was ingenuous, of course. She did feel the
values popularly dubbed 'Bloomsbury' and dreaded their destruction by the war. But it was a recurrence of mental illness and a fear
that she would never be able to write again that caused her to take
her own life.

Her total application to the craft of letters during the inter-war
years had come to mean for creative people of every kind a gauge

by which to measure the depth of the artist's experience. The destruction of the fine mechanism at such a moment was felt by every serious writer like the numbing of part of his own imaginative being.

Novels: *Between the Acts*, 1941.
Short Stories: *A Haunted House*, 1943
Critical and Miscellaneous Writings: *Roger Fry*, 1940; *The Death of the Moth*, 1942; *The Moment and Other Essays*, 1947; *The Captain's Death-Bed*, 1950.

Acknowledgements

For permission to publish or reproduce the material in this anthology, acknowledgement is made to the following:

for W. H. AUDEN: 'Lullaby' and 'Musée des Beaux Arts' from *Collected Shorter Poems* by W. H. Auden, to Faber & Faber Ltd;

for BRUCE BAIN: 'We only see' from *Poets Now 2*, to Favil Press;

for GEORGE BARKER: 'Sacred Elegy', 'To My Mother', and 'To T. S. Eliot' from *Collected Poems* by George Barker, to Faber & Faber Ltd;

for ELIZABETH BERRIDGE: 'Tell it to a Stranger', to the author;

for ELIZABETH BOWEN: 'Mysterious Kôr' from *The Demon Lover and Other Stories* by Elizabeth Bowen, to Jonathan Cape Ltd and the author;

for BRYHER: '1940' from *The Days of Mars*, to Marion Boyars;

for ROY CAMPBELL: 'One Transport Lost' from *Collected Poems Vol. II* by Roy Campbell, to The Bodley Head Ltd;

for CHARLES CAUSLEY: 'Chief Petty Officer' from *Union Street*, to Rupert Hart-Davis;

for WILLIAM CHAPPELL: 'The Sky Makes He Hate It', to the author;

for HERBERT CORBY: 'Missing', from *Hampdens Going Over*, to Nicolson and Watson;

for R. N. CURREY: 'Dam', to Routledge & Kegan Paul Ltd;

for C. DAY LEWIS: 'Ode in Fear', 'Where are the War Poets?', 'O Dreams O Destinations', and 'The Poet' from *Collected Poems 1954* by C. Day Lewis, to Jonathan Cape Ltd, The Hogarth Press, and the author;

for PAUL DEHN: 'The Sweet War Man Is Dead' from *The Fern on the Rock* by Paul Dehn, to Hamish Hamilton Ltd;

ACKNOWLEDGEMENTS

KEITH DOUGLAS: 'Alamein' from *Alamein to Zem Zem* by Keith Douglas, and 'Desert Flowers', 'How To Kill', and 'Aristocrats' from *Collected Poems* by Keith Douglas, to Faber & Faber Ltd and Mrs Marie J. Douglas;

for T. S. ELIOT: 'Little Gidding' from *Collected Poems 1909–1962* by T. S. Eliot, to Faber & Faber Ltd;

for WILLIAM EMPSON: 'Aubade' and 'Ignorance of Death' from *Collected Poems* by William Empson, to Chatto and Windus Ltd and the author;

G. S. FRASER: 'Poem' from *Home Town Elegy*, Editions Poetry London, 1944, to the author;

for ROY FULLER: 'The Middle of a War' and 'What is Terrible' from *Collected Poems* by Roy Fuller, to André Deutsch Ltd and the author;

for DAVID GASCOYNE: 'Walking at Whitsun' from *Poems 1934–1942*, to Oxford University Press Ltd;

for ROBERT GRAVES: 'The Persian Version' from *Collected Poems 1965* by Robert Graves, published by Cassell & Co. Ltd, to International Authors N.V.;

for JAMES HANLEY: 'Sailor's Song', to the author;

for RAYNER HEPPENSTALL: 'Instead of a Carol' from *Poems from the Forces*, edited by Keidrich Rhys, to Routledge & Kegan Paul Ltd;

for RICHARD HILLARY: 'Spitfires' from *The Last Enemy* by Richard Hillary, to Macmillan & Co. Ltd and the Literary Executors of the Richard Hillary Estate;

for GLYN JONES: 'Bowen, Morgan and Williams' from *The Water Music* by Glyn Jones, to Routledge & Kegan Paul Ltd and the author;

for SIDNEY KEYES: 'War Poet', 'Cervières', 'Elegy for Mrs Virginia Woolf', 'Time Will Not Grant', and 'Europe's Prisoners' from *The Collected Poems* by Sidney Keyes, to Routledge & Kegan Paul Ltd;

for ARTHUR KOESTLER: 'The Yogi and the Commissar' from *The Yogi and the Commissar*, to Jonathan Cape Ltd and the author;

for ALUN LEWIS: 'Song' and 'Dawn on the East Coast' from *Ha! Ha! Among the Trumpets* by Alun Lewis, 'All Day it has Rained' from *Raider's Dawn* by Alun Lewis, and 'Ward "O" 3 (b)' from *In the Green Tree* by Alun Lewis, to George Allen & Unwin Ltd;

ACKNOWLEDGEMENTS

for J. MACLAREN-ROSS: 'A Bit of a Smash in Madras' from *Memoirs of the Forties*, to Alan Ross Ltd;

for LOUIS MACNEICE: 'The Conscript' from *Collected Poems* by Louis MacNeice, to Faber & Faber Ltd;

for GEORGE ORWELL: 'In Defence of P. G. Wodehouse' from *Collected Essays* by George Orwell, to Martin Secker & Warburg Ltd;

for MERVYN PEAKE: 'Had Each a Voice' from *Shapes and Sounds*, to Chatto & Windus Ltd;

for F. T. PRINCE: 'Soldiers Bathing' from *Soldiers Bathing*, to The Fortune Press Ltd;

for V. S. PRITCHETT: 'The Saint' from *Collected Stories* by V. S. Pritchett, to Chatto & Windus Ltd and the author;

for JOHN PUDNEY: 'Convoy Job' and 'For Johnny' from *Collected Poems* by John Pudney, to The Bodley Head;

for KATHLEEN RAINE: 'Heroes' from *Collected Poems*, Copyright © 1956 by Kathleen Raine, Hamish Hamilton Ltd, London;

for HENRY REED: 'The Naming of Parts' and 'A Map of Verona' from *A Map of Verona* by Henry Reed, to Jonathan Cape Ltd and the author;

for W. R. RODGERS: 'Awake!' from *Awake! and other Poems*, to Martin Secker and Warburg Ltd;

for ALAN ROOK: 'Dunkirk Pier' from *Soldiers, This Solitude*, to Routledge & Kegan Paul Ltd;

for WILLIAM SANSOM: 'The Wall' and 'Building Alive' from *The Stories of William Sansom*, to the Hogarth Press Ltd;

for FRANCIS SCARFE: 'Conscript' from *Poems and Ballads*, to The Fortune Press Ltd;

for E. J. SCOVELL: 'Days Drawing In' from *The First Year* by E. J. Scovell, and 'Daylight Alert' from *The River Steamer* by E. J. Scovell, to The Cresset Press and the author;

for EDITH SITWELL: 'Still Falls The Rain' from *The Canticle of the Rose* by Edith Sitwell, to Macmillan Co. Ltd and the Literary Executors of the Edith Sitwell Estate;

for STEVIE SMITH: 'A Shooting Incident' from *Harold's Leap* by Stevie Smith, to Chapman & Hall Ltd;

ACKNOWLEDGEMENTS

for JOHN SOMMERFIELD: 'Squadron Move', to the author;

for STEPHEN SPENDER: 'Memento' and 'The War God' from *Collected Poems* by Stephen Spender, to Faber & Faber Ltd;

for DYLAN THOMAS: 'Deaths and Entrances', 'Ceremony After a Fire Raid', 'A Refusal to Mourn the Death, by Fire, of a Child in London', 'Among those Killed in the Dawn Raid was a Man Aged a Hundred', and 'Fern Hill' from *Collected Poems* by Dylan Thomas, to J. M. Dent and Sons Ltd and the Literary Executors of the Dylan Thomas Estate;

for TERENCE TILLER: 'Flare' from *Unarm, Eros* by Terence Tiller, to The Hogarth Press Ltd and the author;

for HENRY TREECE: 'In the Beginning was the Bird' and 'Lincolnshire Bomber Station' from *The Black Seasons* by Henry Treece, to Faber & Faber Ltd;

for W. J. TURNER: 'Words and Ideas' and 'The Young and the Old', to the Literary Executors of the Estate of W. J. Turner;

for FRED URQUHART: 'The Tattie Dressers', to the author;

for VERNON WATKINS: 'The Collier' and 'Two Decisions' from *The Ballad of the Mari Lwyd* by Vernon Watkins, to Faber & Faber Ltd;

for DENTON WELCH: 'Sickert at St Peter's', to the Literary Executors of the Denton Welch Estate;

for VIRGINIA WOOLF: 'The Death of the Moth' from *The Death of the Moth and Other Essays* by Virginia Woolf, Hogarth Press.

Every effort has been made to trace copyright holders, but in a few cases this has proved impossible. The publishers would be interested to hear from any copyright holders not here acknowledged.

*

The Editor would also like to thank Mr J. B. Leishman and The Hogarth Press for permission to quote from his translations of Hölderlin; the Executors of the Estate of the late T. S. Eliot and Messrs. Faber & Faber for 'Little Gidding'; the Estate of the late Cyril Connolly, Mr John Lehmann, Mr Keidrich Rhys, Mr Ian Hamilton, Mr R. N. Currey, Mr Geoffrey Grigson, and many other editors of war-time magazines and anthologies for their assistance; and Professor and Mrs Stephen Garrett, the University Librarian, Cambridge, and Ipswich Borough Library.   R.B.